# Group Travel Operations Manual

by Martha Sarbey de Souto, CTC

DELMAR PUBLISHERS INC.
MERTON HOUSE TRAVEL AND TOURISM PUBLISHERS

0-9160-3220-5

**Publisher's Note:** The purpose of this book is to give general guidance and provide authoritative information on the subject matter covered. It is sold on the understanding that neither the author or the publisher is engaged in giving legal, accounting or other professional advice. If legal or other assistance is required the reader should seek the services of a lawyer, accountant, consultant, or other competent professional. While every effort has been made to include only accurate information, due to the changing nature of the travel industry and the subject matter covered, neither the author or the publisher can be responsible for errors.

ISBN: 0-916032-20-5

Library of Congress catalog card number: 83-61024
Copyright © 1985 by Martha Sarbey de Souto

All rights reserved. No part of this publication may be reproduced, stored in a retrieval system, or transmitted in any way or by any means, electrical, mechanical, photocopying, recording or otherwise, without written permission of the publisher, except for quotations made for the purpose of a review. All inquiries should be addressed to the publisher.

DELMAR PUBLISHERS INC.
Two Computer Drive West, Box 15-015
Albany, New York 12212

**Manufactured in the United States of America**

Other books in The Travel Management Library Series:

BUDGETING FOR PROFIT AND MANAGING BY GOALS
COMPLETE GUIDE TO TRAVEL AGENCY AUTOMATION
THE DICTIONARY OF TOURISM
GUIDE TO STARTING AND OPERATING A SUCCESSFUL TRAVEL AGENCY
GUIDE TO TRAVEL AGENCY SECURITY
HANDBOOK OF PROFESSIONAL TOUR MANAGEMENT
LEGAL ASPECTS OF TRAVEL AGENCY OPERATION
LEGAL FORMS FOR TRAVEL AGENTS
THE TRAVEL AGENCY PERSONNEL MANUAL
TRAVEL AND TOURISM MARKETING TECHNIQUES

*For the wonderful, professional members of the travel industry with whom I have been affiliated through the Institute of Certified Travel Agents (ICTA), The Pacific Area Travel Association (Norcal PATA), and Travellarians . . . who gave me their support through this project*

# Contents

Preface, vii

Acknowledgments, ix

About the Author, xi

1. Undertaking Group Travel, 1
2. Preparing to Handle Group Business, 18
3. Researching and Designing the Tour, 33
4. Negotiating and Booking the Tour, 48
5. Costing and Pricing a Tour, 83
6. The Tour Brochure, 100
7. Marketing the Tour, 115
8. Client Handling, 142
9. In-house Operations and Dealing with Suppliers, 176
10. Tour Manager Preparation and Dispatch, 205
11. Managing the Tour Enroute, 219
12. Posttour Wrap-up, 247
13. Incoming Group Tours, 261
14. And ... for the Experienced Group Operator, 278

Glossary, 291

Index, 306

# Preface

As a student living in Europe in 1954, I grew to abhor those busloads of "Ugly Americans" touring the continent and swore that I would never condescend to be one of *them*—those people who raced through 2,000 years of history on a three week tour consisting mostly of one-night hotel stands and a view of the natives through a tinted motorcoach window.

Strange then that I should ultimately have found group travel to be one of the primary educational forces in the world today and at the same time one of the most exciting business careers possible. Group travel in the '80s is no longer simply hordes of uninitiated travelers being pushed and pulled from country to country. On the contrary, it has become a highly specialized and diversified field encompassing not only the traditional tours, but also a wide variety of group projects for very sophisticated travelers. It ranges from conventions, sales incentives and all kinds of international meetings to trade missions, treks, white river rafting adventures and overseas campus in-residence programs. It might include Christmas shopping junkets to Hong Kong, theater or opera tours, wine-tasting seminars, or study programs at sea. In short, the arena of group travel is today an extremely imaginative and stimulating field, offering a unique opportunity to those entrepreneurs and employees willing to make their way in a group travel career.

Yet, very little exists in the way of formal education or training for this challenging field. Most travel agency preparatory courses devote no more than perhaps a lecture or two to the entire field of group travel, as instructors scurry through weeks of airline ticketing and quick skill preparation in an effort to give students entry level training for typical retail travel agency employment. At the other end of the spectrum, most university programs, while perhaps looking at tourism as it affects the ecology or economy of a country, seem not to train the theorist how to put his or her idealism to work in a practical career in which one can bring together interdisciplinary studies and "do good" in the world and still make a living.

And, if academic institutions (be they at university level or trade school level) have failed in teaching group travel, it may be partially because there have not been the necessary textbook source materials. Teaching group tour packaging myself the first year to a small class, I was able to photocopy sufficient materials from my office to use as samples and was able to call on my own experience and that of friends and colleagues in the group travel field. However, as classroom size grew, this became unwieldy and as inquiries for my classroom materials started coming in from other instructors across the country and from travel agents, tour operators, and outside salespeople I began to realize the need for a text.

This book, then, is designed to be used by both the student of tourism and by members of the travel industry who hope to increase their skills. It is highly personal, being a synthesis of thirty years' experience in the group travel field and of eight years of teaching group travel in the college classroom. Many of the opinions expressed herein are merely that—personal opinions reflecting experiences, both positive and negative, throughout my group travel career. Your experiences may prove different, and as times and techniques change we can all certainly adapt to new ways of thinking and new methods of approaching things. It is hoped you can bear with me through some of the "how-to" practicalities and through some of the necessary pedantics—never losing track of the contagious excitement and personal fulfillment which is the essence of the group travel field today.

Marty Sarbey de Souto<br>
Berkeley, California<br>
February, 1985

# Acknowledgments

I wish to thank the following for permission to reprint materials: Agreement Research, British Airways, Cal-Farm Travel Service, Inc., Gil Ferrer Salon, Golden Bear Travel, Howard Tours, Inc., Jeffrey R. Miller, Olsen-Travel World, Ltd., R & H Voyages, Royal Cruise Lines, and Treasure Tours.

I wish to express appreciation to the many colleagues who helped read the manuscript at various stages along the way, specifically Peter Felleman, Sheila O'Brien, Lynne Sorensen, and Ann Wagner. Thank you to Ralph Davis for his insurance expertise, to Tanya Edgar for assistance with the illustrations, to Jeffrey R. Miller for his legal guidance, to Frances Friedman for sharing up-to-date tour escorting information, to Dorothy Purdie for her common-sense budget guidance, and to Henry Eaton for his marketing and public relations advice.

To employers past and present: Jack Dengler who gave me my start at SITA Tours, Joe Howard of Howard Tours, Inc. who taught me operations, Ken Goy of Cal-Farm Travel who gave me my freedom in marketing, and John Bell who puts up with all my foolishness at Golden Bear Travel. To my students at Cañada College and Vista College on whom I practiced my theories over the years. A special thank you to my 92-year-old mother who read every word to be sure her daughter did her proud, and to my dear husband, José, who virtually went without a playmate for three summers and many's a weekend while I completed this work.

# About the Author

Martha Sarbey de Souto, CTC, brings to her book thirty years' experience in the group travel field. Her background includes handling group operations, group travel sales (both wholesale and retail), frequent tour escorting, itinerary planning and costing, writing tour brochures, editing travel newsletters, and preparing marketing and advertising campaigns.

With a B.A. in journalism from the University of Arizona, she began her career in the area of student travel in New York City. Subsequently she worked with professional medical and dental overseas convention programs, then in the area of academic study tours and overseas campus programs, and then with special-interest agricultural study tours and trade missions.

She teaches a variety of group tour packaging and wholesaling classes at the community college level for Cañada College in Redwood City, California and for the University of California Extension. In 1978 she developed the travel industry certificate program and curriculum for Vista College in Berkeley, California, and is still active there as group travel instructor and as chairman of the travel industry advisory committee for the college.

The author is past president of Travellarians of California, and has served on the Board of Directors of the northern California chapter of the Pacific Area Travel Association (NORCAL PATA). She is a frequent contributor to *TravelAge West,* and was selected as outstanding travel agent in the country by *Travel Weekly* in January 1983.

The author lives with her husband, José, in Berkeley, California. She is Vice-President—Marketing for Golden Bear Travel in San Rafael, a large agency specializing in group cruise and tour business.

# 1
# Undertaking Group Travel

Imagine this scenario.

You have just sold your first group tour. Everyone at the agency is excited. You are proud and pleased and are entertaining visions of satisfied customers as well as extra profits for the agency.

But wait! What if something should go wrong? Suddenly you feel somewhat nervous and apprehensive. After all, when you make a mistake with one client, you have just one complaint, one unhappy customer. When you misprice one individual client, the financial loss to the agency is small. But what happens if the mistake, the complaint, the mispricing are multiplied many times over for a group?

Before becoming too heavily involved in groups, a travel agent should step back and assess the motivations and capabilities of the agency and its staff. The agent will want to be sure that group business is really a wise choice.

## Why Handle Groups?

An agency may decide to handle group business for many reasons. These reasons might include building a list of clients, expanding the base of potential future travelers, developing repeat tour projects, and filling in weak business periods in the office. Other reasons are less directly connected with business, and might include helping a friend or client who is involved with a group or assisting new and inexperienced travelers to attempt that first trip (a trip that they might never be able to take without help!). But the primary fact remains that *group business is attractive because, if handled properly, it offers an agency the greatest profit potential.*

Many agents will refute this statement by saying that if they devoted the same amount of time and involvement to thirty independent passengers that they do to a group of thirty, they would be ahead financially. If this really proves to be the case, it is probably because the tours are not being priced properly. The reason that an agency can make more money on a group of thirty than on thirty individuals is not because of volume handling or because the commission is earned thirty times over. It is because *group tour business allows an agency to establish its own markup on its tours, and frees the agency from working under the commission system.*

No matter how many individual bookings an agency handles, the earnings on those bookings are still limited to those that can be obtained from suppliers. These earnings are usually 11 percent on an air ticket sold in conjunction with a land tour and an itinerary (IT) number. They are a basic 10 percent on tours and cruises, plus whatever overrides accrue because of volume bookings or through tenacious negotiating with suppliers. But even when selling tours and cruises, and even when dealing with volume, the agency's earnings are still restricted to a commission rate that someone else has established. While this commission can be attractive (particularly if overrides are involved) when compared to the commission usually received on individual bookings, these earnings are still not as attractive as they could be if the tour were built from scratch. When designing a tour, an agent is free to work with net rates, then determine the profit needs of the agency, then mark up the net rates accordingly to result in the earnings needed. When an agency builds a tour this way, it steps over the line from selling transportation to selling travel—travel as a total concept.

For obvious reasons, existing packages, such as cruises or published tours, cannot be marked up. Why should a client buy a cruise from one travel agency if its price is $100 higher than the price of the same cruise being sold by another agency down the street? Perhaps if an agency is just beginning in group business it might want to sell a group into an existing product such as a cruise or tour, learning how to handle group business in this way and being content with the commission the supplier will grant.

However, ultimately, as the agency's personnel become more knowledgeable about group handling, and somewhat braver and more adept at the whole group process, the agency will want to package its own tours. Packaging a tour involves custom designing a trip to the particular needs of a specific group or projected clientele. In this way, the agency controls the tour—its components, its quality, its pricing, and so forth. And control of the tour's components means control of potential earnings. Since the agency determines the amount of profit built into the trip, it controls the expenses, and makes the operational decisions that affect the pricing and the profit. This freedom from working under the commission system gives wide latitude to be creative in including noncommissionable features in an itinerary and to design tours that standard tour operators are not offering, or tours that may appear unfeasible or unprofitable to others.

The higher profit potential also gives the agency the freedom to hire personnel—a good operations manager, for example—at a higher salary level, since higher earnings will support higher salaries. It also may allow an agency to be more generous with its commissioned salespeople who are involved in bringing in group business to the agency. Many commissioned salespeople will want part of the *profit* of group business and will not be content with their usual commission split arrangement with the agency. They will want a split of the total earnings on the project (including markup, overrides, volume savings, and so forth), not merely a split of commissions.

## How Handling Groups Differs from Handling Individual Travelers

Group business is indeed good business, big business, profitable business. But working with groups is a unique experience. Agents who have been working as inside retail travel counselors or as commissioned salespersons will find that handling group business is different from previous travel experience in many respects. Some agents love group business; others hate it. Here are some of the aspects of group business that make it unique.

1. A retail travel counselor deals on a day-to-day basis with the potential traveler when planning an individual client's trip. With groups, the counselor may never meet the individual traveler and may miss this personal contact. This is not to say that the counselor will never meet the public. But the public an agent does meet will more than likely be people in the travel trade or key individuals in clubs and organizations for whom tours are being

handled. If the program is being wholesaled, there will also be dealings with other travel agents.

2. A retail travel counselor deals with individuals. A group counselor deals with volume, and everything must be geared to efficient handling of large numbers of people at one time. The agent must forego personal tastes—that charming country inn with only ten rooms, or that elegant restaurant that will not accept a tour group.

3. A retail travel counselor deals with clients planning to travel in the relatively near future. Group handling involves planning for clients who will travel far in the future—at least a year from the first planning stages, often longer. The agent does not experience the immediate satisfaction of happy clients returning and reporting on their trip. By the time a tour finally leaves, many experienced agents find that their interest in it has been all but exhausted.

4. A retail travel counselor does much of the business verbally—either in person or by phone. In dealing with groups it is vitally important to put all transactions and confirmations in writing. Therefore, written communication skills become more important—good composition, good business letters, accurate grammar and spelling, the ability to engender enthusiasm and sell by mail.

5. A retail travel counselor is subject to the flow of the day's pressures; for example, the telephone, incoming mail, drop-in clients, and visitors. In dealing with groups, the agent must get out from under these daily pressures imposed from outside sources and must follow a schedule—a planned calendar. Organization skills are of prime importance.

6. A retail travel counselor sells a product produced by someone else. In dealing with groups, one person often produces the product as well as selling it. This means that the counselor can be much more knowledgeable about the product, because he or she designed the product in the first place and understands how it was put together. But it also means that there is no one else to go to for the answers to difficult questions or to take responsibility for mistakes. The agent ultimately must be responsible for the product.

7. A retail travel counselor demonstrates creativity by selling well, and by knowing the product line of existing tours, cruises, and other products well enough to match the right travel product to the right client. However, the constraints of time and potential

profit on any one client do not afford the luxury of lengthy conversations or extended research when planning a day-by-day itinerary for just one individual. On the other hand, the time frame and profit potential of a group allow the counselor these luxuries—probably even require them. The counselor is much more likely to need a broad experience of the world, since much of the material needed to construct an interesting trip, write an exciting itinerary, or publish brochures that sell cannot always be found in traditional travel industry source books and must therefore be researched elsewhere.

## Designing Tours for Clientele and Community

Many newcomers to the group travel field ask, "Which do you do—plan the trip and then try to sell it to an organization? Or get an organization interested in working with you first and then custom-design a trip to its needs?" The answer is "Both—depending on the circumstances."

Every travel agency should have a mailing list. A mailing list may consist solely of clients who have traveled with the agency in the past, or it may consist of clients as well as prospective clients—people who have requested literature or who have requested that their names be added to the list. Large agencies that have been in business many years may have a list that numbers into the thousands. With such a list, an agency may use the first of several methods of designing tours. It can put together a program of tours for the year—perhaps a few of its own tours, perhaps a few cruises on which it blocks group space, and perhaps several short weekend trips to appeal to younger, new travelers. (The agency should try to keep the mailing list fresh by adding newcomers each year.)

The agency then presents these trips as its annual program to this list of past and potential travelers. It also advertises the trips to the local community. These trips are not developed for a special-interest group or professional organization or church; they are open to the public—preplanned, prebooked, and offered for sale. Under this arrangement, the agency first decides what products it believes its clientele will want, and then takes the risk in expending time, energy, and promotional monies to develop those products. Organizing the annual program might go something like this:

1. Create the tour concept.
2. Plan the itinerary.

3. Book all arrangements—air, hotel, sightseeing, and so forth.
4. Cost and price the tour.
5. Publish the brochure.
6. Market the tour to the agency's own mailing list, run advertisements in local publications, and so forth.
7. Handle clients from the time they first inquire about the trip to the time they depart on tour.
8. Deal with suppliers on periodic review dates and with finalization.
9. Brief the tour manager.
10. Manage the tour enroute.
11. Handle the posttour wrapup.

## Designing a Tour for a Specific Group

The best approach for designing a tour for a specific group would be, to first contact organizations—clubs, schools, businesses, and so forth—to induce them to sponsor a group travel program through the agency. The agency usually designs the itinerary to fit the needs of the particular group. Often on the first sales call the agent does not make a presentation for any specific trip, but simply makes the contact, sells himself or herself and the agency, and then follows up with a specific itinerary. This second method of custom-designing tours might involve a procedure like this:

1. Locate the organization to which to sell the idea; research the organization and its previous travel history, if any.
2. Visit the organization and discuss generalities.
3. Get back to the organization, presenting several ideas with itinerary plans and rough cost estimates.
4. Ask the organization to commit to a specific itinerary and date.
5. Book all arrangements—air, hotels, sightseeing, and so forth.
6. Cost and price the tour, advising the organization of the final price.
7. Publish the brochure.
8. Market the tour to the organization's members.
9. Handle clients from the time they first inquire about the tour to the time they depart on tour.

10. Deal with suppliers on periodic review dates and with finalization.
11. Brief the tour manager.
12. Manage the tour enroute.
13. Handle the posttour wrapup.
14. Continue rapport with the organization's officers toward future tours.

When visiting the organization for the first time it is helpful to have several itinerary suggestions and approximate cost figures so that you can sound knowledgeable about some areas—even if not the area on which the group ultimately settles.

## A Large Operator's Approach

A third method is often used by some extremely large tour companies. Under this arrangement, a seasonal series of tours—perhaps a spring series of back-to-back one-week Rhine River tours—is set up, space booked, and the brochure produced.

Then the company sales representatives call on clubs, university alumni organizations, professional groups, and so forth on a nationwide basis. The sales representative suggests that the group block space on a specific departure date and offers to market the tour to group members via direct mail at the company's expense. Such an approach is usually beyond the scope and financial capabilities of the average retail travel agency. This approach might be as follows:

1. Create the tour concept.
2. Plan the itinerary.
3. Book all arrangements—air, hotels, sightseeing and so forth.
4. Cost and price the tour.
5. Publish a standard brochure.
6. Take the product on the road, locating organizations that wish to block departure dates and selling their group into the existing product.
7. Overprint the standard brochure in quantity, custom-tailored to show the name of the organization and the date that they have selected as their group departure date.
8. Market the tour (usually by direct mail) to the membership of the client organization.

9. Handle clients from the time they first inquire about the trip to the time they depart on tour.
10. Deal with suppliers on periodic review dates and with finalization.
11. Brief the tour manager.
12. Manage the tour enroute.
13. Handle the posttour wrapup.
14. Continue rapport with the organization, with a goal of possible future tours.

Under all three methods described above reservations are booked with all suppliers *before* the product is released for sale to the customer. An agent should never publish a sales piece, promote the tour, collect passengers' deposits (to ascertain if there is enough interest), and then try to book the tour space. This is a dangerous practice. More often than not, the flights and other reservations listed in the sales piece are not available. Then substitutions must be made or the dates changed or the resulting prices set higher than those originally envisioned. Reputable tour companies avoid this type of operation.

**Is the Group Viable?**

The author once became involved in working with a Girl Scout troop that, over a three-year period, carefully and meticulously planned a summer trip to Europe, raising the funds from bake sales. Each girl eventually managed to accumulate $650 to make the trip—a ridiculously low amount by travel industry standards but an astronomical figure for a 15-year-old high school student.

There was no money to be made on the project by the agency, since the trip consisted of a charter flight (which in those days paid only 5 percent commission), a stay at a Girl Scout lodge (noncommissionable), and a do-it-yourself approach to sightseeing, with bread-and-cheese picnics along the side of the road. However, there was no way to avoid becoming involved; the Scout leader was a long-time family friend.

Sooner or later, many travel agents become involved in such projects—and undertake them willingly just because of a genuine desire to help, or because a friend or relative ensnares them, or because they cannot bear the misinformation or bad treatment that the clients are receiving elsewhere. Before they know it they are involved.

However, good business sense dictates that travel agencies cannot afford many of these goodwill projects. Most projects must meet some commonsense criteria. Groups must be examined dispassionately before making a decision to become involved. Groups come in all sizes, shapes, and formats. Since some are more desirable than others, before determining whether the agency should attempt a specific group project, one might be wise to ask the following questions:

- What is the profit potential—does it warrant the involvement, time, energy, and financial risk?
- Is there the probability of an ongoing annual tour or is this just a one-time deal?
- Is there any competition? For example, is this a splinter group of an already-existing large-scale official tour program?
- Is there a certain prestige affiliated with the program—perhaps leading to future tours for other similar organizations?
- Is there enough lead time—at least a year?
- Does the trip fit into the agency's schedule, perhaps filling an otherwise low period in sales or a period when staff is not busy?
- Does the clientele for whom this trip is intended have the financial ability to afford it, or are they being unrealistic?
- Will this group perhaps lead to other groups of a similar nature for which the agency can use the same itinerary and the experience gained on this first trip?
- Will the project require extending credit, or will it be strictly pay-as-you-go business?
- Is there a large enough base of clientele (usually a good mailing list) to warrant any risk?

A *no* answer to any of the above questions does not necessarily mean that the project should be turned down. However, in the complete analysis, it is best to meet as many of these criteria as possible.

## Where to Find Group Business

Some groups simply arrive, a *fait accompli*. These might be the university professor convinced that he or she has a following, the commercial account that the agent knows is holding an overseas meeting, or the agent's daughter's senior class civics trip to the nation's capital. But, mostly, group business is located by diligent research and by going out and asking for the business.

CLOSE TO HOME

Many groups are located through the agency staff itself or through personal contact—friends, organizations to which agents belong, special interests of agency employees, and so forth. If agency employees are members of the local Rotary Club or golf club or Toastmasters Association, then, of course, they will want to be alert to group tour possibilities within these organizations. It is possible that agency staffers are active in a variety of community organizations. Enrolling staff members in organizations and paying their dues and monthly meeting fees may cost the agency money, but ultimately the investment may pay off. (This assumes that belonging to an organization is of interest to agency employees for reasons other than just the lure of potential group business.)

Staff members' interests in a specific sport or the arts offer possibilities to agency business. A staff member who loves classical music and has a knowledge of overseas music festivals may make a better recruiter for cultural tours than the staff member whose idea of a cultural activity revolves around the World Series. Also, the clients the agency has been serving may belong to organizations that are potential group travel accounts. Agency clients often prove to be excellent leads into group business.

IN THE LARGER COMMUNITY

In addition to looking to the agency's contacts, consider the potential from the community, the state, and even the nation. It might be a good idea to spend time at the library or county seat researching various organizations for potential group business.

One excellent source for corporate group travel accounts is Standard & Poor's *Register of Corporation Directors and Executives*. Not only does it list major firms, but it also lists the names of the companies' officers. This list allows the counselor to address a first letter or phone call to a real live individual instead of to the anonymous "Dear Sir."

County offices may be of help, particularly if they have a recreation department used by various community groups of which they may have a record. Senior citizens' clubs, arts councils, or theater groups are all potential clients.

The Yellow Pages of the telephone directory can offer much valuable information, particularly under the heading "Associations." This listing will provide names, addresses, and telephone numbers of such diverse organizations as labor unions, museum associations, chambers of commerce, the United Way, Masonic Lodges, United Nations Association,

YMCAs, and YWCAs. Also country clubs, police officers' associations, educational foundations, life insurance underwriters, Christmas tree growers, medical associations, and athletic organizations can be found here. Some of these may prove to be viable contacts, others useless. Yellow Page listings under churches, schools, universities, fraternal organizations, and professional organizations can also be useful.

The diligent agent will not stop with the telephone book of one city or community, but will try that of the state capital. Many organizations maintain lobbyists in the capital; listings in that city's directory may be more complete.

It may be helpful to contact potential groups by categories rather than going out and randomly calling on individual groups. For example, if the agency has just completed a successful tour for a university, it might be appropriate to use that product as a sample and call on other universities in the immediate area or even out of state. The university for which you just developed a tour may be prepared to give you the name of the contact person at sister academic institutions.

**Sales Call Hints**

When making sales calls, it is important to present oneself to the organization as a group specialist, indicating that the agency is not looking for independent business but group business. Many, if not most, of these organizations already will have a travel agent and will say so. The reply to this should be along the lines of "But of course you do. I would assume that any organization with the stature of yours would have an agency, and I assume that they are doing a good job for you. But we, as group specialists, can do much more than most travel agencies can." With this approach the author once sold a tour to an organization that owned its own travel agency! The agency was a commercial agency and not geared to group tours or to financial risk-taking to secure volume bookings through a direct-mail promotion.

It is also a good idea to learn to think and talk about complete packages, to sell a total idea, not just component parts. Travel counselors, accustomed to selling individual air reservations and hotel bookings, are used to quoting the airfare and the hotel per-night cost—in short, quoting breakdown charges. In selling groups, it is best to stop thinking components and think total package; for example, an agent might explain cost to a client by saying "I estimate we could package a ten-day trip at slightly under $1,500, depending of course, on which hotel we are able to secure for you, time of year you select, and several other factors. There are some attractive airfares in this market and we'd pick the one most advantageous to your organization once I know more about your specific needs. Now, tell me such and such . . ." deflecting the conversation back to the direction desired.

The motivation of a group must also be considered in designing the sales approach. The motivations behind travel are varied and complex. The skilled agency salesperson will quickly perceive which motivations are on target in a given sales call situation and point them out to the potential buyer as a part of the sales presentation.

## Motivation for Group Travel

To sell group trips successfully, the agent must understand the reasons why individuals and organizations choose to participate in group travel programs. After all, everyone in the whole world could conceivably travel independently, never joining any sort of group. Similarly, organizations could decide that they do not want to bother making group travel programs available to their membership or employees, that it is too much trouble and risk. Yet many individuals do travel in groups and many organizations do sponsor group travel programs. Why?

INDIVIDUAL MOTIVATIONS
FOR JOINING GROUP TRAVEL PROGRAMS

The individual may join a group travel program for one of many reasons. A decisive motivation is the *money saved* by traveling in a group—special group airfares or other group rates may offer large savings. In fact, many individuals will buy a package and throw away the land portion just to take advantage of group airfares.

Another motivation might be *companionship*—the desire to travel with others, hoping to meet people of similar interests with whom to share the joy of travel experiences. Also important is a negative motivation, *fear*—the novice traveler's fear of being alone, something going wrong, of not knowing the ropes, of showing his or her ignorance, or of being taken advantage of in a foreign culture or milieu. Many people also join groups because they appreciate the *convenience*. Their luggage is taken care of for them; their sightseeing is planned and prearranged; they are free from daily decisions or problems.

These motivations pertain to both the novice and the somewhat experienced traveler. However, many extremely well-traveled, sophisticated, and experienced travelers also join group travel programs.

One reason might be *destination*. Although experienced travelers may feel comfortable traveling independently year after year in Europe or Mexico, they may not feel as comfortable in places like India or the Orient—in areas where cultural values and language differ radically from their own. They probably also know that in some countries, such as the USSR and the People's Republic of China, group travel is often *the only possibility.*

Another reason experienced travelers join groups might be that they perceive participation in a specific group tour as the *"in thing"* to do. If the tour is a private tour, giving them access to meetings with certain key individuals or entree to private homes or businesses, they will join for these subliminal reasons. There is also the factor of *traveling with the "right" people.* The author has been involved in many professional travel projects, even some totally paid and hosted invitational tours. Often the first thing that the individual will ask when invited, even before asking about the tour content itself, is "Who else is going?" Many experienced travelers want to feel that they are traveling with their peers.

Many people join nontour tours—that is, tours that are not called tours. Everyone has seen the phenomenon in recent years of companies that specialize in the trek, expedition, study program, overseas cultural experience, and so forth. These are not tours in the true sense of the word. To many people, the term *tour* is a negative word implying a different city, a different hotel every night—the "If it's Tuesday, this must be Belgium" syndrome. The physician who says he never takes tours may excitedly say that he is going to participate in an overseas onsite inspection of medical facilities in Timbuktu next summer on a program sponsored by his medical association.

WHY ORGANIZATIONS SPONSOR GROUP TOURS

If individuals have certain motivations for participating in group tours, then so do organizations. Even if the travel agent does all the work on the group travel program for an organization, the officers or individuals within the organization working with the agent on the project are investing time, energy, risk, and other factors. They could easily say that they do not want to be involved in group travel projects. And some do say that. Yet, many more do not. Many are eager to be involved in all aspects of group travel programs for their organizations. What motivates their involvement?

Probably one of the primary motivators is a *personal desire to travel.* Another reason might be *glamor;* most people outside the travel industry still see it as a glamor industry. It is *fun* for them to be involved.

Travel is a happy subject. Deciding about travel certainly is more exciting than the day-to-day decisions many executives face concerning budget, sales quotas, and personnel problems.

Many people see a travel program as being *prestigious*—a university that develops an overseas study program or a professional organization that participates in a foreign meeting may receive recognition within its field. It may also be perceived as *helpful*—making possible a group trip for employees at a lesser cost through group buying. It can also be a way for an organization to *raise funds*. A museum might assess a donation fee to each tour participant. A group tour can offer the sponsoring organization exposure or *publicity,* so reaping recognition and perhaps eventually additional sales or business for that organization. In this way a tour can be a form of institutional advertising.

Many businesses see travel as an excellent *motivational tool* —an incentive for employees to produce or sell. Many salespersons, for example, will exert themselves to make that last sale necessary to qualify for a place on the company's annual incentive trip. Such a trip cannot be measured in monetary terms. It is measured more in terms of personal satisfaction or recognition from peers and employer.

## Types of Groups

Losely categorized, group travel probably falls into one of three major categories:

1. Group travel for pleasure (vacation).
2. Group travel for business.
3. Group travel with a purpose (other than business, often called special-interest travel).

GROUP TRAVEL FOR PLEASURE

This category would cover basic vacation travel in a group. Although pleasure travel can be associated with a business trip or convention, or as a pre-or postconvention pleasure trip, it is conceived as strictly for enjoyment. It can be open to the public or not, as in a private tour or cruise limited to members of a specific club, church, or organization.

GROUP TRAVEL FOR BUSINESS

This category encompasses a variety of different kinds of travel projects. Some of these are more profitable than others, some feasible for the beginner, and others only for the experienced group specialist. In this category one would find incentives, conventions, meetings (for directors, stockholders, and so forth), seminars, trade missions, scientific meetings, and site inspection tours.

GROUP TRAVEL WITH A PURPOSE

This category might be considered an offshoot of either of the former categories, but it is really a category unto itself. It is not only transportation to get somewhere for a business purpose, nor is it travel for travel's sake or for pleasure. Rather, this kind of group travel revolves around a specific purpose or interest. This could be a sport—ski tours, skin-diving expeditions, trekking in the Himalayas, or a golf or tennis package. The trip could be for education—a tour for academic credit or teachers' salary increment. It might be for philosophic or religious fulfillment—the pilgrimage to the Holy Land, or the Buddhist search for a guru in India. It could be a tour with a certain life style—living with the local villagers rather than staying in hotels. It would cover what is loosely called special-interest tours.

## Choosing the Right Group Business

One of the first things the agency will need to consider if deciding to go into group travel is the type of group or groups in which to specialize. With which type does the agency feel most capable and comfortable?

LARGE VERSUS SMALL GROUPS

A large convention may be a possibility, but can the agency handle convention business? Convention and meeting business requires individual air itineraries and individual billings, as opposed to incentive and corporate business for which the agent bills one central source. If it is an offshore meeting (one held in Hawaii, or the Bahamas for example) there may be enough profit in the longhaul airfare, pre-and postconvention tours, and a markup on the basic convention package to make the venture worth the travel agent's while. On the other hand, if the convention is closer to home, if delegates can drive or book their own air trip locally, and if the basic package is little more than a couple of nights' hotel accommodations and a registration fee, is it worthwhile becoming involved?

Large conventions, involving use of many hotels and many block flights, require efficient computer handling with inventory control capacity to keep track of all those hotel beds and airplane seats. Often a special computer program must be written especially for the project. Upfront money is often required and many large conventions are booked four to eight years in advance. Therefore, convention business is not appropriate if the agency's group department is expected to show a profit within a year or two. Nor is it appropriate if cash flow is limited, nor if there are not the needed trained backup staff, computer capacity, and toll-free telephone lines to handle client calls from all over the nation.

However, smaller meetings of forty to fifty people, although not particularly lucrative (unless overseas, and involving longhaul air and a ground package), can be a starting point for any travel agency wishing to become involved with group business travel.

Pleasure-vacation travel, be it for a country club, church, museum, or garden club, is the easiest type of group business for the beginner in the group travel field. Often these tours will be planned for small, manageable groups (one busload of forty passengers or less) and often such tours will center around one key individual—the "Pied Piper." This Pied Piper could be the pastor who takes his congregation to the Holy Land, or the museum curator, golf pro, or club president. Sometimes this person will actively recruit a group; other times he or she may simply be a celebrity who is a "name draw" for the tour but does not do much active sales recruiting. Groups of this manageable size and nature will give the agency the experience necessary to go on to other, more sophisticated projects.

In addition to gaining experience, the agency can sometimes count on a substantial profit from group pleasure travel. A group of forty on a comprehensive three-week tour overseas can generate the same income as a group three or four times that size attending a local convention. Profit must never be judged solely on numbers of passengers nor in commission percentages. It should be measured in terms of earnings per total project.

## Group Ideas

Here is a brief listing of potential group travel prospects that a travel agency interested in group business might want to consider:

    agricultural groups
    bridge-playing groups
    churches (for religious pilgrimage tours)

conventions
country clubs
high schools
incentive groups
jazz fans clubs
literary groups
museum associations
music devotee organizations
opera buffs organizations
professional organizations (teachers, nurses, and so forth)
radio disk jockey listeners (Pied Piper)
sailing clubs
sales meetings
scientific meetings
senior citizens
service clubs (Rotary, Kiwanis, and so forth)
ski clubs
skin-diving groups
stockholder meetings
tennis clubs
trade missions
universities

This first chapter has provided a substantial introduction to the field of group travel. Differences between handling individual clients and handling group clients have been explored. The advantages and types of group travel have been delineated. But many other aspects of this complex business remain to be examined. For example, one might ask how an agency can best prepare itself to manage group business in a proper and profitable way. What type of legal security, insurance, and backup personnel will the agency need? What financial risks and time commitments must the agency assume? Does the agency have the in-house expertise to execute successful group projects, and thereby enhance its reputation? How can the agency be assured of satisfied, repeat customers? Later chapters will address these and other important questions.

# 2

# Preparing to Handle Group Business

Once it has been decided that the agency does indeed wish to handle group business, it is important to make sure that it is really ready to handle such business. Does the agency have access to sound legal advice? Is insurance adequate for group risks? Is the necessary accounting system in place prepared to track group profit or loss? What about financing? Has a structural format for a group division been designed? What about special office layouts, personnel, and supplies? Many decisions must be made.

**Legal Preparation**

In the interest of preventive legal planning, the company attorney should certainly be brought into the picture *prior to* embarking on a major group travel project or before opening a group department. The attorney may wish to call attention to some specific needs and, conversely, should be told that business is going to be expanded in this direction, thus increasing the company risk. An attorney should review necessary insurance coverage and prepare a standard responsibility clause ready for any tour brochures that may be planned. (See the responsibility clause in the sample itinerary in chapter 3).

The decision to become involved with group business may change the agency's status from agent for an existing principal (as when selling a group into an existing tour or cruise) to principal (when packaging one's own tours). The name of this principal must be disclosed in all literature published.

For more information on legal planning see *Legal Aspects of Travel Agency Operation,* by Jeffrey R. Miller, Merton House Travel and Tourism Publishers, Inc.

## Insurance Coverage

The agency's insurance coverage should be reviewed in light of the decision to handle group business. This includes liability protection, errors and omissions coverage, and ways to lessen risk against such things as supplier defaults, employee illness or accident on tour, and suppliers who do not live up to their contracts and commitments.

LIABILITY INSURANCE

As an agency expands into group travel and other more extensive operations, it becomes vulnerable to more kinds of liability situations. For this reason, it is essential that enough liability insurance be carried to anticipate and cover these problems. Liability protects the agency in the event a tour member slips and breaks a leg on tour and claims negligence, or if the motorcoach carrying the group goes over a cliff. While most retail agencies nowadays probably carry a minimum of one million dollars in liability insurance, many agencies involved in groups have increased their coverage to five million dollars or more. Bear in mind that if a motorcoach carrying forty passengers went over a cliff and the responsible agency held only one million dollars in coverage, this would amount to only $25,000 per passenger—not a great amount nowadays.

It should be noted that liability should be *worldwide* liability. Also, it is possible to name a client organization (a club, church, corporation, or the like) as a rider to the agency's insurance policy for the duration of a specific trip.

ERRORS AND OMISSIONS INSURANCE

Errors and omissions insurance, or E and O, as it is often called in the trade, is the travel agent's equivalent to malpractice insurance. It protects the agency in the event agency staff (an employee or even a short term outside contractor, such as a tour manager) makes an error causing a client hardship and expense—for example, ticketing someone on a nonexistent flight or overlooking the need for a special visa or inoculation. It is possible that if a product does not live up to clients' expectations, they might bring suit against the agency for having been negligent in the selection of hotel or reception operator, or for being uninformed, or having used bad judgment. Even if the agency is in the right, just the cost of legal defense can be extremely high. Having an errors and omissions insurance company attorney to work with in settling such problems can prove invaluable.

INSURING AGAINST OTHER RISKS

Other possible risks must be considered. Defaults on the part of wholesalers, airlines, and overseas reception operators are a fact of life in today's economic climate. Yet, at the present time a blanket type of coverage which a travel agency may purchase against this type of risk does not seem to exist. Risks of this sort are often considered part of the cost of doing business. As Jeffrey R. Miller, noted Maryland travel industry attorney, notes in his book, *Legal Aspects of Travel Agency Operation,* "In most instances, the cost of the insurance will outweigh the protection it will afford. The best protection . . . is to know the reputation of the tour operator or supplier you are dealing with. . . . A prudent business man or woman can be the best insurance against many of the risks faced in the travel industry."

It should be noted that a client can purchase individual insurance coverage on an optional basis. This insurance covers everything from medical/accident coverage, baggage loss/damage, cancellation penalty protection and trip interruption, to the default of a tour operator, airline, or cruise line. This type of optional insurance should be offered to the individual client, and, in fact, should be urged. Some travel agencies and tour operators have experimented with purchasing such coverage on behalf of their clients and packaging it into the cost of the trip, but this method has been denied validity by many states' departments of insurance. As Ralph Davis, president of Travel Insurance Services in Walnut Creek, California, recently explained, "In the state of California the client must know he is purchasing this insurance and must be advised of the premium involved and be given the opportunity to refuse the coverage if he so wishes. It cannot simply be forced upon him or her as part of the package price of the tour."

Certainly, if an agency is sending employees or freelance tour managers to escort tours, such risks as their luggage being lost, their becoming ill or injured on the tour, and so forth, must be considered. It is fairly easy to purchase pretrip individual coverage for a tour manager from the same company that is providing client travel insurance. The tour manager may already have medical coverage through the company employee group plan, through a personal medical plan, or simply through Medicare. Do be aware that Medicare is not valid overseas, so if a tour manager is totally dependent on Medicare, a supplemental plan should be in force on any tour leaving the country. It is also wise to consider bonding a tour manager who will be carrying substantial funds.

**Escrow Account**

Another financial safeguard an agency may wish to consider is a special bank escrow account. When money is placed in escrow, two parties agree to a certain payment and compliance arrangement, and then place the monies in question in the hands of a third, neutral party. This third party holds the funds until satisfied that the terms of the agreement are fulfilled. This arrangement is very common in the field of real estate where the monies changing hands between the buyer and the seller of a home remain in escrow until each party is satisfied that the other has lived up to his or her part of their mutual agreement.

A similar arrangement can be devised between a travel agency and a supplier, naming a bank as the third party holding the funds in escrow. For example, if an agency were chartering a plane from an air carrier, it might wish to arrange with the airline in question to make part of the payment for the plane before departure and the balance only after the carrier has provided the return flight sector. This would assure that the agency's clients are not stranded abroad without homeward passage in the event that the air carrier defaults (or at least assures that the clients are not left without financial recompense). Of course, this sort of three-way escrow arrangement is only possible if all parties agree. If the chartering airline refuses to agree to the escrow arrangement at the outset, the agency might wish to select another air carrier.

The same type of arrangement might be set up if an agency were using a tour operator or cruise line to provide services, assuming that the tour operator or cruise line agreed to the arrangement at the outset. As can be seen, this would necessitate a separate escrow account and agreement between the agency and each of the major suppliers used on a given tour.

A number of suppliers may not be willing to agree to such an escrow, because they might need the cash flow monies earlier, or might be afraid the agency would try to quibble over small items at the end. Or a supplier simply might not need the business badly enough to want to bother with escrow. And, if small amounts of money are involved, it indeed may not be worth the trouble. But if an agency has large amounts of money—not to mention faith, trust and reputation—riding on the performance of this supplier, escrow arrangements are certainly worth considering.

Many travel agencies have returned passengers' monies when a supplier defaulted, just to save face with the clients, even though the agency has never recovered the monies from the supplier, or perhaps has only received ten cents on the dollar later in a bankruptcy court. An agency may be able to stand a loss of this nature if only small amounts are at stake, or when individual FIT clients and diversified suppliers are involved. But with a group, when large amounts of money are at risk in the hands of one major supplier, it may not be the kind of financial risk an agency wants to undertake.

## Accounting

An important part of the planning involved before getting into group operations is a survey of the accounting system that will be handling this part of the business. The accounting system should be sufficiently sophisticated to separate all incoming and outgoing payments on a given tour project from the rest of the agency's figures. Then the accountant can, at the end of each trip, accurately analyze each tour project for a true profit picture. If a tour does not make the money that was projected for it, examination of the figures for the actual tour compared to initial projections can show where things went wrong. This could be an invaluable help in properly costing the next tour project. Working in advance, the accountant can demonstrate how to assign a special code number to each tour so that all financial transactions related to that tour carry this number throughout the life of the tour project.

## Financing

Before embarking on any large group project or deciding to open a group department, an agency needs to draw up some rough estimates of startup monies needed and cash flow. In all likelihood, an initial deposit from clients will be required as they join the tours. They will be billed for final payment, which probably will be due sixty days prior to tour departure, although in some cases it may even be earlier. Final payment should never be later than sixty days.

In any event, clients' money will not be available to work with, and the agency will need funds to handle such things as advance deposits to hotels or wholesalers wherever required, printing brochures, direct mail, advertising, and other promotional expenses. Perhaps monies will also be needed for entertaining potential group accounts, for staff travel for onsite inspection, or for promotion. Since most tours need a one-year lead time from inception to departure date, this means that the bulk of the clients' money (final payments) will not be available until approximately ten months after tour startup.

It is good business sense to make up a realistic budget of those monies which will have to be advanced by the agency, clearly identifying those which represent risk monies; that is, monies that will not be recouped should a given tour not materialize. An agency may need to borrow to finance the startup costs for the tour. If so, the cost of borrowing money (interest) should be included in the tour costing. If this amount becomes sizable, it is possible to look into whether the hotels, wholesalers, or cruise lines involved in a large tour project might be willing to accept an irrevocable letter of credit from the agency's bank instead of cold, hard cash. It will not eliminate the need to pay eventually (and the bank will charge interest on such a letter of credit, just as it would for a loan), but it may help the immediate cash flow situation. It also may be a good idea to meet with the agency's banker and establish a line of credit that might come in handy in certain unforeseen circumstances. See Figure 2.1 for an example of a realistic budget.

Always keep in mind that offering to handle a tour or opening a tour division constitutes a financial risk. If a tour fails to operate, the agency must return all passengers' deposits to them. The agency, however, has still paid for the brochure, advertising, promotion, salaries, and time involved. *Group handling is indeed a speculative business.*

## Structuring a Group Division

It is a good idea to give some thought to how a group division will be structured. Basically, tour companies or group divisions of a travel agency are structured in one of two ways: vertically or horizontally.

VERTICAL STRUCTURE

A vertical structure is one in which one person handles an entire tour—plans it, books it, costs and prices it, writes the tour brochure and promotional materials, handles the bookings, prepares final documents, and dispatches it. This person may even accompany the tour and act as tour manager in the field. In other words, one individual grows with the project from bottom to top.

A vertically-structured group division would probably be most likely in smaller companies or tour departments, most notably in a one-person tour department where the group person must do virtually everything,

GROUP DEPARTMENT FIRST YEAR BUDGET

| | INCOME | EXPENSES | EARNINGS |
|---|---|---|---|
| INCOME<br>Premised on operating eight group projects the first year | | | |
| Winter Caribbean Cruise, 30 passengers at average sale of $2,000 per passenger @ 10% commission + 5% override commission ........ | $9,000 | | |
| Fall Foliage Tour of New England, 25 passengers at average sale of $2,800 per person @ 10% commission + 2% override commission.. | 8,400 | | |
| Additional income, promotional assistance funds from tour operator supplier ........................................... | 500 | | |
| Local Four-Day Fun Tour for Senior Citizens, 82 passengers (two bus loads) at $295 per passenger, average earnings $1500 per bus | 3,000 | | |
| European Garden Tour, 17 passengers at $3,700 per passenger @ average earnings $650 per passenger ........................ | 11,500 | | |
| Summer Alaska Cruise, 24 passengers at average sale $2,600 @ 10% commission + 3% override commission ..................... | 8,112 | | |
| High School Senior Civics Class Budget Tour to Washington D.C. by bus, 80 students @ $450 per student @ average earnings $60 per student .................................................... | 4,800 | | |
| Mini-Convention, 3-day/2-night land package only. 50 attendees @ $250 per person. Earnings $40 per person .................... | 2,000 | | |
| Two-week Music Tour to Edinburgh Festival, 32 passengers @ $2,950 per passenger @ $400 earnings per person ............. | 12,800 | | |
| Subtotal...................................................... | $59,662 | | |
| Estimate one failure. Loss of upfront expenditures for brochure printing and distribution, advertising and promotion ........... | -2,500 | | |
| Total First Year Income from Group Department ................. | $57,162 | | |

EXPENSES

| | | |
|---|---|---|
| Group Manager's Salary @ $1,600/month x 12 months ............. | | $19,200 |
| Half-time Assistant (clerical and airline computer handling) @ $650/month x 12 months........................................ | | 7,800 |
| Telephone @ $200/month x 12 months............................. | | 2,400 |
| Proportion of rent/utilities @ $200/month x 12 months.......... | | 2,400 |
| Furniture, 2 each desks, chairs, file cabinets, one selectric typewriter and other miscellaneous items ...................... | | 3,000 |
| Stationery and Supplies ....................................... | | 1,200 |

GROUP DEPARTMENT FIRST YEAR BUDGET

|  | INCOME | EXPENSES | EARNINGS |
|---|---|---|---|
| Monthly Accounting Fees @ $100/month x 12 months ............... |  | 1,200 |  |
| Start-up Accountant/Attorney Fees............................. |  | 500 |  |
| Postage ...................................................... |  | 3,000 |  |
| Entertainment of potential group accounts...................... |  | 1,200 |  |
| Travel Expenses for group department staff .................... |  | 1,700 |  |
| Insurance, additional premium for increasing agency's coverage... |  | 500 |  |
| Printing generic brochure on new group department .............. |  | 800 |  |
| Interest, assuming $10,000 start-up loan and another mid-year $10,000 loan, both at 16% interest ............................. |  | 2,400 |  |
| Miscellaneous ................................................ |  | 1,000 |  |
| Subtotal ..................................................... |  | 48,300 |  |
| Contingency, 5% .............................................. |  | 2,415 |  |
| Total First Year Expenses from Group Department ................ |  | $50,715 |  |

EARNINGS

First Year Earnings from Group Department (of which a portion may
be shared with the Group Manager) ............................... $6,447

**Figure 2.1** An example of a typical operating budget. (This is a sample only.)

perhaps with a little secretarial or clerical help from time to time.

This kind of structure has several advantages. First, the group individual knows the product thoroughly and probably can sell it well and answer almost any question about the tour, since he or she put it together in the first place. Second, the individual has total control of the project. There is no danger of too many cooks spoiling the broth or of an important deadline date slipping through a crack and being totally missed because each one thought someone else was taking care of it. Only one person is responsible for keeping track of deadlines and everything else! Third, a vertical structure allows for area specialization. If an individual group staff member is an expert on the Orient, this person can probably best deal with clients' questions on this area, sounding more convincing than someone who has never been there. In an agency structured vertically, there might be a number of tour consultants, each responsible for a given series of tours, perhaps one for Orient tours, another for Europe, and so forth.

There are, however, certain drawbacks to a vertical structure. The person handling the tour may be an outstanding sales and promotion person, but a terrible operations manager—totally inept at detail. Conversely, an excellent operations manager may be capable within the operational realm, but timid or ineffective when it comes to speaking in public or going out and calling on a prospective group account. There is also the frightening prospect of this individual's becoming ill or being out of town, leaving virtually no one else in the office who knows how to answer calls or how to handle the program.

HORIZONTAL STRUCTURE

A horizontal structure is one in which a tour agency (or tour department within an agency) is set up laterally by function rather than by tour program. This kind of arrangement occurs most often in the larger tour companies. That is, one division or individual may design and plan all tours for the company. A second division would book all space, dealing with hotels, airlines, cruise companies, and other suppliers. In fact, in extremely large companies, this booking division may be broken down into separate air, hotel, and ship departments. Another level would be the sales division. On top of that would be the marketing and public relations division, and perhaps others.

With this type of structure, a salesperson would have to become adept at selling all of the company's tour products—not just those that he or she is handling or the one country or area with which he or she is most familiar. Those who work in operations booking group hotel and air reservations, for example, would do so for all of the company's tours.

Here again, there are advantages and disadvantages. This kind of structure allows a crackerjack salesperson to do nothing but sell and an operations person to devote full time to operational control and dealing with suppliers. However, a tour passes through various strata, so no one person is totally handling that tour. Therefore, it requires careful supervision and checkpoints to be sure that nothing falls through the cracks.

MIXED STRUCTURE

Still other companies, perhaps inadvertently, may arrive at a mix of the vertical and horizontal structures. One person or department may initiate a tour—booking the reservations, costing, and publishing it. Then, once the product is ready to promote, it may be turned over to someone else in the office who totally manages the tour to completion, handling sales, client bookings, finalization with suppliers, and dispatch.

The prime advantage of this method is that it allows one staff person or one department to be removed from day-to-day pressures and to be concerned with tours in the future, constantly working ahead a couple of years. Frequently a tour consultant may be so busy working on this year's tour, that it is impossible to stop the momentum and find time to set up next year's trip. Then, by the time this year's tour is dispatched, it is too late to get reservations for next year.

## Office Layout and Equipment

It may be necessary to rearrange the agency to allow group personnel their own private office. If this is not possible, they need at least a hidden corner where they can work with no interruptions by walk-in clientele, and where they will not have to answer the general agency phones. Those people handling groups must adhere to their own strict schedule; they cannot permit an important option date to slip by because they are too busy that day selling a local sector air ticket to a walk-in client.

In addition, group business personnel will need extra file space, cabinets for storage of brochures and bulletins, work space in which to spread out, and wall space for visual calendar reminders. As departure time draws near, it is better not to have agency clients or other personnel tripping over boxes of baggage tags, flight bags, or departure materials that are being prepared for mailing.

When planning to go into volume group business and to set up a true group department, an agency will also need to consider such expenses as a separate phone line (or number on a rotary line), a photocopy machine for heavy-duty inhouse printing of bulletins and, perhaps, eventually, even a telex or word processor. All of this electrical equipment may require an electrician's advice before it is decided where to locate the group work area.

## Stationery and Supplies

The agency expanding into group business will need special forms and supplies—such things as baggage tags, permanent-style name badges, passport wallets, itinerary covers, mailing labels, and perhaps flight bags. When just starting out with a couple of group tours or cruises a year, it is possible to get by with using such items as are sent to the agency by wholesalers or cruise lines the agency is using.

However if a permanent group department is planned, an agency will want to build its image by giving out a nice packet of final documents, all with the agency's name on them. Some agencies even give their line of tours a special name and logo and file for a registered trademark on this name—for example: "Holiday Tours, a Division of LSI Travel Agency, Inc." They have a special letterhead, matching envelopes, business cards, and office forms all designed and color-coordinated with the new name and logo.

Because many of these items, flight bags for instance, are often made in the Orient and shipped in it can take several months to get them, so they should be ordered well in advance. Also, there should be adequate shortage for such supplies and facilities for handling, packing, and shipping to clients.

## Personnel

Selection of the right personnel for group handling is crucial to the success of the program. Sometimes an agency manager will simply assign a group to its lead agent or to the staff member perceived to have the most experience in the industry or the most free time available in the daily schedule. At other times, the agency manager will attempt to handle the group alone, with some operations and secretarial assistance from staff.

### GROUP OPERATIONS MANAGERS

Neither of these arrangements usually work successfully, as the staff person selected, even the manager may not have the group operational expertise required. *The primary requirement for a good group department is a strong operations manager.* Unless someone on the staff has had this strong group *operational* experience (not group sales experience), it is best to hire someone from outside. The kind of person who is likely to succeed should be able to do the following.

- Plan all itineraries.
- Negotiate with suppliers.
- Book all arrangements—air, hotels, ships, ground services.
- Meticulously control a tour project, keeping in touch with all suppliers, cutting space where necessary, finalizing all rooming lists, flight manifests, and so forth.
- Handle all client bookings, dealing with each client graciously, by phone or in writing.

- Cost and price group travel projects.
- Prepare all written materials that the company distributes to tour clients: billings, pretrip information bulletins, departure instructions, final documents.
- Select and brief/debrief tour managers.
- Write promotional material to sell the tour—brochure, ads, flyers (or work closely with someone else on the staff more adept at this specialty).

Because of the responsibility resting on this individual's shoulders, the previous experience required, and the specialized expertise needed, it is necessary to search thoroughly, and to interview and screen carefully. It is best to advertise for a group operations manager openly, perhaps getting applicants from tour companies or cruise lines that operate large air/sea package programs. The usual retail travel counselor, either from the retail side of the agency or from the outside, is not usually the best choice.

It will be necessary to pay this individual a salary considerably higher than might be paid in individual retail sales. Good group people know that group business is priced on net plus markup (and therefore can be marked up enough to cover a good salary). A group department's earnings are not restricted to commission sales, as in the retail end of the company. Many operations managers may also be interested in getting a percentage of the profit (not a percentage of the commissions) attributed to the group division at the end of the season. They will expect to have access to all financial figures related to their group division. As well, they will want to have a certain amount of input into management decision-making over expenses and risks related to their division, since their income may very well depend on these expenses and risks.

WHO SOLICITS GROUP ACCOUNTS?

The agency that decides to open a group division is faced with deciding who will solicit the groups. Although some groups simply fall into the agency's lap, others require a planned program of attack, and the usual inside counselors or outside salespeople may not know how to generate group sales effectively. Calling on groups requires a certain amount of assertiveness, self-confidence, elegance, business training, and group product knowledge. The inside group operations manager may be out of his or her element in making sales presentations, and the dynamic salesperson may not have enough operational knowledge to do a good job. Of course, some lucky agency may find that rare combination—the individual who makes a good operations manager as well as a good salesperson. For most agencies, however, an alternative arrangement might be to have the operations manager accompany the salesperson on certain key sales calls to lend an air of authority.

Some agencies will hire special secretarial and clerical help for the group department. In other agencies, the new group operations manager will be asked to use front-office clerical help. If this is the case, the front office personnel should be so advised by management in advance, to avoid possible resentment when the new group operations manager asks them for help.

Present staff should also understand that group personnel will have their own hours, their own professional lives and schedules to follow. They will not be available for lunch hour fill-in or vacation backup, nor can they answer telephones when front office sales counselors are busy

Since the new group division represents a promise of volume business, suppliers may suddenly start wooing the group people with luncheon invitations, familiarization trips, and site inspections—perhaps invitations that were previously directed to others, either in the front office or the owner or manager. Jealousies and resentments on the part of those staff members suddenly left out can be a sore spot and should be anticipated, not left to be handled defensively after the fact. Perhaps staff members need to be reassured by management that they still will receive their accustomed quota of goodies.

## Operating Procedures

Several major decisions must be made about the way in which a new group division or department will be operated. These decisions determine setup arrangements.

BOOK DIRECT OR THROUGH WHOLESALERS?

One of these decisions is whether to act as a primary operator and book the ground services of the tours directly—writing to hotels and reception ground operators—or whether to book ground services as a total unit through a major wholesaler in the United States.

Buying from a wholesaler can save time, provide the advantage of the wholesaler's bulk buying and reputation overseas, and provide the agency with his or her expertise. This can be particularly helpful when the agency staff is unfamiliar with the countries on the itinerary. And, thinking defensively, in case of a lawsuit against the agency, it means that one more company in the United States would share the defense. Buying through a wholesaler cuts down on the work that must be done in the agency's office—the amount of typing, correspondence, and mailing. So, if most of the agency's programs will be booked through wholesalers, fewer group personnel will have to be hired and the group staff will be less burdened with the operational work load, meaning they can handle a higher client load.

Working through a wholesaler has several disadvantages, however. Among these are loss of identity and recognition of the agency's name; a total dependence on one source; and a lack of that feeling of being in control—that feeling of confidence that comes when one knows that reservations at a given hotel are confirmed because one holds a letter of confirmation on the hotel's letterhead, signed by the hotel manager, rather than having to take the word of a third party. There is also the fact that with the spectre of more and more bankruptcies looming on the horizon, it is wise to pick wholesalers with extra caution, probably sticking with the tried and true, with reputation and financing behind them.

In the long run, it is not only possible but probable that an agency will use a mix of booking methods. Perhaps a wholesaler will be used on some tours, particularly tours to areas with which the agency is unfamiliar, but other tours, particularly to areas well-known to the agency, and with which it feels comfortable, will be booked direct.

WHOLESALING TO RETAIL AGENTS

Still another decision needs to be reached as to whether tour programs will be wholesaled once they are put together. Many retail agents who have packaged a tour have discovered that they had inadequate marketing power. They have gone to other agents to solicit their cooperation in selling it. The problem was that a commission for that other selling agent had not been costed in! It is important to anticipate every possibility from the outset. Think it through. Are you a retail group operator selling directly to the public (even if through a club or organization), or are you a wholesaler selling through other agents?

Sometimes semantics get in the way. Many large group operators refer to themselves as *wholesalers,* meaning that they are large, bulk group operators dealing in volume, or they are of the "I can get it for you wholesale" mentality. In the true sense of the word, however, wholesaling implies selling through a retailer, not selling direct to the public.

If an agency is setting up as a true wholesaler, this affects all of its later actions. Tour brochures will be prepared for retail agents' use as a sales tool with an appropriate empty space on the back, where retail agents can put their agency name and address. Advertisements will be designed for travel industry publications, with the sales pitch directed to agents—not to the public. Even the public advertisements will direct readers to their local travel agent rather than to the wholesaler. And, an agency that is truly wholesaling will not be competing with retail agents, but rather will be backing them, helping them, cooperating with them—perhaps showing films for *their* clients, perhaps sharing promotional expenses for *their* mailings, perhaps promising not to use *their* clients' names and addresses for future trips circumventing them.

One way or another, an agency must decide. It cannot effectively work both ways.

# 3
# Researching and Designing the Tour

No part of the tour process is as exciting as the designing phase. This phase allows the imagination to roam and gives the planner freedom to bring into existence travel programs that both agents and clients want to see but can rarely find on the market.

**The Tour Designer**

The professional who has been working as a travel counselor before going into group tour planning is experienced in booking clients on an *existing* travel package, such as a tour or cruise, and then individualizing it with pretrip and posttrip independent arrangements. Such an agent probably has not been heavily involved in true itinerary design unless he or she is one of those rare creatures, few and far between in the industry today, who knows how to create a complete independent custom-designed trip from scratch—an FIT (Foreign Independent Tour).

In some ways, working as a travel counselor is like selling dresses in a department store. Salespeople in a dress department might help a customer select from the rack dresses that fit the customer in size, style, and personality. Creative salespeople might even go as far as to help their customers choose accessories that are just right and that promote a total effect or image. Nevertheless, no matter how much creativity and energy salespeople bring to the job, they are limited by the merchandise in the store; that is, they are restricted in their sales efforts by the available stock.

Similarly, today's average travel agent (who is not usually a travel designer) is selling the travel industry version of available stock—predesigned tours, cruises, packages, and similar products—rather than planning elaborate individually-designed itineraries, which can be very costly and time consuming.

Designing, however, as opposed to creative selling, expands the realm of possibility. Imagine the difference between a salesperson at the local department store and Christian Dior, Yves St. Laurent, or Pierre Cardin—designers all, be it of one custom-designed dress for a special client and a special occasion, or of an entire new fall line.

This difference between the person who sells dresses and the person who designs them is no greater than the difference between the usual retail travel agent and a travel designer. The dress designer brings to the drawing table a combination of business know-how, practical craftsmanship, understanding of clientele, and inspiration from many sources. Similarly, the true tour designer brings to the task a rich background of knowledge, including travel industry skills, good business sense, marketing, and costing. Just as important, this person usually has a strong cultural base—an eclectic background of history, geography, psychology, art, architecture, music, cuisine, archaeology, anthropology, and so forth. The genuine tour designer is a true Renaissance person—an artist, a creator—much more than someone who merely throws an itinerary together by combining flights, hotel overnights, transfers, and standard city sightseeing tours.

In the tour designer's hands, itineraries become potential travel experiences with interesting themes that answer the psychological needs of a certain type of client. The first-time traveler on a seven-day Caribbean cruise does not have the same expectations as the experienced traveler visiting Mongolia. Similarly, the motivations behind an incentive tour for insurance salespeople would dictate an entirely different type of itinerary than would those behind an educational tour for a group of teachers, although both trips might be to exactly the same destination. By understanding the clientele for whom he or she is designing, the tour designer is able to combine the proper ingredients into a rich, vibrant, exciting trip, the whole of which is greater than the sum of its parts.

The competent designer also understands that features included in the itinerary do not have to originate within the travel industry and be commissionable. The designer knows that custom-designed group tours are priced on net and then marked up, so it does not matter if a given tour feature is commissionable or not. One is, therefore, free to include in the itinerary fashion shows, cooking demonstrations, wine-tasting events, lectures, tours of private industries, or visits to private homes—all experiences often not available to the average traveler.

A tour designer must be knowledgeable about sources—whom to contact for enroute enrichment lectures on a given subject, or which reception tour operator overseas specializes in a certain type of program, or who moves volume groups well as opposed to who is best at handling small, deluxe, intimate groups.

## Research Aids

Many of those who work year after year in tour planning and design often become shortsighted and rely totally on travel industry source materials. It is, of course, necessary to be practical and to know the hotels, air schedules, and sightseeing attractions.

But good tour planning is more than just referring to the *Official Airline Guide,* the *Hotel Index,* or other dependable travel industry publications. It is important to remember that many other resources exist, a number of them outside the travel industry. Here are a few ideas about where to find additional information.

1. *One's own knowledge*—from personal travel, familiarization trips, seminars, and so forth.
2. *Tariffs of reception tour operators*—of the countries and cities the tour will visit.
3. *Brochures from other companies*—read what others are doing. If the majority of tour companies are including a certain tour feature in their itineraries, it may be because there is merit to it.
4. *Airlines*—specifically those serving the countries on the itinerary.
5. *An encyclopedia*—unfortunately, few travel agents have one in their office. Background information from this source can be invaluable in writing interesting brochure copy.
6. *Government tourist offices*—of the countries on the itinerary or the consulate if there is no government tourist office.

7. *Pan Am's Encyclopedia of Travel*—although the confines of this small book make indepth information on any one country impossible, this reference does manage to give a synthesis: weather, population, government, language, principal sights and noteworthy shopping. The information is primarily current and practical, not historical or cultural.
8. *United States government*—for example, the United States Department of State publishes a series of pamphlets entitled "Background Notes" on each country. These inexpensive pamphlets may be purchased from the Superintendent of Documents, United States Government Printing Office, Washington, DC 20402.
9. *Organizations*—such the Organization of American States, the United Nations, Pan American Union, World Health Organization, Pacific Area Travel Association, and others.
10. *A world almanac*—a vast store of knowledge on different countries, their size, population, ethnic makeup, economy, education, agriculture, and arts
11. *The library*—learn to use the Periodical index to look for articles in magazines such as National Geographic or leading travel magazines
12. *Bookstores*—browse through sections under travel, history, geography, and political science. Some bookstores also classify by area: Latin America, Eastern Europe, the Middle East, and so forth.
13. *An academic course*—at a local college. Cultural background, history, or geography courses can be particularly helpful. Although offering long-range rather than immediate help, academic courses can be useful to the tour designer who has an eye to the future.

Of course, few travel agents have the time or budget to research fully all of the above sources for just one tour. However, the creative agent can begin to assemble an office source library and learn from one year to the next, building on information gleaned previously.

## Sample Itinerary

Let us suppose that a tour designer has been asked to put together a short European itinerary for a local country club. A sample day-by-day itinerary plan and accompanying conditions sheet might look something like the European Highlights Tour in Figure 3.1 at the end of this chapter.

## Lead Time

Because a tour designer invests time, energy, and often personal promotional monies in a tour, it is important to have a realistic timeframe in which to organize a successful tour. A minimum of one year's lead time is usually required for most group tours. A year's lead time allows three months to research, plan, negotiate, book, and price the tour, as well as to produce the tour brochure and promotional materials. It allows the next six months for a promotional and sales campaign, and then leaves the final ninety days for billing, dispatch, and wrapup. However, conventions or tours that revolve around a major event such as the Rose Bowl or the Olympics may require as much as a five-year lead. And short weekend trips such as those that might be marketed to a club, church, or a similar preformed target group can be organized in less than one year.

Nevertheless, always keep in mind the one-year lead time rule of thumb. This rule should help a tour planner reject those tours that have little or no chance for success because of insufficient time to plan, book, promote, and finalize. It should also help keep in perspective the pressures generated by deadlines, financial need, or anxious agency owners, who tend to demand a shorter timeframe.

Unfortunately, many new agencies and many outside salespeople hired to generate group business are placed under pressure to produce tours and generate income within six months of startup. It may be possible to secure a group commitment for a tour within six months and have it on the books for the future, but it usually is not possible to have passengers' money coming in and the group departing within six months.

## Itinerary Planning

This is the exciting yet frustrating part of tour packaging—converting the idea into a practical itinerary that works—laying out the day-by-day program with all flights, sightseeing, social activities, special meals, and other components. How does one begin such an awesome task?

## START WITH THE AIRFARE

Rather than arbitrarily starting out with an itinerary and then checking with the airline as to the fare, the wise tour planner researches the various airfares *first* and selects the fare to be used *before* plotting the itinerary. The fare will define the conditions and restrictions of the itinerary. In other words, the itinerary is planned around the airfare, not the other way around.

For example, after researching several airfares, it might appear that the Group Inclusive Tour (GIT) airfare is the most suitable for a particular itinerary. But the GIT might restrict passengers to a total of five stops (two outbound, one at turnaround, and two inbound). Therefore, the itinerary must be planned around that restriction. Furthermore, the airfare might require that the group travel online, that is, on the same air carrier throughout the entire itinerary. This requirement would eliminate any plan to include a city not served by that particular carrier.

Other restrictions dictated by airfares might be blackout periods when a certain airfare is not in effect or the limitations in number of days that excursion fares require. A certain airfare may not be in effect as, for example, during the Christmas holiday season. Or a fare may be limited, for example, to fourteen/thirty-five days. Such a fare would not be workable for a group wanting a one week tour, nor would it be suitable for those who want to spend more than thirty-five days abroad. It is essential that the tour planner be aware of the ramifications and restrictions of all of the promotional fares.

Imaginative airline sales representatives, accustomed to working with group tour planners recognize the importance of special promotional airfares as a sales tool. When calling on these group operators they bring such fares to the attention of the tour planner. Other airline sales representatives, however, seem oblivious to the importance of fares and the manner in which the designer may plan an entire itinerary around a particular fare.

Of course, in certain itineraries cost may be no object, and the desired itinerary cannot be planned within the confines of the special promotional airfares. In these cases, an agent may decide to use a higher airfare to allow the needed latitude and flexibility.

## PROBLEM AREAS FIRST

Once the type of airfare has been established, it is time to consult an *Official Airline Guide* and plot a rough itinerary, working around existing flight schedules. These rough itineraries sometimes look wonderful on paper, but when flights are actually selected for the group, some of the realities of the tour business may emerge: infrequent flights in certain areas, undesirable departure or arrival times, and so forth. If the type of airfare planned restricts an agent to using a certain air carrier throughout, it will be necessary to plan the entire itinerary around that carrier's schedules—even if it means that clients will have to stay in one city longer than desired and will have to shorten their stay in another city.

If the plan includes a short cruise within the itinerary, it is necessary to make sure that space is available on the desired sailing date *before* plotting out the entire air schedule.

It may take some juggling to include a visit to a local market that only operates on Sundays, to avoid Tuesdays in Paris when the museums are closed, or to schedule a certain flight which operates only twice a week.

If the plan includes chartered motorcoach service, it is important to know coach originating points. For example, an excellent airfare to Amsterdam may be available, but if the motorcoach company to be used for the land tour in Europe is based in Switzerland, the airfare savings into Amsterdam may very well be cancelled out by motorcoach deadhead charges. *Knowledgeable tour operators start with the difficult spots first and work around them.*

CHARTING THE ITINERARY

One of the easiest ways to plot out an itinerary is to use a daily chart with areas for morning, afternoon, and evening activities. Of course, a yellow pad can also be used, with one line representing each day. It is important that, whatever method is used, the itinerary indicate days of the week as well as dates. This serves as a double check that no days have been skipped and also that any free days allowed for shopping, for example, are not on Sundays or holidays when all the shops are closed.

*Pacing.* This is an important factor in planning an itinerary. Pacing is how quickly or slowly the itinerary moves, how full or empty each day is, and the sequence of events. If a group arrives at the hotel at 1:00 a.m., it is best not to get them up for an early sightseeing tour the next morning. If a morning of sightseeing and an evening function are planned for the same day, then perhaps the group needs the afternoon at leisure.

So often, because of a tour planner's desire to show the group everything, too much is packed into the trip. Everyone needs time to sit in a cafe, write postcards, shop, take an occasional nap, or visit the barber or beautician. If tour members are not given this time, they may either become ill or may begin to avoid tour activities. It is best to plan for free time at the outset. Remember, sick or overtired tour members do not make happy tour members. A planner should mentally walk through the tour plans day by day and ask, "Would I be overtired?"

*Balance.* Another important aspect of itinerary planning is balance—introducing a variety of activities into the trip: some serious, some frivolous, some lighthearted, some intellectual. Even though a group may be on a professional study tour, no one will want to study all the time. After an intense morning of sightseeing, almost any group would enjoy a relaxing lunch with music. Similarly, it is best to plan some daytime events and some evening functions: a little music and dancing in the evening might best complement a daytime historical tour. An evening of theater or folklore or just plain frivolity might be needed to lighten the tone after a day's touring in an extremely poor country or drab area. Variety is the key to balance.

*Evening activities.* Bear in mind that many people join tours because they want to travel with others, make new friends, and have companionship, particularly for evening activities. An itinerary should never offer group sightseeing all day and then solitary evenings. If evening activities are not planned as an integral part of the tour, at least some evenings on the itinerary chart should be set aside for Dutch-treat events that the tour manager can organize, so that no one in the group ever feels left out or lonely.

*One-night stands.* One-night stands can be tiring. The itinerary may not look tiring on paper, but the act of moving in and out of hotels, buses, and airports—of packing and unpacking—takes up a great deal of time and energy. After a couple of days on the road and a different hotel each night, tour members begin to look forward to a three-night stay in the same hotel. This will give them the opportunity to organize their suitcases, to do some hand wash, perhaps even to sleep late one morning.

FIRST AND LAST DAYS

The two most important days on any tour are the first two days and the last day. Even if the organization for whom the trip has been planned indicates that it does not want meals included in the tour (perhaps to keep the price down) do plan welcome and farewell parties. The agency representative will have to explain to the organization the psychological reasons why such events are important to the success of the tour.

The first forty-eight hours are important because this is when first impressions are made, friendships are initiated among passengers, and a relationship of trust and respect is cemented between the tour manager and the passengers. For these reasons, the wise tour planner pays particular attention to the first two days of the tour to be sure that the itinerary can operate smoothly. Time should also be allowed for a briefing the first day (or if arriving late after a full day's travel, the next day). An opening social event, such as a welcome dinner party or cocktail reception, is a good icebreaker.

Memories of the tour are cemented on the last day of the tour. A wrapup social event, such as a farewell gala dinner party, is a festive way to end a vacation, leaving everyone with memories of happy times, a sense of camaraderie, and the desire to travel with the same agency again.

**Figure 3.1** A sample tour, "European Highlights" shown on the next page, designed following the guidelines in this chapter.

Itinerary

EUROPEAN HIGHLIGHTS TOUR

Specially prepared for the Rosemont Country Club

Day 1, Friday, Sept. 6              DEPART CHICAGO/NEW YORK
Depart from O'Hare International Airport via TWA Flight No. 746 at 12:50 p.m. arriving at New York's Kennedy Airport at 3:57 p.m. local time. Transfer to TWA's international check-in counter, where other tour participants join the Chicago group. We all depart together via TWA Flight No. 814 at 6:45 p.m. Dinner and overnight in-flight.

Day 2, Saturday, Sept. 7              AMSTERDAM
Arrive at Amsterdam's Schiphol Airport at 7:05 a.m. local time. Here we will be met by our local hosts and transferred to the world-famous Krasnapolsky hotel. Balance of the day at leisure to rest and adjust to jet lag. This evening we'll meet for welcome cocktails and our first dinner party together.

Day 3, Sunday, Sept. 8              AMSTERDAM
Dutch buffet breakfast at the hotel, followed by a tour briefing where we'll learn more about what we can expect in the days to come. Then we head out on an introductory tour of the city. The afternoon is at leisure to visit the Rijksmuseum or for optional independent sightseeing. In the evening we enjoy a cruise along the illuminated canals of Amsterdam.

Day 4, Monday, Sept. 9              AMSTERDAM/HAGUE/DELFT
Dutch buffet breakfast at the hotel and full-day excursion to Aalsmeer with the largest flower auction in the world, the Hague (seat of the World Court), and Delft for a visit to the famed Blue Delft pottery works. We'll stop enroute for a typical Dutch lunch. Late afternoon return to Amsterdam. Independent dinner and evening at leisure.

Day 5, Tuesday, Sept. 10              AMSTERDAM/PARIS
Early breakfast at the hotel and then transfer to the rail station for a 9:15 a.m. train to Paris. First class compartments reserved. We can purchase lunch aboard prior to arriving at the Paris Gare du Nord railroad station at 1:00 p.m. Our French hosts will be awaiting us and we depart directly from the rail station on an afternoon introductory city tour of the "City of Light" visiting the Champs Elysees, Notre Dame Cathedral, the Eiffel Tower and all the spots we've dreamed of seeing. Late afternoon

check-in at our hotel, the Meurice Intercontinental, conveniently located on the Right Bank near the fashion houses, the Tuileries, and the Louvre. Evening at leisure

Day 6, Wednesday, Sept. 11          PARIS/VERSAILLES
Continental breakfast at our hotel and morning excursion to the Palace of Versailles. The afternoon is at leisure for shopping and independent interests. Tonight we enjoy a Night on the Town at the famed Lido nightclub, noted for its beautiful showgirls and spectacular show. Champagne and fun for all!

Day 7, Thursday, Sept. 12          PARIS
Continental breakfast at our hotel and then a walking tour through the Louvre to see this great museum with its vast collections. Afternoon at leisure to spend more time on our own at the Louvre or for other interests such as shopping, further sightseeing, or just cafe sitting and watching the world go by. Tonight's a free evening to sample one of the city's many gourmet restaurants.

Day 8, Friday, Sept. 13          PARIS/ROME
Continental breakfast at our hotel and early transfer to the airport for morning flight to Rome. We stay at the Hotel Ambasciatore on Via Veneto. Afternoon tour of the city including the Roman Forum, the Colosseum, the Pantheon, Trevi Fountain, the Spanish Steps and other landmarks. Evening at leisure.

Day 9, Saturday, Sept. 14          ROME
Continental breakfast at our hotel. This morning is purposely at leisure while the city's major stores and boutiques are open. Afternoon visit to the Vatican Museum with the magnificent Sistine Chapel and Michelangelo's "Ascent of Man."

Day 10, Sunday, Sept. 15          ROME/TIVOLI
Continental breakfast. Today we see something of the Italian countryside as we make an excursion to Hadrian's Villa and the lovely Villa d'Este with its terraced gardens and dancing fountains. Country lunch enroute. Return to the city in time to pack and get ready for tonight's festive dinner party. We head across the Tiber River to the old section of Trastevere for an Italian farewell dinner complete with wine, folklore, and Italian songs well into the night.

Day 11, Monday, Sept. 16          ROME/NEW YORK/CHICAGO
All good things must come to an end and we head for the airport for our homeward flight, TWA Flight No. 845 leaving at 11:00 a.m. and arriving in New York at 2:10 p.m. local New York time. We say goodbye to our East Coast tour participants who leave us here.

Chicago-bound members continue on via TWA Flight No. 757 at 4:30 p.m. arriving at O'Hare International Airport at 5:56 p.m. local Chicago time. Welcome home.

<u>Terms and Conditions</u>

Included in the tour price:

1. Round-trip economy class airfare from Chicago, via APEX (Advance Purchase Excursion) Airfare, basic season.
2. Nine (9) nights' hotel accommodation at hotels listed in the itinerary, or similar, based on two persons sharing a twin-bedded room with private bath throughout. A few single rooms are available at a surcharge of $000. Single rooms offer privacy, but do not necessarily mean better accommodations. Requests for single rooms must be made at the time of booking, however, single rooms are not guaranteed.
3. First-class rail fare, with reserved seating, between Amsterdam and Paris, as indicated in itinerary.
4. A total of ten (10) meals, including six breakfasts (two Dutch breakfasts and four Continental breakfasts), two enroute luncheons, welcome and farewell dinner parties; (all meals are table d'hote basis in accordance with local custom; in addition are such inflight meals as may be served by the airlines when flying at appropriate mealtime).
5. Sightseeing by private motorcoach, as shown in the itinerary, including all entrance fees, with English-speaking guide.
6. Transfer between airports, rail stations and hotels for tour participants arriving and departing with the group.
7. Baggage handling for maximum two suitcases per person at airports, rail stations and hotels for all group arrivals and departures.
8. All local taxes on hotels, meals, and other tour services as well as the United States departure tax.
9. Tips to chambermaids, local guides, waiters and <u>maitre d'</u> at included tour meals, motorcoach drivers, porters at airports and rail stations, and hotel bellmen.
10. Services of a tour manager representing LSI Travel Agency, Inc.
11. Social events and special activities as listed in the itinerary, specifically the welcome party, Amsterdam evening cruise, Lido nightclub evening in Paris, and farewell party in Rome.
12. One complimentary trip, shared-room basis, to be granted to Rosemont Country Club, to be assigned by the club at its discretion to one club member to travel with the tour group as club representative (all tour services granted to other tour members will be granted to the complimentary member; items and services not provided to other tour members are not included in the complimentary trip).

# RESEARCHING AND DESIGNING THE TOUR 45

13. Three thousand (3,000) copies of a detailed tour brochure, to be prepared and printed by LSI Travel Agency, Inc. at no expense to Rosemont Country Club.
14. Direct mail charges to include bulk-rate postage, envelopes, cover letter, brochure, and labor charges for circulating the Rosemont Country Club membership of approximately 3,000 members with one mailing.
15. Three quarter-page advertisement/announcements in the Rosemont Country Club Quarterly Newsletter not to exceed $275 per advertisement, plus advertisement production charges.
16. One promotional evening to include room rental, refreshments, invitations, program of speaker and/or films.
17. All necessary planning and operational charges, including liaison with overseas contacts, Rosemont Country Club, and tour passengers.
18. Packet of departure materials including all necessary documentation, canvas flight bags, and our special "Welcome to Europe" information booklet.

Not included in the tour price:

1. Personal expenses such as laundry, liquors, wines, mineral waters, phone, valet, coffee at lunch or dinner.
2. Expenses due to flight delays, strikes, bad weather or other irregularities.
3. Travel insurance.
4. Excess baggage charges, such as overweight charges or handling for more than two suitcases.
5. Individual services apart from the group.
6. Increase in tariffs or dollar exchange rate after publication date.
7. Refunds for hotel accommodations, meals or any other tour services not used.
8. Any expense for a la carte meal items not included in preplanned menus under local custom, or for eating in other dining rooms or at other hours not authorized.
9. Any increase in airfares after publication date.
10. Cost of obtaining a passport.
11. Transportation between home city and Chicago.
12. Luggage handling in the United States at beginning and end of tour.
13. Those meals not specifically listed as included.
14. Customary gratuity to the tour manager at the end of the tour.

Conditions

Registration and deposits: An initial deposit of $200 per person is required to secure definite reservations. We regret that no space may be reserved without a deposit.

Final payment: Balance of payment is due 60 days prior to departure.

Cancellations and refunds: Full refund is guaranteed for all cancellations received up to 61 days prior to departure. Cancellations must be made in writing; verbal cancellations, whether in person or by telephone, are not valid. For cancellations received 60 days or less prior to departure, cancellation charge will reflect any cancellation penalties incurred by airlines, hotels, ground operators, and other suppliers involved. A special optional trip insurance policy will be available to protect against such cancellations.

Tour price: Price of the tour is premised on a minimum of 25 adult, paying participants. Should the final membership fall below this number, LSI Travel Agency, Inc. reserves the right to increase the tour price. All rates for land arrangements are based on the value of the U.S. Dollar in relation to foreign currencies and on tariffs in effect on    (date)   , and are subject to adjustment prior to departure. Airfares are also subject to change.

Special note regarding airfare: In an effort to keep the tour price as reasonable as possible, a special APEX (Advance Purchase Excursion) airfare is being utilized and the tour price is calculated accordingly. This special fare can save one a great deal; however, it does not permit the flexibility of a full-fare air ticket and changes or cancellations in flight plans after the ticket is issued can cost a $50 per person airfare cancellation fee.

Responsibility: This tour is operated by LSI Travel Agency, Inc. by contracting for services from other suppliers. LSI Travel Agency, Inc. and/or its agents, acting as agents for the tour members, shall be responsible to tour members for supplying services and accommodations as set forth in the brochure, except to the extent such services and accommodations cannot be supplied due to force of nature, delays, or other causes beyond the control of LSI Travel Agency, Inc. If the service and accommodations set forth in the tour brochure cannot be supplied due to delays or other causes beyond the control of LSI Travel Agency, Inc., best efforts will be made to supply comparable services and accommodations. If such services and accommodations cannot be provided due to the above reasons, or if the services are not used due to voluntary omission by the tour member, refunds will not be granted.

By becoming a member of the tour, a participant waives any claim against LSI Travel Agency, Inc. for any damages to or loss of property, or any injury to or death of persons due to any act of negligence of any hotels or any other persons rendering any of the services and accommodations included in the ground portion of the itinerary. LSI Travel Agency, Inc. shall not be responsible for any delays, substitution of equipment, or any act or omission whatsoever by any air or surface carrier, its agents, servants, and employees; and a participant, by becoming a member of the tour, waives any claim arising therefrom.

No refund will be made for any unused portion of the tour unless agreed to in writing prior to departure of the tour. The right is reserved to decline to accept or retain any person as a member of the tour at any time. While no deviations from the printed itinerary are anticipated, the right is reserved to make changes in the itinerary with or without notice where deemed necessary, with the mutual understanding that any additional expense will be paid by the individual passenger. LSI Travel Agency, Inc. reserves the right to cancel the tour prior to departure if circumstances permit it, in which case full refund will constitute full settlement to the passenger. The price of the tour is based on tariffs and exchange rates in effect at the time of printing the brochure and is subject to change in the event of any change in tariffs and exchange rates.

The issuance and acceptance of tickets and vouchers shall be deemed to be consent to the above conditions. The air carriers and their agents and affiliates shall not be held responsible for any act, omission, or event during the time passengers are not on board aircraft or air carrier conveyances. The passenger contract ticket in use by the airlines, steamship lines, and/or other common carriers concerned, when issued, shall constitute the sole contract between the carrier and the purchaser of this tour and/or the passenger. The services of any IATA carrier may be used for this tour, and the transportation within the United States may be provided by any member carrier of the Airline Reporting Corporation.

Printed 5/26/85

# 4
# Negotiating and Booking the Tour

The airfare has been selected, the itinerary designed around it, and a rough day-by-day plan of the tour sketched out. The next step is to actually book the reservations to see if the desired itinerary will really work out. Very often, schedules look wonderful on paper but when they are put into operation the itinerary may not work out as planned.

So, where does one start? Which comes first, the air reservation or the hotel? What if the tour planner books everything at once, and then discovers that the air reservations are available but the hotel space cannot be confirmed? What if the hotel rooms are available, but there is no space on the flights desired? In short, what if all the pieces of the puzzle do not fall into place easily—as they most likely will not?

**Start One Year in Advance**

As mentioned earlier, one rule of thumb, which should avert some problems later, is to begin no later than one year in advance. Of course, there may be times when an exception is required. There may be occasions when the passengers are all presold and, therefore, the lead time for sales is not necessary. But ninety-nine percent of the time a minimum of one year's lead time will be necessary to get all reservations and prices confirmed, the costing and pricing done properly, and to have adequate time for promotion and sales.

**Booking Order**

The usual booking order is:

1. air
2. hotels
3. reception ground operators and finishing touches

Of course, with all rules there are exceptions. One exception would be if a cruise is included in the itinerary. If there is, then this should be booked first to be certain that the desired cruise date is available. Once the cruise space is confirmed, the balance of the itinerary can be built around it.

A similar situation would exist if working around a convention date and the convention hotel were crucial to the tour. In that case the hotel should be reserved first and then the air reservations and other arrangements made. If working around a major sporting event or show, it would be necessary to confirm that the tickets were available, and then plan the itinerary around the dates or other requirements. For example, to obtain Carnival in Rio parade seats, it might be necessary to agree to buy a one-week package tour from the Brazilian reception operator. If the agent has already scheduled a group to be in Rio three days only, it would be necessary either to throw away the other four days or totally rework the itinerary.

Another exception would be the case in which the hotel reservations are booked through a reception ground operator overseas. In that case, steps two and three would be combined; the agent would then book the hotels and a reception ground operator in one step.

If an agency had designed a tour that includes a cruise, and if the agency had decided to book the hotels direct, the booking order would look like this:

1. cruise
2. air
3. hotels
4. reception ground operator and finishing touches

## Handling a Group Cruise

If this is the agency's first group, one of the easiest ways to begin is to book the group on a cruise. A cruise is nothing more than a preexisting floating tour package on which the agent may place a group. And cruise lines usually want group business. A cruise can also be included as an integral part of a tour—perhaps a Greek island cruise as part of a European tour, or a cruise to the Galápagos in a South American itinerary. A short cruise gives variety and pacing to an itinerary composed of nothing but flights, airport transfers, and motorcoach trips. Of course, cruises also have some disadvantages. Following are lists of the pros and cons of choosing to book the group on a cruise.

ADVANTAGES OF CRUISES

- Agents can block varying amounts of space, sell what they are capable of selling, and return any unsold space to the cruise line with no further obligation to fill the space.
- Agents can operate the trip even if they produce only a small volume of bookings. It is not necessary to cancel the entire tour because of only a few bookings.
- There is one easy booking source—simple to operate if an agent is unfamiliar with the intricacies of booking overseas hotels, sightseeing tours, guides, and transfers.
- Agencies probably can make as much money on a small group booked on a cruise as they could in handling an entire charter flight or other large-volume but small-markup project.
- Cruises are a popular product and the public is presold on cruising by such shows as "The Love Boat," through friends who have experienced cruising, and so forth.
- Travel agencies receive their commission quickly. When they pay the cruise line, they simply deduct their commission from the remittance.
- It is possible to negotiate with cruise lines for a free trip for the group's tour organizer.
- It is also possible to negotiate with cruise lines for special extras, such as a welcome-aboard cocktail party, a tour of the ship's bridge, engine room, or galley, wine served at dinner and other festive touches. This type of treatment sets the group apart from other passengers and gives tour participants an incentive to travel with the agency again.

- There is excellent potential for success and for happy passengers. If you select the right ship for the right clientele, you are almost certain to bring home a group of repeat clients.
- A cruise is seen as an all-inclusive vacation package incorporating transportation, accommodations, all meals, social activities, sports facilities, and entertainment features. Clients perceive a cruise as a product that permits them to have a preset vacation budget, without a great deal of unexpected expenses along the way.

However, despite the many advantages and the popularity of cruises, there are also a number of disadvantages. It is important to be aware of some of these disadvantages before undertaking a group cruise venture.

DISADVANTAGES OF CRUISES

- No autonomy. The group is getting the same trip, the same itinerary, as all of the other passengers. The only way to have the group feel special is to arrange for extra features on their behalf (as mentioned above), provide an escort or "name" leader, or arrange for a special onboard enrichment program of lectures, seminars, meetings at sea, and other activities.
- No flexibility. It is necessary to take the cruise as is—the dates, the ports, and the rates as scheduled by the cruise line. It is impossible to custom design the cruise to the individual wishes of the agency or one group.
- Not all groups are right for cruises. Although cruising is an excellent vacation product for many people, for the non-touristy individual, the person who wants to see one country in depth, the intellectual who wants to get off the beaten track, or the person who hates groups, a cruise is probably not the right product.
- An agency cannot mark up the cruise price as it would when packaging its own tour. It would be imprudent to do so, since participants could buy the cruise at its tariff price elsewhere. However, it is possible to package pre-and postcruise arrangements with some markup. These additional arrangements, when added to the cruise, make for a total package sold at a total package price.
- One is limited in the amounts of promotional funds or complimentary trips to those that can be negotiated from the cruise line, since the tariff price cannot be marked up to cover these items.

Sometimes a demanding tour organizer who insists on a salary or an honorarium or on taking the family along free will be a problem. There is no way to provide for these demands unless the cruise line will go along with them, or unless the additional expenses are absorbed out of the agency's earnings.

- Early closeout. Many cruises fill quite early. Therefore, the cruise lines will pressure the agent to sell the group space early and return all unsold space space early. This precludes late promotion and late sales. The best that can be expected is to be able to hold the space up to ninety days before cruise departure. In the case of lightly-booked cruises or off-season cruises, a cruise line might tend to be more accommodating and permit the agency to hold the space up to sixty days before departure, and in some cases even thirty days.

- Cruise lines will not allot all the space in the same category or at a single price level. The agency will be assigned a variety of cabins in a range of prices. When a cruise is sold by itself, this range is not a problem. Clients may be offered a variety of cabin categories at various price levels, letting the client choose. However, when packaging a short cruise as an integral part of a longer tour, the variety of cabins and prices can make it difficult to standardize the total tour price.

- The cruise line will keep passengers' names and addresses and will solicit them directly after the cruise, as part of a "club" made up of their past passengers. Some cruise lines will automatically commission the agency if the passengers book another cruise direct with the cruise line, provided the booking does not come from another travel agency. Other cruise lines will simply advise agents that they are soliciting their clients and will leave it up to the agency to get the booking. They will not commission the agency if the client books direct with the line. Be sure to ask the cruise line its policy before booking a group—business is hard enough to come by without having it intercepted by aggressive cruise lines. Of course, many cruise lines do not accept direct bookings.

## Negotiating with the Cruise Line

The key word in dealing in cruises for groups is *negotiate*. The primary role of the travel agency representative will be that of a go-between, trying to obtain the most favorable arrangements for the group. The clue to successful negotiation is to go into any negotiating sessions well informed about the cruise line, its ships, and its competitors, but at the same time to be open-minded and without any preset ideas of demanding a specific sailing date.

The best starting strategy is to investigate several cruise lines and several itineraries. It is necessary, first, to determine the length of cruise and price range suitable for the particular group. It is also important to know the "personality" of the ship under consideration. Does it cater to honeymooners? Swingers? The over-sixty crowd? The best way to find out the answers to such questions is to ask. If the agency staff is not familiar with the various lines and ships available, an excellent source of information is Cruise Lines International Association (CLIA). CLIA will be happy to provide information on its member carriers and also provide information to help the agent calculate such important factors as cabin size, ratio of crew to passengers, and other important information to help sell and promote cruises. CLIA's information is thorough, even down to the history of a given ship. For example, how many travel agents automatically know that the *Pearl of Scandinavia* formerly was the *Finnstar,* that Royal Cruise Line is of Greek registry, or that Sun Line markets its cruises both in the United States and Europe and so carries an international passenger list (as compared to some lines that market strictly within the United States and carry an all-American passenger list).

Once several cruise lines have been selected, the next step is to contact them and request written information on their policy for group bookings. It is essential to read the policy and understand it before starting negotiations.

The best strategy is to enter negotiations by asking the cruise line to indicate which sailings *they* need help in promoting and thereby getting a selection of the lightly-booked sailings (known as "soft sailings" in the trade) from which to choose. Do not accept an unpopular sailing date or an inferior ship just to strike a deal. Often, however, by having the flexibility to be able to move dates by several weeks you can both accommodate the cruise line and perhaps gain more benefits for the agency, as well as some tempting amenities for the group members.

SOME BENEFITS OF CRUISES FOR THE AGENCY AND ITS CLIENTS

1. *Higher commissions.* Although the standard commission in a cruise is 10 percent, a cruise line might be willing to offer up to an additional 5 percent, or even more to large volume wholesalers.

This could be straight commission, expressed as 15 percent across the board (15 percent on all bookings from the first to last). Or it could be 10 percent commission plus a 5 percent override, retroactive to the first booking, but payable only after the group has reached a specific number of bookings—for example, 25 bookings. This means that if the group finalized at 20 participants, the agency would receive only the basic 10 percent commission. An override is not something to be counted on; but it is an incentive.

Some cruise lines may offer a percentage override, others a flat dollar amount per person. Which is more advantageous: a $25 per head flat fee or a 1 percent override? This depends on the fare. For example, if the average cruise fare is $4,000, a 1 percent override of $40 is better than a $25 per person flat fee. Conversely, if the cruise fare is $1,500 then one would be better off with a flat $25 per person. Do not be misled by percentages. Remember that old saying: 100 percent of zero is still zero.

Another approach that some, but not all, cruise lines use is to offer the agency a percentage reduction for the group. Although cruise lines frown on the word discount, this is what it really is—a reduced rate for members of an affinity group. This is an offer that can be used effectively as a sales tool in the sales presentation to the group. Any group likes to feel special and know that it is getting a lower rate than nongroup passengers.

2. *More generous tour leader complimentaries.* On a popular sailing, the cruise line might offer one complimentary berth for every forty bookings. But on a less popular cruise, the line might be willing to grant one complimentary berth for every ten bookings. This could be a decided advantage, particularly if the agency is faced with selling the cruise to an organization whose board of directors is looking for as many complimentaries as possible. Complimentaries can also be helpful in generating additional income since, in many cases, the agency has the option to sell them.

3. *Brochures or shells.* Many cruise lines have shells available from which the agency can develop its own brochure. Some lines also have standard brochures on which can be overprinted the name of the organization, the agency involved, and other basic information. With the high cost of producing original brochures, this help can mean sizable savings to the agency, especially so if it plans to circulate a large mailing list. Often the cruise line has photographs, graphics, deck plans, and other materials that can be used to help produce a professional-looking brochure or mailing

piece. Sometimes, if an agency prefers to develop an original brochure rather than use the standard shell, it can convince the line to pay a share of the production costs such as typesetting, artwork, and printing.

4. *Other promotional assistance.* This might take the form of cooperative advertising, sponsoring a cruise night, or sharing direct-mail expenses.

5. *An offer to waive early berth deposits.* This offer can be helpful to agencies in holding large blocks of space without the need to advance large deposits. Large deposits, of course, inhibit cash flow. Never hesitate to ask the cruise line to waive a deposit—at least to do so until clients' deposits start to come in. Whenever possible, try to work with clients' money, not the agency's.

6. *An amenity package for group members.* This package could consist of such items as champagne in the group members' cabins, a gift certificate good for drinks at the bar or a gift in the ship's boutique, a special welcome aboard cocktail party, or an offer to pay the expected tips to shipboard personnel on behalf of the group.

7. *Free meeting room space on board.* Meeting rooms make it possible to arrange seminars, classes, or enrichment lectures exclusively for the group. Most ships have a theater, and since this is often unused in the mornings many times it can be reserved for the group.

Perhaps after all of the negotiating it will appear that these extra benefits do not justify moving the group to a sailing or a departure date that is not best for the group. Some groups, such as teachers' groups, are confined to the academic year; teachers have to travel during the summer months, or during the Christmas break or spring break. In the case of a postconvention cruise, it will be necessary to search for a cruise that immediately follows the convention dates; the convention cannot usually be scheduled around the cruise date. But even then, when limited in the choice of dates, it is still possible to query several cruise lines and compare their respective offers to see which one will work best.

It is quite possible that the cruise line will want to know something about the agency's track record. The line will want to know what group cruise projects the agency has done before: destination, ship, price level, and degree of success. If the agency is a newcomer to group cruises then the line will want information on other types of groups the agency has handled, such as air/land tours. Bear in mind that the cruise line is taking something of a risk in setting aside a block of cabins on behalf of an agency it might never have worked with before. It will want to know something about the agency in whose hands it is placing its product. Similarly, the cruise line will want to know the travel history of the group: where they have traveled before, price level, and success or failure of their efforts.

Remember also that the economics of the times will play a role in the negotiations. If times are good, if many people are traveling and spending, or if there are few ships in a given geographical area, the market belongs to the seller, and probably the best the agency will be able to negotiate will be the cruise line's standard written group policy. But if people are not traveling frequently or spending heavily, or if there are too many ships cruising a given area (a phenomenon known as overtonnage), such as the Caribbean in winter or Alaska in summer, the chances of negotiating a better deal are improved.

THE CRUISE CONTRACT

When the cruise line has been selected and the sailing pinned down it is time to put everything in writing. Most cruise lines have a standard contract, but if for some reason the line selected does not have such a contract then it is essential to have a letter of agreement signed by both parties and spelling out in detail all of the contracted-for services. This contract should specify the following:

- date of departure and date of return
- name of ship
- name of itinerary and/or ports
- basic commission
- override commission, whether percentage or flat dollar amount, and number of paying passengers necessary to qualify for the override
- number of cabins in each price category
- complimentary policy—how many free for how many booked. Whether complimentaries are shared cabins or single-cabin basis, and whether cruise only or air/sea
- amenity package offered
- number of shells or overprinted brochures promised
- promotional expenditures promised to cover advertising, cruise nights, and so forth

## GROUP BOOKING ACKNOWLEDGEMENT
## GOLDEN ODYSSEY

**Royal Cruise Line**
One Maritime Plaza
San Francisco, California 94111
Reservations: (415) 788-0610
 (800) 792-2992 (California)
 (800) 227-4534 (Other U.S.)

Sales Office: (415) 956-7200
 (800) 622-0538 (California)
 (800) 227-5628 (Other U.S.)

Departure Date: July 11, 1985
Itinerary: Baltic
Sales Manager: Marlene Evans

| | | |
|---|---|---|
| Agency: LSI Travel Agency, INc. | Contact: Marty Sarbey de Souto | Phone #: 312-668-7410 | IATA #: 56321 |
| Street: 1234 Fifth Street | City: Anywhere | State: U.S.A. | Zip: 00921 |
| Organization: Lovers of Archaeology | Address: % Elaine Whittaker, 167 Rose Court, Kansas City, Missouri 64106 | | |

**Stateroom Allocation**

| Category | Type | Deck | |
|---|---|---|---|
| 1 | Deluxe Suite | Riviera | |
| 2 | Deluxe Outside | Marina/Riviera | |
| 3 | Deluxe Outside | Marina | 2 |
| 4 | Deluxe Outside | Laguna | 2 |
| 5 | Deluxe Outside | Marina | 5 |
| 6 | Deluxe Outside | Laguna | 5 |
| 7 | Deluxe Outside | Coral | 5 |
| 8 | Deluxe Outside | Laguna | 5 |
| 9 | Deluxe Outside | Coral | 4 |
| 10 | Deluxe Inside | Marina | 4 |
| 11 | Deluxe Inside | Laguna | 2 |
| 12 | Deluxe Inside | Coral | 1 |
| | **Total Staterooms** | | 35 |

Lower category cabin space will not be released without a fair proportion of higher category sales

**Promotion Arrangements**
Estimated Date of Mailing/Promotion: October 11, 1984
Promotion Review Date: November 11, 1984
Allocation Option Date: April 11, 1985
Unsold Block Space will be released as of this date
Quantity/Type of Brochures: 8,000 our overprints
Type of Postage: bulk rate, at our expense
Printing: at our expense
Mailhouse: at our expense
Advertising: will co-op 3 ads in "Lovers of Archaeology" magazine, not to exceed $600 commitment by RCL.

**Remarks**
(1) Welcome cocktail party on board courtesy of RCL.
(2) Commission: 10% + 3% override retroactive to booking #1 when group reaches 25.
(3) Complimentary concessions: 30+1, 45+2 air/sea basis. Note tips, shore excursions, and incidentals at escorts' own expense.
(4) Reserved room space for two onboard lectures -- time and room to be determined later.

**Conditions**
Confirmed bookings must be accompanied by a $400 deposit per person, within 7 days of date confirmed. Full payments are required 60 days prior to departure. If not fully paid by due date, bookings are subject to cancellation. Within the 60 day period to departure, standard cancellation policy applies.

AGREED UPON THIS 11th DAY OF July 19 84

BY John Jones Approved Max Smith
 Director of Passenger Operations
BY Marty Sarbey de Souto, CTC TITLE Reservations Manager
 Travel Agent

RETURN TOP COPY/RETAIN SECOND FOR YOUR FILES.

**Figure 4.1** A typical cruise line contract. (This is a sample only and does not reflect Royal Cruise Lines policy.)

- option/review dates by which time percentage of unsold space must be turned back to the cruise line
- deposit requirements—amounts and due dates
- final payment dates
- whether or not shore excursion package, if presold, is commissionable

Be sure to review the contract carefully, correct any errors, and write in anything missing. It is quite possible that something promised by the sales department was not communicated to the reservation department issuing the contract, so it is important to call any omissions to the cruise line's attention. When all is agreed and in written form a copy of the contract should be signed and returned to the cruise line; another copy should be retained in the file. But before filing it away be sure to note all option dates on the master calendar so that no important payment or review date will be overlooked. See Figure 4.1 for an example of a cruise line contract.

**Handling Group Air Reservations**

As described in chapter 3, it is important to check airfares with several carriers before starting to plan the itinerary. Once the airfare has been checked, the itinerary planned, and the flights selected, it is time to begin booking the actual space.

The first step is to confer with the airline account executive (also called a sales representative) at several air carriers and determine which carrier the agency wishes to use as the principal carrier on this tour. This carrier will be designated as the coordinating carrier (also called the originating carrier). The coordinating carrier will book all the group air space, whether it is online space on its own airline, or interline space on other carriers. It is the coordinating carrier that will quote the airfare, advise of any flight changes, issue the itinerary (IT) number for the brochure, and register the tour number with the International Air Transport Association (IATA). It is the coordinating carrier that will provide shells for the brochure, assist in a promotional evening, and on whose ticketing plate the group's air tickets will be issued.

The coordinating carrier does more than book the air. It becomes, in effect, a cosponsor, a working partner in the tour venture. It is important to have a good working relationship with this carrier and its personnel so that the parties have a sense of mutual respect and an understanding of each other's role.

When selecting an air carrier, there are some important questions to consider.

- Does the carrier have good inflight service, scheduling, and equipment, or is the agency compelling the group to accept inferior passenger service in order to earn a higher commission or strike a better deal? If the service of two carriers is comparable, it is to the agency's advantage to accept the best deal possible. But the clients can be expected to be angry about enduring a five-hour wait at Heathrow Airport in London enroute to Geneva if they discover there was a direct flight to Geneva five hours earlier on another airline. Obviously, such a situation, no matter what financial savings it offers, is to be avoided.
- Does the airline have a group desk with which to work directly or will it be necessary to work through a go-between or deal with a one-person local sales office?
- Does the airline have fast and accurate airfare quote capacity or is its rate desk piled high with a three-week backlog?
- Will the airline provide group flight confirmations and fare quotes in writing willingly? (It is essential to have a written fare quotation in the file before publishing a brochure.)
- Does the agency staff work well with the personnel at the airline selected? Key personnel on whom the agency will depend will be the account executive from the sales office as well as people on the group and rate desks.
- Does the airline have suitable and attractive shells available in the quantities the agency will need? Travel agencies and tour operators have been known to select a certain carrier solely because of its attractive shells or other promotional pieces.
- Does the airline want the business on this particular routing and at this particular time of the year? Or does the airline give the impression that, since this is the peak season, group business is not needed for a route that is already heavily booked? Does it appear that the airline is not interested in booking low-cost APEX-fared passengers or does not want short-sector bookings?
- Can the agency negotiate an override commission or other form of supplemental income and promotional monies with the carrier?

## Booking Air Reservations

The golden rule of group tour operations is *put it in writing*. It is also essential to *get it in writing*. Start by requesting all of the group space in writing from the coordinating carrier. At present, it is not possible to book group space through an automated reservation system, but this policy may very well change in the future. Although many airlines are willing to take group bookings on the telephone, this is not a good idea unless the phone call is followed up with a letter.

Since each airline has its own system for handling group reservations, it is best to check with the airline account executive first to ascertain if the booking letter should be sent to the sales department or direct to the group desk. In some cases, sending a letter to the account executive may delay it, since he or she may be out on sales calls and may not forward it to the group desk promptly. In other cases, the airline may require that the booking letter go through the sales department before it can be processed by the group desk. (Note that it is important to distinguish between *group desk* and *tour desk*. The group desk is the department that will process the group air reservations; the tour desk is the department that sells that particular airline's inhouse tour packages.) If contacting the group desk directly, be sure to send a copy of the letter to the account executive as a courtesy.

Before writing to the airline, however, it is important to prepare either a reservation card or a group air booking form. See Figure 4.2 for an example of a booking form. A group air booking form is used inhouse to record replies from the controlling airline as they are called in to the agency. It is quite likely that the airline will call today with confirmations on one or two flights, tomorrow with another, and so forth. These can easily be recorded manually on the master group air booking form as they are called in, since the written recap of space confirmation probably will not arrive until considerably later when the bulk of the flights are confirmed. Note that this form should contain spaces to record flight dates, flight numbers, and total number of seats desired on each flight sector. It should also have a space to record the date each flight is confirmed, the name of the airline employee confirming the space, and the exact status of each flight: confirmed, waitlist, unable, and so forth.

As a check list it is important to include all of the following information in the booking letter to the airline:

- name of tour, departure date, and year—at the top of the letter for easy identification.

NEGOTIATING AND BOOKING THE TOUR 61

**Figure 4.2** Sample group air booking form and control sheet.

- number of seats and class of travel for each sector.
- airfare status (APEX, GIT, and so forth). Many flights are capacity controlled; there may be space on the plane but not in the fare category requested.
- flight by flight, a list of each flight desired, using the proper two-letter airline codes and three-letter airport codes. For example PA 001Y SA 02 APR JFK/LHR 19:15/08:05+1. (Translation: Pan American flight No. 1, economy class, on Saturday, April 2nd from New York, Kennedy airport, to London, Heathrow airport, departing at 7:15 p.m., arriving at 8:05 a.m. the following date, April 3rd.).

Note that flight numbers are expressed in three digits, even if two of them are zeros. Airport codes are used, not city codes. This becomes extremely important in cities that may have more than one airport, such as London with Heathrow and Gatwick, New York with Kennedy, La Guardia, and nearby Newark. Even worse is the case of Iguassú Falls; the code IGU means Iguassú, Brazil, whereas IGR means Iguassú, Argentina located on the opposite side of the falls, and no easy feat to get across when the waters are running high.

It is important to use the twenty-four-hour time system. Although many airlines and computers now are on twelve-hour times, the professional travel agent knows that only the twenty-four-hour time system can truly guard against what could turn out to be a mammoth error. If the agency staff is unfamiliar with this system it is essential to have them take the time to learn it. Figure 4.3 illustrates the twenty-four-hour clock.

If several legs of the itinerary are via surface (train, ship, or motorcoach), it is necessary to indicate this in the booking letter so that there are no open sectors in the continuity of the flight itinerary.

At the end of the letter be sure to indicate what the airline should do next. It should never be assumed that the airline will automatically send a written confirmation and fare quotation; ask for it. The airline should also be asked to put in writing such things as the basic commission, overrides, shells, promotional assistance, policy on tour conductor tickets (complimentaries), and whatever else is pertinent.

It is important to have all details confirmed in writing in the file before starting to promote the tour so that there are no misunderstandings later. It also develops good work habits to have neat, clean, and orderly files so that anyone on the staff can pick up the file and

NEGOTIATING AND BOOKING THE TOUR                63

| TIME | 24-HOUR TIME | PRONUNCIATION |
|---|---|---|
| 1:00 A.M. | 01:00 | oh one hundred |
| 2:00 A.M. | 02:00 | oh two hundred |
| 3:00 A.M. | 03:00 | oh three hundred |
| 4:00 A.M. | 04:00 | oh four hundred |
| 5:00 A.M. | 05:00 | oh five hundred |
| 6:00 A.M. | 06:00 | oh six hundred |
| 7:00 A.M. | 07:00 | oh seven hundred |
| 8:00 A.M. | 08:00 | oh eight hundred |
| 9:00 A.M. | 09:00 | oh nine hundred |
| 10:00 A.M. | 10:00 | ten hundred |
| 11:00 A.M. | 11:00 | eleven hundred |
| 12:00 NOON | 12:00 | twelve hundred |
| 1:00 P.M. | 13:00 | thirteen hundred |
| 2:00 P.M. | 14:00 | fourteen hundred |
| 3:00 P.M. | 15:00 | fifteen hundred |
| 4:00 P.M. | 16:00 | sixteen hundred |
| 5:00 P.M. | 17:00 | seventeen hundred |
| 6:00 P.M. | 18:00 | eighteen hundred |
| 7:00 P.M. | 19:00 | nineteen hundred |
| 8:00 P.M. | 20:00 | twenty hundred |
| 9:00 P.M. | 21:00 | twenty=one hundred |
| 10:00 P.M. | 22:00 | twenty=two hundred |
| 11:00 P.M. | 23:00 | twenty=three hundred |
| 12:00 MIDNIGHT | 24:00 | twenty=four hundred |

Examples:

(1) 8:05 P.M. would be "twenty oh five"
(2) 2:15 P.M. would be "fourteen fifteen"
(3) 11:59 P.M. would be "twenty-three fifty-nine"  (Note that many midnight flights are listed this way to be sure of date)
(4) 9:10 A.M. would be "oh nine ten"

Notes Regarding Crossing Dateline or Time Zones

(1) Plus one (+1) means one date later. For example, if one says "The flight leaves Tuesday at 14:00 (fourteen hundred) and arrives at 17:00+1, this means it arrives at 5:00 P.M. on Wednesday

(2) Minus one (-1) means one date earlier. For example, if one says "The flight leaves Tuesday at 14:00 (fourteen hundred) and arrives at 17:00-1, this means it arrives at 5:00 P.M. on Monday

All flight times listed in airline schedules always are the local times observed in the cities specified.

**Figure 4.3**  The twenty-four hour clock.

work from it without having to ask a lot of questions. It is conceivable that one person might negotiate and book the tour but then turn it over to someone else to operate, or that the person who booked the tour might be ill or out of the office. Hand-scribbled notes and word-of-mouth promises from the airline should be avoided.

LSI TRAVEL AGENCY, INC.

Date

Mr. Jeffrey Whelan
Trans World Airlines

RE: Rosemont Country Club
European Highlights Tour
Departing Sept. 6, 1985

Dear Jeffrey:

This will reconfirm our telephone request today for the following group space, 32 seats, economy class, APEX fare basis, throughout:

```
TW 746   Fri.   Sep. 06   ORD/JFK   12:50/15:57
TW 814   Fri.   Sep. 06   JFK/AMS   18:45/07:05+1
------   Surface------   AMS/CDG   ------------
AF 630   Fri.   Sep. 13   CDG/FCO   08:35/10:35
TW 845   Mon.   Sep. 16   FCO/JFK   11:00/14:10
TW 757   Mon.   Sep. 16   JFK/ORD   16:30/17:56
```

Now, here's what we'll ultimately need from your office to "wrap up" this project:

(1) Space confirmation, in writing.
(2) Current fare quote, in writing - both for ORD and JFK originating passengers.
(3) IT number.
(4) Your policy on override commissions.
(5) Sample shells (after seeing what you have available we'll either decide to use your shell or do our own original brochure. We'll need 3,000 shells, if we do decide to use them, and would need to know the cost, if any).
(6) Policy on tour conductor.

We look forward to working with TWA on this group and hope the tour will sell well.

Cordially,

Marty Sarbey de Souto, CTC
Group Manager

MFS/s

**Figure 4.4** Airline booking letter.

An example of a properly prepared booking letter will be found in Figure 4.4.

NEGOTIATING WITH THE AIRLINES.

Before deregulation, airfares were standardized on all carriers, and negotiating was nonexistent, at least as it related to commissions and overrides. Airlines did help tour operators and travel agencies by "buying" large quantities of nonexistent brochures, supposedly for airline promotional use. Many other under-the-table schemes were elaborately conceived to circumvent the rules and regulations.

Today, this situation no longer exists. Today negotiations are all open and up front. An agency can negotiate almost anything. But bear in mind that the agency representative will probably be going up against experienced airline personnel who are much more sophisticated at negotiating than many travel agents. Therefore, before going into negotiations with an airline, it is important to be familiar with some of the terms and concepts of group travel.

*Upfront monies.* This term refers to money that an airline may be willing to pay the agency up front (before the fact) to assist in promotional expenses—that is monies paid to the agency before any sales result. Obviously, this is more useful for the agency than after-the-fact monies, such as override commissions. If an airline is giving an agency up-front help, it is sharing the risk; if the tour sells well, both benefit; if it fails, the airline loses, too, as it already has expended the money, just as the agency has, on a lost cause. If the airline is putting money up front, then it can be more demanding of the agency. For example, it can insist that the promotional piece be mailed by a certain date, or that it have sole occupancy of the envelope.

*Override commission.* This term can be confusing as there actually are two overrides involved in an air booking. If an agency sells an international air ticket without an accompanying tour package, the agency receives a base commission of 8 percent and deducts this when making its weekly ticket sales report. If the air ticket is issued in conjunction with a bona fide tour package and an assigned IT number is written on the ticket, the agency receives not only the base 8 percent commission but an additional 3 percent override, for a total of 11 percent. The agency also deducts this additional 3 percent when making its weekly ticket sales report. The total 11 percent is paid on the full gross value of the ticket, including all sectors, regardless of which carriers are involved as interline carriers.

In addition, it is now possible to negotiate with a carrier for a further override. The amount may vary from airline to airline. In some cases it may be granted as a percentage and in other cases it may be a per-passenger flat dollar amount, such as $25 a head.

This second type of override is not deducted from the weekly airline sales report. The sponsoring airline pays it separately, directly to the agency, after the tour has returned home and there is proof that the group actually did travel on the flights ticketed. The airline may require that the agent sign a contract before the tour is promoted. It is important to find out if a contract for this override commission is required. It should never be assumed that once the tour is over the agency can ask the airlines for an override commission that was not agreed upon earlier. This override usually is paid on the net online revenue only, not on the gross price of the ticket and not on the sectors flown by other airlines.

Let us assume that the agency is working with an Around South America itinerary at a per person airfare of $1,000, using Varig Brazilian Airlines as the originating carrier. Varig has offered to pay the agency a 5 percent override on the net online Varig flight segments. Out of the $1,000 total gross fare, $600 is on Varig; the other $400 is on interline carriers such as Avianca, Argentine Airlines, and so forth. The override would be calculated as follows:

| | |
|---|---:|
| Value of air ticket | $1,000 |
| Flights of other carriers | −400 |
| Value of Varig's flights | 600 |
| Less basic 11% commission on $600 (8% + 3%) | −66 |
| Net value of Varig's flights | $ 534 |

The agency is paid 5 percent on the $534 figure, or $26.70 per passenger. This is quite different from 5% on the $1,000 gross ticket value, which would have been $50 per person.

CHECKING THE CONFIRMATIONS

Once the confirmation of space and the rate quote are received they must be examined carefully. Information must be doublechecked to make sure the flights confirmed are those requested and that the times of departure and arrival are as requested. Also to be checked are option dates and any special sales cutoff date, special deposit, or ticketing date pertinent to the specific airfare. Before filing the airline correspondence away, all important dates must be recorded on the master calendar for action on the appropriate date. Even if the airline does not require that certain dates be adhered to, it is wise to write on the calendar the 90/60/30 day review dates so that the agency can take the initiative and contact the airline group desk with a progress report rather than waiting for them to follow up. Such efficiency sets a professional tone.

## Handling Group Hotel Space

Once the flights are confirmed (or at least most of them), the next step in the booking order is to obtain hotel reservations. There are four ways to book group hotel space:

- Booking each hotel directly, by letter, telex, or telephone.
- Booking through a hotel chain's sales office such as Hilton, Sheraton, Intercontinental, and so forth—if the hotel desired belongs to such a chain.
- Booking though a hotel representative (also called a hotel "rep"), such as John A. Tetley, Utell International and so forth.
- Booking with the overseas reception operators who will be handling the tour in each country and having them include the hotels as part of their package in that geographical area.

If the itinerary is complicated, with fifteen to twenty different hotels, booking methods might be combined within the same tour; certain hotels might be booked directly and others not. Following are some of the advantages and disadvantages of the different methods.

ADVANTAGES AND DISADVANTAGES
OF CONTACTING THE HOTEL DIRECTLY

Following are some of the advantages of direct contact with the hotel:

- Information comes directly from the source. There is a confirmation on hotel letterhead signed by an hotel official. There can be no dispute later as to whether the hotel space was confirmed or not; the letter proves it.
- Rapport and agency reputation are established with the hotel. The hotel people will grow to know the agency. Your group will not be just tour number 6704 of a given wholesaler.
- There is no middle man to interpret details (or perhaps misinterpret them). The agency will not have to depend on someone else for information on whether rates are net or gross, if breakfast is continental style or American style, when deposit is due, or what the hotel's complimentary policy is.

Disadvantages of contacting the hotel directly include the following:

- Staff time is taken up in corresponding with each hotel property, not only at time of booking, but later when submitting booking reports, final rooming lists, payment, and other items.
- There can be waiting time for answers, particularly if done by mail. If space is requested by telex, waiting time is not such a problem.
- The hotel may not know the agency and may not give priority on space or its best rates.

- If the hotel people do not know the agency's track record, they may demand more in terms of early deposits, final payments, and option cutoff dates than they would ask of an established group operator.

ADVANTAGES AND DISADVANTAGES
OF USING A CHAIN SALES OFFICE

When a hotel chain's sales office is used, the agency can gain the following advantages:

- The agency can build credibility with a given chain. Even though the agency may be totally unknown to the management of the Sydney Hilton, were it to contact that property directly, it might have booked the Hong Kong Hilton heavily in the past. The agency's record would be known at the Hilton International sales office. As a solid client of Hilton, the international entity, the agency would have more influence.
- Speed. One phone call does it all. The hotel chain's sales office will telex its individual property and get back with a quick answer. (Most hotel chain offices do not have a sell-and-report policy for immediate confirmation of group space. Even they have to go to the specific property in question to request group space.)
- Answers are available to questions about the property. The chain office should know its own properties well enough to answer questions on such things as location, meeting room facilities, and current rates. They may, however, have to telex the property for advance rates or for answers to more detailed questions.

The disadvantages of using a hotel chain's sales office include the following:

- The decision to use a hotel chain's sales office often means that the agency is limiting itself to the larger, more expensive hotels—hotels that can support an elaborate marketing and reservation system. Perhaps the property that might be best for the group will not be selected, in the interests of speed and efficiency.
- Even if rooms are booked initially with the hotel chain office locally, later correspondence will nevertheless be with the hotel personnel at the property itself; probably with the sales manager or the front office manager. Once the group space is confirmed, booking status reports, deposits, or final rooming assignments would not be made through the chain office.

ADVANTAGES AND DISADVANTAGES
OF BOOKING THROUGH A HOTEL REP

The following are some advantages of using a hotel rep:

- Speed is an advantage if the rep, in turn, books the space by telex or phone. (If all the rep does is write a letter, then the agency might as well book directly.)
- The rep can answer questions about the property if he or she really knows the property well.

There are also some disadvantages of booking through a hotel rep, such as the following:

- Many reps act on behalf of so many different hotels that they are not truly knowledgeable about the details of any one of their properties. Similarly, many are so busy handling independent bookings that they are not geared to group bookings, and they do little more than act as a go-between for the agency.

ADVANTAGES AND DISADVANTAGES
OF BOOKING WITH A RECEPTION OPERATOR

Many agencies find it best to let their overseas reception ground operator simply include the hotels as part of their overall package of sightseeing, transfers, and so forth in their country. This is particularly convenient in rural areas. An agency representative may not know the pros and cons of a hotel in, for example, interior Brazil, whereas he or she may know the hotels in Rio. If it is a crucial time of the year (New Year's Eve in Acapulco, Carnival in Rio, the Olympics), the only chance of getting hotel space may be through a reception ground operator who already has large blocks of space reserved for his own packages.

Booking hotel space through a reception operator has the following advantages:

- It may be the *only* chance of getting space at certain key times of the year.
- Overseas operators know the local properties better; they have probably developed rapport with the right personnel at each hotel; and know which hotels are appropriate for which clientele.
- Overseas operators can monitor the reservations. If it appears that the hotel is heavily oversold, they can put in a deposit for you and keep the tour group's name in front of the hotel staff.

There are, of course, disadvantages of booking through a reception operator. These include:

- The time lag is the same as if booking the hotel directly.
- The ground operator will keep a portion of the commission, or if getting a net group rate perhaps will mark it up before quoting a price.
- You must have absolute trust in the reception ground operator and must be sure that you are working with a reputable and financially sound operator. Should the operator go out of business you will be in trouble.
- The reception ground operator may try to force you into using a hotel that you do not like—perhaps because the operator has a good relationship with that particular hotel, or perhaps because the company gets a good override from the hotel, or perhaps because the company owns the property itself. This happens more frequently than one might think.

CHOOSING THE RIGHT GROUP HOTEL

Regardless of what method is used to book the hotel space, it is important to select the right type of hotels for each specific group. Sometimes tour members are unpredictable. When they first buy the tour they may say that a hotel room is not really that important, that they are not going to do anything other than sleep in the room, and that all they really want is a clean and comfortable bed and a hot bath at the end of a weary day. Yet, these same clients sometimes end up complaining bitterly if the hotels do not live up to some subliminal expectations. Although clients may say that it is the "travel experience" that is most important, the two things that can most quickly ruin a trip are bad hotels and a bad motorcoach. So it is important to give serious consideration to the hotels that are selected before they are booked, and to evaluate them objectively and professionally. Here are some factors to be considered when deciding on a hotel for a group:

- Location. Is the hotel centrally located in town so that the tour members can get out to shops and cafes? A central location is not as important for a quick overnight stop. However, no one wants to be stuck in a motel alongside the highway for a three-day stay. If a hotel is out of town, take into account the coach availability and costs for transfers in and out of town.

- Type of clientele. Do families, swingers, honeymooners, or conventioneers frequent the hotel? Group members should feel comfortable and in step with the other hotel guests.
- Does the hotel cater to groups? Some hotels may surprise you. They may not want the group! Many groups are noisy. Groups mean suitcases lined up all over the lobby and massive check-ins and check-outs all at once.
- Image. Some hotels are just a place to sleep. Others are cozy country inns. Some are resorts and can be sold on the basis of their beach, golf course, or tennis courts. Some hotels are slick and modern; others pride themselves on an old-world atmosphere with afternoon tea served in the lobby
- Standard level of hotels throughout the tour. You do not want a wild swing from a luxury hotel one night to a rundown one the next. An ultramodern hotel and an old-world one might be included in the same itinerary, but they should be comparable in class.
- Lobby. Be sure that the hotels have lobbies; lobbies are a great place for a group to meet for sightseeing in the morning or to gather over a drink in the evening. Some less expensive hotels forgo lobby space in the interests of economy.
- Dining room/coffee shop. Some quite lovely hotels, particularly smaller ones, may not have dining facilities, requiring that the tour members go outside the property even for a cup of coffee. Similarly, many hotels may have a formal dining room requiring coat and tie, but no quick informal coffee shop.
- Dining plan. Many hotels require that guests take meals at the hotel. Acapulco during the winter season is an example. When planning a tour without meals, it is important to research the policy of mandatory meals first.
- Ease of baggage handling. Can the hotel move baggage quickly and easily? Some charming colonial hotels in Yucatán, for example, can handle a maximum of one busload of passengers at one time. If two busloads arrive at the same time, with only two small elevators and one bellman on duty, the group may not get its luggage until the wee hours.
- Motorcoach loading space. Is there a place for a tour bus to park to load and unload passengers and baggage? Trying to unload forty passengers with a traffic policeman threatening to ticket your driver can be unpleasant.

- Special facilities. If you plan to have a welcome cocktail party or briefing or farewell dinner, does the hotel have private dining rooms available? What about meeting rooms? If meetings or a convention are involved in the trip, are there necessary facilities—audiovisual, microphone, translators, photocopy, and secretarial services?

REQUESTING THE HOTEL SPACE

Once the first choice of properties has been selected and the decision has been made on how to book them, it is time to request the reservations. What information does the hotel need when the booking is made? And what information must be received from the hotel in its reply to allow the tour to be priced properly?

The booking letter should include the tour name, the arrival date, the departure date, and how much space is needed. It is important to specify not just the number of rooms or people but a breakdown of how many twin-bedded rooms and how many singles are required. In some cases, when families are involved, triples may be needed. The term *twin* and not *double* should be used. *Double* implies one double bed, which might be acceptable to some of the couples on tour, but not to two ladies who are strangers to each other.

The letter must specify the date of arrival and departure, termed the *in date* and the *out date*. It should say "in January 5, out January 7," not "January 5 to 7." Meal arrangements desired should be specified. It is also helpful to the hotel to advise them of the arrival flight number and the name of the reception ground operator who will be transferring the group to the hotel. That way, if the group is late, someone will be able to find out what happened to them.

It cannot be assumed that the hotel will automatically give all the needed answers in its reply. It is best to ask direct questions and delineate what answers the agency is expecting in the reply letter. See Figure 4.5 for an example of a hotel booking letter.

ANSWERS NEEDED FROM THE HOTEL

- Written confirmation of space, indicating how many twins and how many singles the hotel is confirming.
- Written confirmation of rates—rate per twin and per single, per night. (If the hotel does not have rates available for the following year the current rates should be requested and a percentage added to cover anticipated increase.)

```
                    LSI TRAVEL AGENCY, INC.

                                              Date

Mr. Hans Van der Hooten
Sales Manager
Hotel Krasnapolsky
Dam 9, 1012 JS
Amsterdam
The Netherlands

                    RE:  Rosemont Country Club
                         European Highlights Tour
                         Arriving: Sept. 7, 1985

Dear Hans:

We would like to book another tour with you.  Kindly confirm 14 twins,
4 singles for a maximum total of 32 passengers, for a three-night stay,
in Sept. 7, 1985 and out Sept. 10, 1985.

The group will arrive Amsterdam at 07:05 via TW 814 from New York and
will be transferred to your property by our ground operator in Amsterdam,
Transbus.

With your confirmation, please advise rates per twin and per single, and
specify if net or gross and if in U.S. dollars or Dutch guilders.  Also
indicate any taxes or service charges applicable, as well as your policy
regarding complimentary for the tour manager.

Rooms are to be reserved European Plan.  Any meals taken at the hotel
will be at passengers' own expense and should be charged to their personal
accounts, not to the master account.

Should you have your '85 room rates available now, we would appreciate them.
If not, please just confirm the space and give us current '84 rates for
now.

Thank you, and awaiting word ....

                                        Sincerely,

                                        Marty Sarbey de Souto, CTC
                                        Group Manager

MS/s
```

**Figure 4.5** Hotel booking letter.

- Clarification as to whether rates quoted are gross (commissionable) or net (noncommissionable) group rates. This is important, since all tour costings are done in net figures.
- Percentage of tax.
- Percentage of service charge, if any, to cover gratuities to hotel staff.

- Policy on complimentaries for tour manager(s). Remember that there is no standard worldwide policy; each hotel will have its own. Complimentaries can range from one free bed with each fifteen booked up to one free bed for each forty booked. Sometimes complimentaries are based on a free room for so many rooms booked, sometimes on one bed for so many beds booked. Sometimes the complimentary includes group meals; sometimes it does not. The exact nature of complimentaries should always be clarified.
- Any special services such as meeting rooms, welcoming drink and so forth.

Many hotels, when sending their confirmations, may specify review dates and payment dates. It is important when the confirmation comes in to record all those dates on the master calendar so that important review dates do not slip by. There may be option offerings; that is, a hotel may offer the space *on option* but expect the agent to reply by a certain option date, or sign a contract, or submit a payment to pick up the option. If these expectations are not met, the hotel may cancel the offer automatically.

Most larger hotels today will make clear what they expect; that is, when they want payment, when they need a rooming list, and so forth. But it would be wise to anticipate this at the time of requesting the space. For example, the agency letter might say: "Our company policy is to send you booking status reports at 90, 60, and 30 days prior to the group's arrival, with final rooming list and one night's deposit 30 days prior. Our tour manager will pay the balance of the account at time of check-out. If this arrangement is not satisfactory, please advise." This gives the agency credibility with the hotel as a serious operator. Nine times out of ten, the hotel will agree with the policy. However, there will always be times when the hotel will want one night's deposit at once to prove that the agency is serious, or, in some cases, such as the Olympics, it might even ask for a 50 percent upfront payment, but these times, fortunately, will be rare. Many hotels, particularly the large chain hotels, may reply with a formal contract. See Figure 4.6 for a sample hotel confirmation.

In communicating with hotels, the agency staff will encounter jargon peculiar to the hotel industry. Any unfamiliar terms should be looked up, to avoid misunderstanding. The standard glossary is *The Dictionary of Tourism,* edited by Charles J. Metelka, published by Merton House Travel and Tourism Publishers, Inc.

```
                    MARTY'S INTERNATIONAL HOTEL
                         Paris, France


                                                    Date

LSI Travel Agency
1234 Fifth Street
Anywhere, U.S.A.

                    RE:  Rosemont Country Club
                         Arriving September 10, 1985

Dear Ms. de Souto:

Thank you for your request of reservations for your Rosemont Country Club
group, 42 maximum for three nights in September 10, out September 13, 1985.
We are pleased to confirm 18 twins, 6 singles.

Our rates are 860 francs net per night per twin and 760 francs net per night
per single.  In addition there is an 18.6 VAT and 15% service.  Rates
include continental breakfast.

We will be happy to provide one complimentary for your escort with a
minimum of 40 paying passengers in the group.

An initial deposit in the amount of 10% is due March 10 with final payment
and rooming list 30 days before arrival.

With all best wishes for success in your sales endeavor.



                                        Sincerely,

                                        Pierre Lapin
                                        Pierre Lapin
                                        Sales Manager

PL/mg
```

**Figure 4.6**  A typical hotel group booking confirmation.

HOTEL TERMS YOU SHOULD KNOW

Most hotels will assume that the travel agent knows their terminology. Here are some of the most frequently used phrases:

- Rack rate. This is the highest rate for a hotel room, the rate published on their public rate sheet and posted in the rack for the guest who walks in the door. As a group operator you should *never* settle for this rate! It is for the individual guest.

- Gross. The rate before commission has been deducted. A gross rate assumes that the hotel pays a commission, usually 10 percent—but always check. For example, in Germany the commission can often be only 8 percent; in some areas, when business is slow, it can be 15 percent; and there are still many hotels that pay no commission.
- Net. Rate after commission has been deducted.
- Net net. Rate after any commission has been deducted and any taxes or service charges have been added.
- VAT (Value Added Tax). A government tax straight across the board on top of the rate quoted. Not applicable in all countries.
- Run of the house. A flat rate for all rooms used by the group. Theoretically, the hotel is supposed to assign the best available rooms in the house at the time the group checks in. This may mean that some of the group gets better rooms than others.
- Service charge. Refers to a flat fee charged to cover gratuities to hotel staff—room maids, bellmen, telephone operators, and others. In many hotels this is a mandatory charge and takes the place of tipping.
- European plan (EP). Without meals.
- American plan (AP) With three meals. Often the lunch and dinner will be restricted to a specific dollar amount or to meal coupons or to a given dining room.
- Modified American plan (MAP). Same as American plan, but usually without lunch. Born of beach resorts for guests who did not wish to come in from the beach and dress for lunch.
- Full pension. Full board, the European version of American plan. Usually implies continental breakfast rather than full American breakfast plus lunch and dinner on a *table d'hote* basis (set menu), often in a specified dining room and sometimes at a specified time when the group is served together.
- Half pension (also demi pension). Half board, the European version of modified American plan. Usually implies continental breakfast rather than full American breakfast plus choice of lunch or dinner with the same restrictions as full pension.

PRICING HOTEL ACCOMMODATIONS

The hotel may quote gross rates (commissionable) or net rates (non-commissionable). Regardless of which is quoted, it will be necessary to convert the rates into net rates, since net rates are the common denominator of the group tour business. Group tours are never costed on a gross basis. Three sample hotel rate quotations are outlined below.

*Sample One.* A hotel quotes a rate of $100 per night gross for a twin-bedded room, plus 10 percent tax and plus 15 percent service charge. They pay 10 percent commission. Therefore:

| | |
|---|---|
| Basic gross rate for two | $100 |
| 10% tax on $100 | 10 |
| 15% service charge on $100 | 15 |
| Total gross per night per twin | 125 |
| Less 10% commission | −10 |
| Net net rate per twin per night | 115 |

The figure of $115 is divided by two in order to arrive at the per person cost of $57.50 per night. If the group were staying at this hotel for three nights, the per person cost would be a total of $172.50. Remember that this is *net net;* that is, what the tour operator, will be charged for the client's hotel stay. This is not what the client pays the agency. For more complete information on costing see chapter 5.

*Sample Two.* A hotel quotes the agency a net rate from the outset and, therefore, it is not commissionable. The hotel quotes a rate of $90 per night per twin room plus 10 percent tax plus 15 percent service charge. Therefore:

| | |
|---|---|
| Basic net rate for two | $ 90.00 |
| 10% tax on $90 | 9.00 |
| 15% service charge on $90 | 13.50 |
| Total net net rate per twin per night | 112.50 |

The figure of $112.50 is divided by two in order to arrive at the per person cost of $56.25 per night. If the group were staying at this hotel for three nights, the per person cost would be a total of $168.75. Here again, this is *net net,* what the agency pay the hotel and not what the client pays the agency.

As one can see from the above examples, if the agency is quoted rates in gross, the client is costing the agency $57.50 per night. On the other hand, if the agency is quoted rates in net, the same client is costing the agency only $56.25 per night—a savings to the agency of $1.25 per night. It is always advantageous to secure quotations in net group rates whenever possible.

Experienced tour operators request quotations in the currency of the country concerned. That way, you can watch the dollar exchange rate and you can decide when the foreign exchange is advantageous to buy. A retail travel agency may not be accustomed to dealing with foreign exchange, since, for one or two clients, there rarely is sufficient profit to be made. But in dealing with groups, it often is possible to earn an extra few thousands of dollars per group just by carefully watching foreign exchange rates and buying foreign currency drafts at the appropriate time. Here is a sample quote in foreign currency.

*Sample Three.* A French hotel quotes 300 French francs per twin plus 8 percent tax and 20 percent service charge. At the time of the quotation, the exchange rate is eight francs to the United States dollar, therefore:

| | |
|---|---:|
| Basic net rate for two in French francs | fr300 |
| 8% tax | 24 |
| 20% service charge | 60 |
| Total per twin per night in francs | 384 |

To arrive at the per-person cost per night 384 French francs are divided by two, or 192 French francs. If the exchange rate were 8 francs to the dollar, the cost in United States dollars would be $24.00 net net rate per person per night.

If the group were staying at this hotel for three nights, the per person cost would be United States $72 net net.

**Booking Reception Operators**

Once both the air reservations and the hotel space are confirmed, it is time to fill in the gaps, to add the missing ingredient, to consult that company whose services can make or break a tour—the ground or reception operator. This is the company on whom the agency will depend for good motorcoaches or bad, knowledgeable and helpful local guides or mediocre ones, gracious and personalized services or just average ones. It is this company which will help the tour manager when there is a sick passenger, or when someone has lost a tourist card enroute, or when the tour manager needs help in reconfirming air reservations enroute. It is through this source that the agency books sightseeing, transfers, local events, special motorcoach charters, cultural activities, special meals, visits to museums, and night life. In short, the day-to-day operation of the tour in the field will depend very much on the quality of the reception ground operator selected. So, the least expensive is not necessarily the best choice; anyone can bid low for the first chance to operate a tour. But experience and competence are necessary to handle emergencies and unforeseen events; and these attributes are worth paying for.

If the agency has not worked with a reception operator previously, it might want to investigate the services of several operators in each city or country. Since it is often difficult to select an operator simply from a catalog listing or from a tariff, several sources should be checked.

The airline account executive may have useful information on who the top operators are. Consult particularly with the airlines that service the cities into which the group will be flying. KLM is certainly a better source of information on Dutch reception operators than Alitalia. Several of the leading United States wholesalers can be called and asked who their operator is in a particular city or country, and the various government tourist offices can be helpful. Once a list of names and addresses of operators is compiled, agency staff can write and request their tariffs and suggestions and ideas for the tour. Obviously an operator who replies quickly and seems to be responsive is the kind of operator that will be good to work with. Often, the tone of the operator's reply and the nature of the tariff will provide enough information for a decision. Did the company reply quickly? Did it provide easily understood rate breakdowns? Did it answer all the questions that were asked, so the tour planner can go on to cost and price the tour from the information sent? See Figure 4.7 for a sample excerpt from a reception operator's tariff.

A reception ground operator's tariff will outline specific services. However, existing services can be modified to meet the group's needs. There is no hard and fast rule that, just because Colonial City Tour No. 101 operates every morning at 9:00 a.m., it cannot operate at 2:00 p.m. for your group. But there also may be a good reason why a tour operates at a specific time—perhaps a certain museum on the tour is only open in the morning.

As in the letter to the hotels, the name of the tour, arrival date (including year), flight, and maximum anticipated number of passengers should appear at the top of the letter to the operator. The letter should describe the itinerary day by day, outlining the services that the operator is to provide: transfers, city tours, package tours outside the city, meals, and other features such as baggage tips, social events or cultural activities. See Figure 4.8 for an example of a booking letter to a ground operator.

It is essential to be explicit about what the company is expected to do, and what the agency will be responsible for. As an example, the reception operator should be told if the hotels have already been booked directly. Otherwise, the operator may assume that they are to book

# TREASURE TOURS INTERNATIONAL

Government Licence n. A 447

Head Office: **PARIS**    15 rue de l'Arcade, 75008 Paris, France
Telephone: (33) (1) 265 05 69 (Nightline 265 61 17).
Cables: Treasure Paris. Telex: 290415 F Treas.
Open 9am to 6pm Monday to Saturday.
Bankers: Union de Banques à Paris, place de la Madeleine 75008 Paris.
Account No. 80-137 855 004. Telex: 640664.

## TRANSFERS

**PARIS** — Arrival & departure

| | Individuals, Private Car | | | | | Private Coach | | | | |
|---|---|---|---|---|---|---|---|---|---|---|
| | 1 | 2 | 3 | 4 | 5 | 6/10 | 11/14 | 15/19 | 20/29 | 30/39 | 40+ |
| City Terminals (Bus/Rail/Air) | 280 | 165 | 135 | 115 | 105 | 124 | 87 | 69 | 59 | 50 | 45 |
| Airport Charles de Gaulle | 430 | 230 | 165 | 160 | 130 | 140 | 104 | 82 | 64 | 59 | 53 |
| Airport Orly | 340 | 190 | 150 | 140 | 120 | 140 | 104 | 82 | 64 | 59 | 53 |
| Charles de Gaulle to Orly airport or v.v. | 620 | 340 | 240 | 220 | 190 | 240 | 140 | 116 | 94 | 88 | 79 |

## SIGHTSEEING AND EXCURSIONS

**Paris Complete Tour**
Duration 3 hrs
No interior visits, but this is the most complete sightseeing itinerary. Daily departure by double-decker bus with taped commentary.
Departures at: 9.30 am, 10.00 am, 10.30 am, 11.00 am, 11.30 am, 1.00 pm, 1.30 pm, 2.00 pm, 2.30 pm, 3.00 pm
Winter: 10.00 am, 11.00 am, 1.30 pm and 2.30 pm
Rue de Rivoli, Place de la Concorde (stop), Tuileries, Louvre (stop), Carrousel, Pont Neuf, Ile de la Cité, Notre Dame Cathedral (stop), Hôtel de Ville, Place des Vosges, Place de la Bastille (stop), Ile St. Louis, Left Bank, St. Julien-le-Pauvre, Sorbonne University, Quartier Latin, Panthéon (stop), Jardins de Luxembourg and Palace (stop), St. Germain des Près (stop), Assemblée Nationale, Les Invalides (stop), Eiffel Tower (stop), Palais de Chaillot, l'Arc de Triomphe (stop), Champs-Elysées, Grand Palais, Elysée Palace, Madeleine, Montmartre, Sacré Coeur (stop), Opéra, Rue de la Paix and Place Vendôme (stop).

| Indiv. Gross | Indiv. Net | 16–20 | 21–29 | 30–39 | 40+ |
|---|---|---|---|---|---|
| Frs 115.00 | Frs 103.50 | Frs 125.80 | Frs 100.60 | Frs 97.95 | Frs 86.25 |

**Louvre and the Treasures of Paris**
Duration 3½ hrs
Departures at: 9.30 am Wed, Fri, Sun
Winter: Wed, Sun
Tuileries, Saint Roch, Palais Royal (visit gardens), Saint-Eustache, National Archives, Museum of the City of Paris, Place des Vosges, Eglise St. Paul, Hôtel de Sens, Jewish Memorial, Sainte Chapelle (visit), Pont Neuf, Louvre Palace and Museum (visit).

| Indiv. Gross | Indiv. Net | 16–20 | 21–29 | 30–39 | 40+ |
|---|---|---|---|---|---|
| Frs 155.00 | Frs 139.50 | Frs 169.50 | Frs 135.60 | Frs 131.75 | Frs 116.25 |

**Versailles Palace and Gardens**
Duration 3½ hrs
Daily departures at: 9.30, 10.30 am, 1.00, 2.00 pm
(except Mondays)
Winter: daily at 10.00 am and 2.00 pm
(except Mondays)
Drive past the Palais des Arts Modernes, the TV/Radio Building, and the Bois de Boulogne to Versailles. Visit the magnificent 17th and 18th Century Palace with its Chapel and the famous Hall of Mirrors (where the Peace Treaty was signed in 1919) and the gardens.
On the regular excursion the interior visit is unaccompanied but there is a historical commentary on the way to and from Versailles.

| Indiv. Gross | Indiv. Net | 16–20 | 21–29 | 30–39 | 40+ |
|---|---|---|---|---|---|
| Frs 120.00 | Frs 108.00 | Frs 131.25 | Frs 105.00 | Frs 102.00 | Frs 90.00 |

**Chartres**
Duration 6 hrs
Departures: 1.00 pm Tues, Thurs, Sat – all year round.
Drive via Sèvres and Ablis through rich farmland to the ancient city of Chartres. Visit the Gothic Cathedral – one of the finest in the world, and see the superb sculpture and stained glass windows (12th and 13th Centuries). Return via Maintenon with its pretty château and Rambouillet – summer residence of the French President.

| Indiv. Gross | Indiv. Net | 16–20 | 21–29 | 30–39 | 40+ |
|---|---|---|---|---|---|
| Frs 156.00 | Frs 139.50 | Frs 169.50 | Frs 135.50 | Frs 131.75 | Frs 116.25 |

**Cabaret + Moulin Rouge**
Departures: 9.00 pm every evening – all year round.
Parisian cabaret followed by show at the Moulin Rouge (complete with "Can-Can") – ½ bottle Champagne included.

| Indiv. Gross | Indiv. Net | 16–20 | 21–29 | 30–39 | 40+ |
|---|---|---|---|---|---|
| Frs 505.00 | Frs 454.50 | Frs 568.10 | Frs 454.50 | Frs 441.80 | Frs 429.25 |

**Figure 4.7**   Ground operator tariff excerpt.

LSI TRAVEL AGENCY, INC.

Date

Mr. Jean Claude Murat
President
Treasure Tours
15 rue de l'Arcade
Paris 75008, France

                        RE:   Rosemont Country Club "European Highlights Tour"
                               Arriving Paris Sept. 10, 1985
                               Maximum 32 passengers

Dear Mr. Murat:

We would like to book the above-mentioned new tour with you. Kindly confirm arrangements and give us a cost quote on the following services:

   Sept. 10 -- Meet and greet at Gare du Nord for arrival via train which leaves Amsterdam at 09:15 and arrives Paris 13:00. Immediately depart on your three-hour "Paris Complete Tour" and drop at Hotel Meurice at the conclusion. Include baggage transfer for maximum two bags per person. (We will instruct the group to have lunch on the train prior to arrival, so you will not have to make a lunch stop).

   Sept. 11 -- Versailles morning tour including private motorcoach and guide. Return drop at hotel in time for lunch on their own. Afternoon Paris Gastronomique Tour on an optional basis. Evening Lido tour -- late show without dinner, including roundtrip private motorcoach transfers, champagne, entrance and tips.

   Sept. 12 -- Morning walking tour of the Louvre including local guide. No coach transfer needed.

   Sept. 13 -- Departure transfer Meurice/CDG Airport via private motorcoach, including baggage transfer, for AF 630 at 08:35 to Rome.

Please note we have booked the Meurice Hotel directly through Intercontinental Hotels' local office, so do not include hotel costs in your price quote. Similarly, we hold the air CDG/FCO and will ticket this sector here.

Although we hope to have 32 passengers, kindly quote with permutations of 15+1, 20+1, and 25+1, specifying if quote is net or gross. The optional Gastronomique Tour should be quoted as a separate entity at 15+1. If you do not have your '85 rates established yet, please give us '84 rates and we will add an anticipated margin for '85 increase.

For continuity's sake, we would prefer to have the same guide assigned to our group throughout the Paris stay if possible. On our last group with you we enjoyed Monique Savin very much and would like to request her again if available.

Hoping to have your confirmation of services and price quotes as quickly as possible and looking forward to working with you again.

                                                        Cordially,

MFS/s
                                                        Marty Sarbey de Souto, CTC
                                                        Group Manager

**Figure 4.8**  Ground operator booking letter.

the hotels. Similarly, the operator needs to know which flights are being booked and ticketed as part of the international ticket, and which flights the operator must ticket locally. The operator should also be told what information is expected in a reply letter, and on what number of passengers prices should be based. If the agency's letter is not specific about numbers, the operator will price the services based on the maximum number of passengers anticipated in the group. It is smart to ask for graduated prices, for example 20 + 1, 30 + 1, 40 + 2, and so forth. If the following year's prices are not available, the operator should be asked to quote in current prices, and a margin for increase will have to be included when costing the tour.

Once confirmations have been received from the various operators that will be used, the various review and payment dates should be noted on the master calendar. The correspondence then can be filed away. The reception ground operator's reputation with suppliers as an organization that makes reliable commitments depends on the accuracy of the information it receives from the agencies using its services. How the operator handles deposits and how it plans the availability of guides, to name just two factors, are governed by that information. It is vital to make sure that that information is kept current by periodic progress reports.

# 5
# Costing and Pricing a Tour

All the planning and negotiations described in the previous chapter will be wasted if one point is not kept in mind: *The purpose of a tour is to make money!* That may sound hard and cold, but it is true. Some travel agents may feel that a tour has one or more of the following purposes:

- A way to effect volume savings for a group, allowing members to travel less expensively than if they traveled alone.
- A way to get public relations exposure for their agency in the community.
- A way to build a base of future clients, who will return as individuals or who will refer other business to the agency.
- A way to start an annual ongoing tour project.
- A way to fill an otherwise slack period in the office.

Although all these purposes may be valid, the fact remains that unless a tour makes money, it is not successful. It may bring back a planeload of happy clients, promises of future business, and passengers who think very highly of the agency. But this is not enough to justify the work of planning and handling the tour. If the tour was not profitable, it has failed—it is as simple as that.

It is likely that an unprofitable tour was incorrectly costed and priced to begin with. Effective costing and pricing are crucial to a successful group travel operation.

## Costing versus Pricing

The discussion of costing vs. pricing should begin with definitions of these terms. *Costing* is the actual, laborious job of analyzing what each item on the tour really will cost the travel agency out of pocket. *Pricing,* on the other hand, is the process of determining what the agency will charge the customer for the tour. The difference between what the client pays (what comes in) and what the tour costs the travel agency (what goes out) is earnings, or *profit.*

Costing might be considered an operational duty; the costing for a given tour may be prepared by the agency's operations manager. Pricing, on the other hand, should be considered the duty of management, after receiving costings and suggestions of those involved in the operational details of the tour.

## Costing a Tour

The travel industry has no sacrosanct method of costing. Ask a hundred different tour operators how they cost their tours, and there will be a hundred different answers.

Some tour operators use elaborate systems, charts, or percentages to calculate breakeven points. Others have been at it for so long that they can virtually calculate in their heads and come up with a figure so close to the real thing that it is uncanny. Still others are mispricing, and have been doing so for years. The fact that they are still in business is purely a coincidence.

But here are some basic points about costing that are pertinent to any effective costing procedure and which are common to the industry.

- Tours should be costed in net figures, not gross.
- Tours should be costed on minimum enrollment expectations, not maximum.
- Most earnings come from markups, not commissions.
- A group tour project must be thought of as an entire unit, and earnings must be thought of in terms of per project rather than per client.

Figure 5.1 shows a sample costing worksheet. The following discussion tells what information is needed to obtain the figures that appear on such a worksheet.

## Variable versus Fixed Costs

Tour costs may be segregated into one of two major categories: variable costs and fixed costs.

*Variable costs.* As the term implies, *variable* costs vary with the number of passengers in the group. These are best thought of as costs related to the individual passenger. Samples of variable costs are meals, hotel accommodations, taxes, tips, airfares, admission fees, and sightseeing tours. Note that these are items for which the travel agency is not charged unless the passengers are present to use them.

*Fixed costs.* Fixed costs do not vary with the number of passengers in the group. They are best thought of as costs related to the project as a whole. Some samples of fixed costs are promotional charges (brochures, printing, advertising, direct mail); free trips for the organizers; the tour manager's salary and expenses; and charters of planes, motorcoaches, or ships. Miscellaneous lump sum payments such as a museum donation would also fit into the category of fixed costs.

Many fixed costs, particularly promotional costs, are referred to as *upfront costs*—costs that must be paid for in advance of the tour. Because these items are paid for before it is known whether the project will be a success or not, they are often thought of as risk factors.

## Specific Variable Costs

### HOTEL CHARGES

Whether hotel reservations are booked through a wholesaler in the United States or through a reception ground operator overseas, the hotel accommodations will be included in the total package price. However, if hotel accommodations are booked directly with the hotels, it will be necessary to calculate those costs on a night-by-night basis. This is fairly easy for a short, single-destination tour. However, if the itinerary is complicated, costing hotel charges becomes a lengthy process.

Most advertised tour prices are based on a share-room basis—half the twin-bedded *room* rate. The quoted per night twin-bedded room rate should be divided by two to arrive at the per *person* nightly rate. If working with student groups or ski packages based on minimum-share dormitory or share chalet accommodations, it may be preferable to cost the tour on three or even four to a room.

LAND TOUR EXPENSES

|  | VARIABLE (PER PERSON) EXPENSES | FIXED (PER PROJECT) EXPENSES |
|---|---|---|
| Quote from Amsterdam reception operator | $280.00 |  |
| Oneway rail ticket AMS/PAR | 64.00 |  |
| Quote from Paris reception operator | 367.00 |  |
| Quote from Rome reception operator | 325.00 |  |
| Flight bag and departure packet | 7.00 |  |
| Total per person land tour expenses |  | $1,043.00 |

FREE TRIP FOR SPONSORING ORGANIZATION

| Airfare for club president, as no comp air | $800.00 |  |
| Land tour expenses Amsterdam operator, comp | 0 |  |
| Rail ticket AMS/PAR comp at 15 | 0 |  |
| Land tour expenses Paris operator, comp | 0 |  |
| Land tour expenses Rome operator, comp | 0 |  |
| Flight bag and departure packet | 7.00 |  |
| Total expenses for club president |  | $807.00 |

TOUR MANAGER EXPENSES

| Salary, 11 days at $75 per day | $825.00 |  |
| Variable land tour expenses from above | 1,043.00 |  |
| Single room supplement, net | 130.00 |  |
| Airfare - no comp air | 800.00 |  |
| Miscellaneous - extra meals etc. | 300.00 |  |
| Total expenses for tour manager |  | 3,098.00 |

PROMOTIONAL EXPENSES

| Brochure, 3000 copies | $750.00 |  |
| Direct mail | 1,394.00 |  |
| Promotional evening | 300.00 |  |
| Advertising | 925.00 |  |
| Total estimated promotional expenses |  | 3,369.00 |

| TOTALS | $1,043.00 | $7,274.00 |

RECAPITULATION

| Per person variable expenses | $1,043.00 |
|---|---|
| Fixed expenses per project of $7,274 divided by 15 persons minimum in group | 485.00 |
| Total net land costs per person | 1,528.00 |
| Markup - to make 25% profit on the gross, divide net $1,528.00 by .75 = gross land price | 2,037.00 |
| Plus gross airfare | 800.00 |
| Total retail price, land and air | $2,837.00 |

PROFIT PICTURE AT 15 PARTICIPANTS

| Retail land price per person | $2,037.00 |
|---|---|
| Less net land costs per person | -1,528.00 |
| Per person land profit (markup) | 509.00 |
| Per person land profit of $509 per person x 15 persons minimum in group = per project land profit with minimum 15 | 7,635.00 |
| Plus commission on airfare, 11% on $800 gross fare = $88 per person x 15 persons minimum anticipated participants = total airfare profit | 1,320.00 |
| Total profit at 15 persons ($7,635.00 land plus $1,320 air) | $8,955.00 * |

PROFIT PICTURE AT 30 PARTICIPANTS

| Retail land price per person | $2,037.00 |
|---|---|
| Less net land costs per person | -1,528.00 |
| Per person land profit (markup), | 509.00 |
| Per person land profit of $509 per person x 30 persons in the group = per project land profit when group reaches 30 passengers | 15,270.00 |
| Plus commission on airfare, 11% on $800 gross fare = $88 per person x 30 persons | 2,640.00 |
| Plus savings on fixed expenses for 15 passengers (that is for passengers #16 through #30), since the project's fixed expenses have already been covered by passengers #1 through 15. $485 x 15 | 7,275.00 |
| Total profit at 30 persons ($15,270.00 land plus $2,640.00 air plus $7,275.00 savings on the last 15 passengers to join the group) | $25,185.00 * |

* Note at 30 passengers, tour membership has doubled but profits have virtually tripled, since tour was priced on minimum expectations from the start

**Figure 5.1** Sample costing worksheet.

As an added check, a mental walkthrough of the trip night by night ensures that sleeping accommodations have been costed in for each and every night (except when spending the night on planes, ships, or trains).

*Single room supplements.* Although most tours are priced on the share room basis, it is also common practice to publish in the brochure the tour price of a single room. This is frequently called the single room supplement—that is the additional amount a passenger must pay to have a room for single occupancy. This is usually shown in the brochure as:

Tour price, per person, from New York,
    share-room basis ........................................ $2,995.00
Single room supplement ....................................... 389.00

Or, it may be expressed as:

Tour price, per person, from New York,
    share-room basis ........................................ $2,995.00
Tour price, per person, from New York,
    single room basis ....................................... $3,384.00

The amount of the single room supplement night by night must be calculated, or a quotation requested from a wholesaler if one is being used. It is usually possible to obtain the single room supplement quotation in net figures, which then may be marked up.

Of course, there may be certain tours on which single rooms are not offered or cannot be guaranteed (China, for example). There may also be tours on which a tour operator does not wish to offer passengers traveling alone the option of sharing with a stranger, thus forcing such passengers into singles at the higher fare. Such decisions are strictly management policy decisions; they vary from agency to agency.

*Taxes, service charges, and foreign currencies.* Any quoted taxes and service charges should be added to the hotel charges, because these costs can be sizable in many countries. In the best circumstances, hotel rates will be quoted on a net (noncommissionable) basis. But if they are quoted gross (commissionable) the net figure can be found by deducting the commission. The net per person figure is used on the costing sheet, When deducting commissions, keep in mind that commissions are not paid on taxes or service charges.

When foreign currencies are involved, they should be converted into United States dollars at the exchange rate of the day. It is a good idea to jot down the exchange rate used and the date when the hotel calculations have been completed.

## MEALS

The variable individual cost of meals may be handled in a number of ways. In some cases, meals will be included with the hotel accommodations (or when booking American Plan basis or full pension). However, the budget may still be augmented by costing in for extra tips to waiters and the *maitre d'* or for additional meal items not included in the hotel meal plan. In other cases, it may be decided to keep the tour price low by omitting all meals. On more deluxe, all-inclusive tours, all meals may be included, perhaps even on *à la carte* basis. In this case, an *estimated* per meal or per diem figure, based on what the current rate is in the various countries or cities concerned, can be used. *A la carte* meals that passengers do not eat or that they undereat (not spending as much as budgeted) constitute a savings to the agency and are what is called *breakage*—an item budgeted for but not used.

## TIPS

Tips, or gratuities, come in all forms: those to waiters, *maitre d's*, or wine stewards; those to local sightseeing guides; and those for luggage handling at airports, piers, trains, and hotels. It is important to determine specifically which tips already have been covered in the services quoted, which tips must be costed in, and which tips the passengers must pay for out of pocket themselves. Again, a walkthrough of the tour day by day, move by move, meal by meal, will ensure that no tips have been overlooked. Taking a wholesaler's word that "all tips are included" can sometimes result in a costing error of $50 or more per passenger. When this is multiplied by forty passengers, it could be a disastrous reduction in the project's profit.

## SIGHTSEEING TOURS

In many cities the agency will be contracting for city sightseeing tours. These may have been quoted as part of the overall per person package or they may have been itemized. This is another breakage item; if the reception operator quotes sightseeing on a per person basis (not a chartered coach basis), the agency should not be charged for passengers not present on sightseeing tours. To be safe, determine whether or not the quoted price is based on a stated minimum number of passengers.

ENTRANCE OR ADMISSION FEES

Entrance or admission fees include fees charged by museums, castles, and other similar attractions on the itinerary, special church donations to allow the tour into the inner sanctum, and so forth. Many tour brochures promise, "Today we see the XYZ Museum." And that is exactly what the travelers do. They see it—from the outside. If the tour leaves the motorcoach and goes inside, an entrance fee is paid. Be sure to determine if the quotation given includes the entrance fees, and if the guide actually escorts the group inside and explains what they are seeing (or hires a local guide to take the group around), or if the tour members are merely turned loose to explore on their own. There is a big difference in the cost of these two approaches.

TAXES

National or regional governments may impose taxes on a variety of services, such as hotel accommodations, meals, and other items. In some cases, these taxes may be included in the quotation. In other cases, the taxes may be quoted as a certain flat amount or as a percentage. In this case, the actual amount must be calculated. For example, a hotel may quote a twin room rate of $100 plus 10% tax and a 15% service charge. That total of 25% on top of the $100 makes the room rate, in reality, $125.

AIRFARES

Airfares are usually quoted on a gross basis and traditionally are not marked up by the tour operator. Usually the land portion is priced separately, net, then markup is added, and last the gross airfare. If and when net airfares become a reality, tour operators may change this traditional approach.

## A Closer Look at Fixed Expenses

*Brochure.* Producing a tour brochure is a fixed cost because the price of printing a certain number of them remains constant whether 13 people or 113 people join the tour, In fact, even if nobody joins the tour, the cost of producing the brochure remains. Production costs include typesetting, layout, pasteup, art, and photography.

*Advertising.* The cost of an advertising campaign for a tour project is also considered a fixed cost. Here again, the charges are not related to the number of people who join the tour. Advertising costs are a constant, and are related to the project as a whole. This category of costs includes production costs for the ads, such as typesetting, art, layout, and pasteup, as well as the actual publication costs.

*Promotional evenings.* Another fixed cost of the tour is a promotional evening. This category includes such things as invitations and postage, room rental, food and drink, and miscellaneous costs such as slide projector rental and paying for the door prizes or gifts.

*Direct mail.* No matter how small the mailing list, direct mail costs are considered fixed costs. This would include the cost of envelopes, cover letters and postage, and labor charges for stuffing and sealing envelopes, running off and affixing address labels, and bundling and delivering the envelopes to the postoffice.

*Tour manager's salary and expenses.* Still another major fixed cost is the cost of the tour manager. Obviously, if the tour organizer is qualified, experienced, and willing to be the tour manager, that will keep the tour cost down, since such an individual will usually accept the responsibility in exchange for nothing more than a complimentary trip. On the other hand, it is unrealistic to expect to have a professional tour manager without being willing to budget properly for such an individual. Most smoothly operated tours budget for a real pro, and cost in accordingly for the tour manager's salary and enroute expenses.

A tour may carry both a professional tour manager *and* an organizer who earned a free trip. There will not be enough complimentaries from the hotels, airlines, and other suppliers to take care of both individuals; therefore, it will be necessary to use the complimentaries accrued for one of these individuals and prorate the full cost of the other individual's trip over the amount charged to members of the group.

*Organizers.* Free trips for tour organizers are fixed costs. In many cases, the organizer can be unreasonable. Spouse, children, and secretary may be expected to travel on a complimentary basis. Never say no! Just point out that as many free trips as desired can be costed in simply by prorating them over the amount charged to the other members of the group. When the organizer realizes that the tour price is increasing by $300 or so for each free trip, he or she will understand the economics of the situation, which require that the tour price remain competitive so that it will sell. Otherwise there is no tour and no free trips for anyone. Usually, organizers want one free trip for fifteen paid passengers and two for thirty, but hotels rarely give one for less than forty, and many airlines do not give any free air tickets anymore—at least not when the lower-priced promotional airfares are used.

*Charters.* Whether it is a chartered airplane, boat, motorcoach, or villa, the basic fact remains the same: the entire entity must be paid for whether or not it is filled. Charters may be considered the ultimate fixed cost. The airline that charters an agency an aircraft is not interested in whether that plane is filled or not; the charge will be exactly the same amount whether there is one passenger aboard or 300. Most tour operators who handle charters frequently figure their costs on the assumption that they will only partially fill the plane. They never prorate the cost of the aircraft over the 100 percent occupancy figure—that is too risky.

Not only is there a risk factor of filling or not filling the plane, but there are also stiff payment deadline dates that must be met, often dates after which the flight cannot be cancelled if the tour membership falls off. Or, if the flight is cancelled, the agency may risk incurring sizable financial penalties. Therefore, charters should be prorated on a minimum or average membership expectations, not on maximum. The same would hold true on motorcoaches, chartered yachts, and so forth. If the motorcoach holds forty-three passengers, prorate over twenty-five or thirty passengers.

*Miscellaneous lump sum expenses.* A multitude of miscellaneous expenditures are usually costed on a group project basis, rather than on an individual passenger basis. An organization might have been promised a $1,000 donation. Or perhaps there will be a large reception on tour, with fifty foreign guests invited to meet the tour group. Maybe there was an agreement to buy a certain painting for the museum sponsoring the tour.

One tour operator specializes in tours to remote South Pacific villages. He budgets whole village projects, such as a new town sewer, into the tour costs, since the villagers will not accept payment for home hospitality offered to his group tours. These items, whether gifts or donations or goodwill social gestures must ultimately find their way into the costing of a given tour or series of tours. They are considered lump sum expenditures in the category of fixed expenses.

## Markups

Markups are no great mystery. They are the lifeblood of any tour. There is no right or wrong amount of markup. Perhaps we should say that the right amount is a markup that allows the agency to make a reasonable profit necessary to justify the time, expense, and risk that went into the project. And perhaps the wrong amount of markup is one that is either so low as to have inadequately compensated all involved or so high as to make the tour noncompetitive and nonmarketable. A markup may also be so low that it does not give the operator any room to move, any room to do what is right by a group to cover an error or to surprise them with a nicety. Some operators may mark up the net land cost as little as 10 percent; some as much as 40 percent.

A 25 percent markup usually is adequate cover for the agency, while still being fair to the customer. (Bear in mind that a 25 percent markup on the net is not the same as 25 percent earnings on the gross. For example, if the net land costs were $1,000 per person and the markup were 25 percent, adding $250 to the $1,000, then the published tour price would be $1,250. On the other hand, $250 is not 25 percent of the $1,250 published land tour price. That $250 is only 20 percent of $1,250. So, to a certain extent, pricing is a matter of semantics. In this example, there was a markup of 25 percent on the net, but it works out to 20 percent on the gross.)

Sometimes the person costing the tour may not care what the percentage is on the net. Rather, he or she may wish to be assured of making a certain percentage on the gross (retail price). For example, an agency may wish to make 25 percent so as to keep 15 percent and pass 10 percent commission on to other selling travel agents through whom it is wholesaling. If, in this case, the net costs were $1,000, the net would be divided by .75 to arrive at a retail price of $1,333.

The formula is to divide the net price by a percentage which is 100 percent minus the percentage of markup required. To make a 35 percent profit on the retail price, subtract 35 from 100 to arrive at 65, and then divide the net cost by .65.

Bear in mind that it is not customary to mark up airfares. Therefore the earnings of a tour come from a markup on the land portion of the tour, plus whatever commissions and overrides are received from the airlines.

ESTIMATING WHEN PRICES ARE NOT KNOWN

There may be occasions when the actual costs for a given item on the tour are not available. For example, a hotel may not have next year's rates established and may quote this year's rates. Often it is not possible to hold up promotion on the tour while waiting for that one hotel to make a decision. In this case, it may be necessary to take this year's rate and pad a reasonable amount, say 15 percent. This is the "pad and pray" method. Never price a complete tour this way—it is far too risky. However, occasional items within the framework of the tour may have to be costed on this basis when nothing more accurate is available.

NONCOMMISSIONABLE ITEMS

Note that because the tour operator's earnings are not premised on commissions but rather on markups over the project as a whole, the agency is free to utilize noncommissionable resources and services. For example, university dormitories, private homes, country inns, theater performances, lectures, cooking demonstrations, and fashion shows could be components of a fine tour. Yet none of these pays commission. One agent turned down a group that was to utilize university accommodations overseas because "he couldn't make any commission on it." Obviously, this agent was thinking individual client handling, not group handling. Subsequently, a local university bought the idea of doing an overseas summer campus program based on this very concept—utilization of university dormitory accommodations not normally in use during the summer months. The project spawned several such far-flung campuses, at a profit to the tour company behind the idea.

## Sample Tour

The following is a sample tour that demonstrates how the costing and pricing theories work. Please note that the figures in this sample are for demonstration purposes only.

SCENARIO

The agency is planning an eleven day, ten night tour to Europe for the Rosemont Country Club (see chapter 3 for details of the itinerary and conditions). Although the tour has been booked for a maximum of forty passengers, the agency has decided to price it on a minimum of fifteen passengers and has guaranteed to operate it if the club has at least fifteen participants. The club president has been offered a free trip for herself at fifteen paying passengers, but since she is not an experienced tour manager, the agency has offered to send a professional tour manager along. All promotional expenses are to be paid by the agency.

The airfare selected is the Advance Purchase Excursion (APEX), on which the airline does not grant a complimentary air ticket. A sample costing sheet for this tour is shown in Figure 5.1. As Figure 5.1 shows, the airfare is not entered into calculations until the end, as it is not marked up. Note that the reception ground operators in Europe have quoted their prices on the basis of 15 + 1, that is, one complimentary for fifteen paying participants. If the one complimentary is used to give the president of the country club a free trip, it means costing in the trip for the professional tour manager since the suppliers do not give enough complimentaries to pass along two free trips—one to the club president and one to the professional tour manager.

Another solution might have been to ask the European reception operators to quote on 15 + 1 and 30 + 2. In that case, the first complimentary accrued at 15 could be used for the professional tour manager and the country club could be told that their president would receive a complimentary trip at 30 tour participants.

## Other Costing Considerations

The costing sample shows a basic tour with no complicated factors to be costed into the tour price. Bear in mind that each custom-designed tour may have its own needs. If the agency is required to make large deposits in advance to hold reservations, it might be necessary to cost in interest on borrowed money. If sending a member of the agency staff as tour manager instead of hiring an outside professional, it might be necessary to cost in the fee for hiring a temporary worker in the office while the regular staff member is out on tour.

In addition to looking at other miscellaneous cost factors like those mentioned above, one should also look at other sources of profit potential for every group. These could include commissions to be made on domestic air reservations to connect to the group flights, sale of travel insurance, and most importantly override commissions from airlines, cruise lines, or other suppliers.

## Evaluating the Price

Once the tour is costed and a price has been decided upon, it might be wise to review a number of competitive tours in the marketplace to see how pricing compares. Undoubtedly yours will be more expensive. Major tour wholesalers with multideparture programs have certain savings not available to the smaller ad hoc operator. They are buying on a volume basis and probably receive lower wholesalers' rates. Many of their fixed expenses such as advertising and brochure publishing can be prorated over a series of monthly tours instead of being attributed to one single tour departure. Perhaps they keep tour managers stationed overseas and do not have to pay air transportation to send them back and forth.

On the other hand, one should not feel obligated to meet the price of these giants. If a small operator is offering a product that is unique to the marketplace and if this product includes special features such as a renowned leader or private entree to peoples and places to which the average traveler does not have access, then the price cannot even be compared.

WAYS TO REDUCE THE PRICE

If it appears that the tour price is totally out of line and that it must be brought down, the planner faces a number of choices. Obviously it is necessary to settle on less earnings to the agency or to brings costs down. The following are a few alternatives.

- Cost the tour on a higher minimum expectation. If it was previously costed on 15 passengers, consider redoing it based on 20 (thus operating it with a minimum of 20 instead of 15).
- Go back to the bargaining table—can lower rates or higher overrides be negotiated from any suppliers?
- Consider using a tour manager who lives overseas.
- Convince the sponsoring organization that its demands for complimentaries are unrealistic, and are forcing the tour price up into a nonsalable price bracket.
- Lower the hotel category by one level throughout.
- Drop all meals except, perhaps, a welcome and farewell meal function.
- Plan on a plainer, less-expensive tour brochure.
- Look at other profit possibilities surrounding the project—sale of optional tours, travel insurance, or pretour and posttour arrangements.
- Piggyback the mailing if doing direct mail. Can the brochure be mailed in the same envelope along with another brochure to a different, noncompetitive destination? Although this divides the reader's attention, it also divides the postage and other mailing expenses.

- Publish more than one tour in the same brochure and thus prorate the cost of the brochure over more than one tour. For example, if the agency is selling three winter programs—a Caribbean cruise, a golf week in Hawaii, and a Mexico tour—package them all in one brochure under one umbrella theme such as "Winter Sun Getaways."

Usually, the major price savings are to be found in the fixed costs, including brochures, promotional costs, complimentaries, and leadership rather than in the variable cost category.

## Decision Making Based on Costing

As sometimes happens, down the road toward departure date it may become apparent that the tour is not going to "make it." Perhaps it was costed based on twenty passengers, but only seventeen have enrolled. At this point it becomes necessary to make a quick decision as to whether to operate the tour or cancel.

Such a decision should be reached by going back to the drawing board, reviewing cost sheets, and reconstructing the tour price from scratch, based on seventeen passengers instead of the hoped-for twenty. Never make an emotional decision to operate or cancel a tour, without looking at the total financial picture.

Of course, there are considerations other than financial ones, such as:

- Loss of credibility with passengers.
- Possible loss of sponsoring organization as a future client for a future tour product.
- Loss of credibility and reputation with suppliers.
- Low staff morale at failure of the project.

As a general rule of thumb, if a great deal of money has already been expended on promotion—say several thousand dollars on the tour brochure, advertising, and direct mail—it is probably best to operate the tour. Even if the agency only breaks even, the books will not show a large loss for promotional expenses already paid. However, if operating the tour puts the agency further into the red, that is another matter.

If it is a losing proposition, here are some alternative suggestions.

- Cancel the tour and protect the people on an existing tour departure of another tour operator—as close in dates and itinerary as can be found.

- Operate the tour without diminishing the features promised the tour members. They will not be happy if they arrive abroad to find that hotels were changed to a lesser category to save money because the group was small.
- Perhaps change from a fully escorted tour to a locally hosted basis in each country or city. Advise passengers about this ahead of time, however.
- Consider operating by van or minibus instead of a large coach. (In this case it may be necessary to stop promoting and selling to fit the group into the confines of the smaller van. Also limit luggage to fit.)
- Consider sending an agency staff person as tour manager —someone who can travel on a 75 percent agent's discount air ticket. (Be sure that the needed airline pass allotments for the airlines that the group is using have been set aside. It is best to put a "hold" on these until it becomes obvious how the tour is selling.)

**Summary**

This list of do's and don'ts recapitulates the important points to be remembered when costing a tour:

DO'S

- Do cost the tour on the minimum number of participants anticipated, not the maximum.
- Do include a safety margin to cover errors, increases, or simply maneuvering room if needed.
- Do keep good, clean records as to how figures were calculated, should staff members have to refer to them months later. If converting foreign currencies, jot down the exchange rate, the source, and date. Similarly, on airfares, keep track of airline, fare quote number, and date. Better still, have it in writing from the airline.
- Do walk through the tour mentally, day by day, tour feature by tour feature, to be sure that something important has not been forgotten.
- Do cost in adequately for good tour leadership—it can make or break a trip.

- Do calculate upfront risk monies that the agency will lose if the tour fails to materialize. Do the potential earnings warrant the financial risk?
- Do consider the "up front" time expenditure that the agency will lose if the tour fails to materialize. Do the potential earnings warrant the time invested?

DON'TS

- Don't quote a firm price to an organization until the agency has had time to price the tour accurately, based on actual confirmed services. If giving an advance quote, be sure that it is understood by all concerned that it is only a ballpark figure.
- Don't be too optimistic on sales and promotion results. Budget more than enough time for these items to ensure the tour's success.
- Don't forget the unseen costs—interest on borrowed money, loss of sales revenue from the sales staff who may be taken out of the office to operate the tour in the field, and so forth.
- Don't be afraid to compensate the agency adequately by providing a large enough markup.

# 6

# The Tour Brochure

Once the tour has been planned, booked, and costed it is time to publish the tour brochure. "Nothing to it," says the unwary planner; "I'll just get a shell from the airlines and get together with the printer." (A shell, of course, is a brochure that contains illustrations but no type; the planner would provide the information. See Figure 6.1 for a sample shell.)

If there is "nothing to it," however, the planner will not be presenting the best visible proof of the tour product. After all, clients are expected to pay perhaps thousands of dollars for a product they cannot see, touch, or take home. They cannot even be sure that it really exists until they first hold their air ticket in their hand or first taxi down the runway. Why should they trust the travel agency? Why should they be convinced that all the promised services will be provided—the transfers, hotels, social events, good times, camaraderie, experienced tour manager?

Clients are entitled to more than just vague promises, more than just a hastily thrown-together itinerary and responsibility clause, more than pretty pictures of glamorous hotels with sparkling swimming pools and bikini-clad girls beckoning them to warm waters. They are entitled to a complete, clearly-written, no-nonsense brochure.

And, if clients do not know that they are entitled to this kind of brochure, the courts certainly do. More and more, when travel agencies or tour operators are brought to court by disgruntled clients, judges are looking at the tour brochure for honesty and forthrightness rather

THE TOUR BROCHURE 101

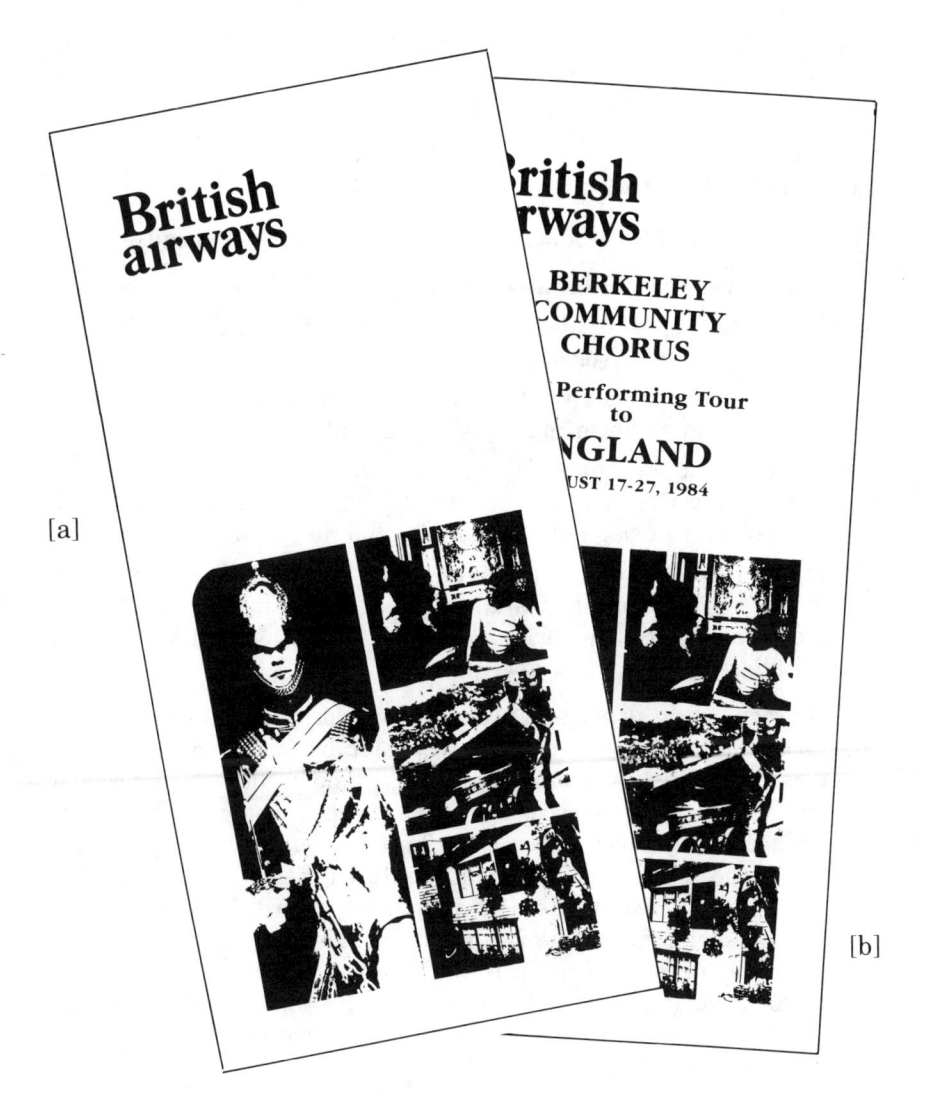

[a]

[b]

**Figure 6.1** Sample shell (a) as it comes from the airline, and (b) after imprinting.

than for intricate interpretations of the responsibility clause. For these and other reasons it is essential that one take the time (and the money) to produce a thoroughly professional brochure.

## Reasons for Printing a Brochure

A brochure should be produced for every travel project because:

- It forms a contract between the agent and the client.
- It standardizes the sales presentation by assuring that each client in the group receives exactly the same information.
- It gives the client a product that can be seen, touched, taken home, analyzed, and shown to family and friends.
- It carries an itinerary (IT) number, which provides for override commission from the airline (the 3 percent difference between 8 percent and 11 percent on international air).
- It gives the airlines, hotels, and other suppliers proof of the operator's professionalism and an indication that the agent's promotional efforts are serious and that space blocked with these suppliers is not unduly speculative.

The brochure need not be an expensive, glossy, full-color job. It is quite possible, with the help of a good layout artist and some effective graphics, to produce a visually attractive and well-written product without going to the expense of four-color process. Generally speaking, the average retail travel agency can afford a full-color brochure (called four-color process in the printing trade) only if a shell is used. Producing such a full-color brochure from scratch, using color transparencies, is financially viable only if one is a major wholesaler planning to print 100,000 copies or more. But if printing small quantities (between 1,000 and 20,000 copies) the four-color process will be well beyond the budget of the small tour operator. See Figure 6.2 for an example of an effective one-color brochure.

## To Shell or Not to Shell

The basic decision, then, is whether to use an existing shell or whether to produce an original brochure. A shell certainly has advantages—primarily simplicity and the availability of an attractive full-color product at low cost. Shells can be obtained from airlines, cruise lines, government tourist offices, and several other sources.

**Figure 6.2** Sample one-color brochure cover.

In some cases, however, shells can turn out to be more expensive than an original brochure done from scratch, and they can be extremely restricting. The following questions should be considered:

- Which method is most advantageous for the agency? Is the supplier charging the agency for the shell? If so, which will be less expensive—paying for good graphics/art and layout for an original brochure or buying the shell? For small quantities (2,000 or so), buying the shell is probably less expensive. But if 10,000 or more copies are to be produced, prorating the cost of a good art/graphics/layout person is probably the better investment.
- Is the shell suitable? Does it have enough white space to allow for your needs or is a whole column devoted to describing the wonders of the sponsoring airline? Does the theme coincide with the image that you want to portray? A cover showing a couple with champagne glasses in hand may not be appropriate for a tour to the Girl Scouts' World Leadership Conference. And a shell with beach and bikini scenes may not be businesslike enough for a travel seminar project intended to be tax deductible and having to pass the scrutiny of the Internal Revenue Service.
- Are enough shells available? Often an airline can provide 2,000 to 5,000 shells, but if larger quantities are needed they may not be available, even if the agency is willing to pay for them.
- Can more shells be ordered later? If it later becomes necessary to reprint midstream in the promotion, can more of the same shell be obtained? Usually not.
- Do you mind not having exclusivity? Bear in mind that other travel agencies may very well be using the same shell for other tours.
- Is the shell's layout easy to work with? Or is it necessary to adopt an unnatural layout, squeezing some subjects to fit and expanding others to fill white space?

**Planning the Layout**

Once it has been decided whether to use a shell or to do an original piece from scratch, it will be necessary to plan a layout and then write the copy to fit it, not the other way around. If an eight-panel brochure is planned (four panels on one side, four on the other) the panels will probably be used as follows: one panel for the cover, one for a reservation form, three for the itinerary (with photos interspersed), and one for the tour costs (and what is included/not included in that cost). A panel will also be needed for general information such as deposits, cancellation policy, clothing, baggage, passports, and the like. The last panel (usually the back page) will be for the responsibility clause. This eight-panel layout should work well for a tour of two weeks or less. For a longer tour the next size will probably be necessary—a ten-panel brochure (five panels on each side) to provide room to write a longer itinerary.

When first learning to write a brochure, it is wise to keep to a standard size brochure instead of going into exotic formats. A standard brochure is one that folds to 9" x 4" to fit a No.10 size business envelope. If several brochures will be mailed in one envelope, cut the brochure size down to 8 7/8" x 4" to have a little extra clearance at the end of the envelope. Another easy, standard size is 8 1/2" x 11", a size which may be mailed flat in a 9" x 12" envelope or folded in thirds to fit a No. 10 envelope.

Remember—be sure to plan how the brochure will fold and check the fold with the printer before completing the layout. Be sure the fold desired can be handled by machine. The author once mistakenly had 13,000 copies of a brochure printed and then discovered that it had to be folded by hand. The bill was well over budget, to put it mildly!

## Getting a Printer's Bid

Once a decision has been reached on whether to use a shell or not, and once the size, folds, number of panels has been decided, it is time to approach a printer (or several printers) for a bid. In order to quote a price, the printer will need to know the following: number of copies to be printed, number of halftones (printer's term for photos), number of maps or drawings (line art), and weight and color of paper stock. Figure 6.3 is a "spec" or specification sheet showing the information the printer will need. Brightly colored paper stocks, imported papers, and fancy textures increase the price. The two main expenses are the typesetter's time and the paper stock, so small printing runs of several thousand brochures will be proportionally expensive. The more copies printed, the less expensive each brochure becomes.

Another important factor is the number of colors—the least expensive being what is termed a one-color job, that is, one color ink and one color stock. Black is considered a color, so black ink on white stock is a one-color job just as is blue ink on yellow stock. If a second color ink is added, for example, both red and black ink on white stock, this

LSI TRAVEL AGENCY, INC.

SPEC SHEET FOR PRINTER

| | |
|---|---|
| NAME OF PRODUCT/JOB NO: | Travel brochure |
| QUANTITY: | 3,000 copies |
| SIZE, FLAT: | 9" x 16" |
| FOLD: | To 9" x 4", to fit a #10 size envelope |
| STOCK: | Coated, white, 70 pound, Flokote or similar |
| INK: | Two colors: Black and red PMS 199 |
| ART: | One map, two line drawings, two half-tones |
| PROOFS REQUIRED: | One blueline |
| PREPARATION: | You are to provide typesetting, pasteup, art and all separations |
| | or |
| | Typesetting, pasteup and art being done elsewhere. You will receive mechanicals camera-ready |
| DELIVERY: | 100 to our office |
| | 2,900 to our mail house: Best Mailing Services, 1234 Seventh Street, Anywhere, U.S.A. |
| SPECIAL NOTES: | Please advise if quote includes any delivery charges and taxes, or not. |

**Figure 6.3** Sample spec sheet for printer.

is termed a two-color job, and the added color will mean about a one-third increase in the cost of the brochure. (Be sure that the ink is sufficiently dark to form a strong contrast on the paper. Black ink on pale yellow stock is fairly easy to read, but red ink on yellow becomes difficult to read if there is a lot of small type.)

Even after obtaining a firm price quote from the printer, it is a wise precaution to add a margin to the printing budget to allow for error, misunderstandings, and author's corrections. Printers do not charge when they make a mistake and have to correct it, but when the customer changes copy, changes layout, or changes his or her mind, printers *do* charge—and on an hourly basis.

Also, allow extra time in the schedule. If a printer promises that a brochure will be off the press in two weeks, add at least two weeks more to allow for holidays, paper delivery delays, strikes, and so on. Usually thirty days is the shortest period in which one can expect a truly professional-looking brochure to be completed. Besides, there should be time to read at least three sets of printer's proofs. The first set, called *galley proofs,* are long strips of type that are read just for content and spelling errors but without headlines or layout. Second proofs are called *page proofs,* that is, proofs submitted after the corrected type has been pasted onto a layout page complete with headlines, borders, and so on. The third and final proof is usually called a brownline, dylux, or other such term, and is presented after all the pages have been photographed and negatives have been made. Corrections should be made at stages one and two and never at stage three; it is costly to change once film has been made because it means rephotographing the entire page.

## Art and Layout Assistance

If a shell is to be used, an artist or layout person will probably not be needed. All that is necessary is to block out the appropriate panels, measure the amount of copy that will fit, and, in consultation with the printer, select proper typefaces and sizes. It is best to keep to a simple, readable typeface for the body type, saving any fancy styles for headlines. For continuity and visual clarity, stick to one type style throughout the brochure; do not jump from one style to another. Also, be sure to select a body size large enough for easy reading.

If the brochure is to be produced from scratch, an artist/layout person will probably be needed. Such charges should be costed in to the tour price from the outset. Some full-service printers have such a person on the staff or available on a freelance basis. If not, an independent graphic artist should be consulted. If such a professional is not available, or if attempting the do-it-yourself approach, stay with a simple layout, an attractive type style, a couple of good photos, and decorative line drawings or silhouette art. Probably the most difficult job will be locating good *black-and-white* glossy photos. Although sources such as airlines and government tourist offices may be able to supply photos of buildings, ships, and planes, it is sometimes hard to find good human interest photos. If setting up a permanent tour department in the agency, and if a number of tour brochures will probably be produced by the agency in the future, members of the staff and tour managers should start carrying a camera loaded with black-and-white film on trips to build a library of good human-interest and action photos. Using photos of recognizable people requires their written permission. If photos are obtained from outside sources, a credit line must be published with each photo. A credit line identifies the individual photographer or organization that gave, sold, or lent the photo.

Do not rely solely on travel-related organizations as a source of good photos. Commercial photo houses or museums are good sources. The author once obtained permission from the Norton Simon Museum of Art in Pasadena for one-time reprint rights to a black-and-white photo of a Paul Gaugin painting in their collection; it was used as the cover of a Tahiti brochure. The search for good photos requires creativity. Photos for brochure use must be distinct, focused properly, and not too dark. This is particularly important when using textured papers, as they tend to absorb a lot of ink and thus darken photos.

## Use a Map

A map is a must in any brochure, because many clients may not have a good idea of where they are going or where *there* is in relation to *here*. Many clients are amazed to find that South America is actually southeast of North America, not due south, or that Hong Kong is as far south of Japan as it is, and hence the difference in weather and clothing requirements. A map will help the potential client to understand the itinerary, the routing, the distances, and the flight times involved.

A simple map outline or silhouette can be drawn by a commercial artist, and the printer can then typeset and position the names of cities in their proper location on the map. But one cannot simply reproduce an existing map in, say, a Rand McNally atlas. Some basic silhouette maps may be available in clip art catalogs

## The Cover

Remember that the cover of the brochure is the gateway to the tour. Be sure that it *attracts* the client and that it will draw him or her to open and read the brochure. The cover need not give the full story—just enough to answer the basics: where, when, and with whom (the agency? a local club? a famous tennis pro?). Do not forget the year! Price need not be on the cover unless it is such a low price as to be an outstanding feature that should be emphasized.

If the tour is going to be wholesaled through retail travel agents and displayed in an agency's brochure rack, the cover should be visually

**AGRICULTURAL**

# Travel Seminar Program

to the

## SOUTH PACIFIC

including

**FIJI**
**AUSTRALIA**
**NEW ZEALAND**
**SAMOA**

JANUARY 12 - FEBRUARY 1, 1974

*Professional Farmers of America*

In cooperation with
**AMERICAN AIRLINES**
and
**FARMER-TO-FARMER TOURS**

**Figure 6.4**  Sample study tour brochure cover.

bold and simple, easy to pick out from among other brochures on the rack. If, on the other hand, it is going to be merchandised primarily by direct mail, perhaps it can be a bit daintier or designed to be pulled out of an envelope or as a direct-mail piece in itself to be sent through the mail without an envelope.

## The Itinerary

Nothing sells as does a day by day, blow by blow, well written itinerary, showing clients all the features that they will be getting each day. Beware of overblown terms such as beautiful, gorgeous, unbelievable, and unforgettable. Why is San Francisco beautiful? Because the itinerary keeps saying so? Or because a picture is formed for the reader, letting him or her visualize San Francisco's steep hills, shrouded in fog, and streets lined with brightly-colored Victorian houses?

Write the itinerary in the language of the potential customer. An educational study tour to London with class sessions in the morning and afternoon sightseeing might more accurately refer to "afternoon field trip to Windsor Castle and Runnymede, site of the signing of the Magna Carta," than "afternoon sightseeing tour." Teachers and students take field trips, not sightseeing tours. And a program for the local dental association to the annual meeting of the American Dental Association could refer to "morning session of essays and table clinics" instead of "morning convention session."

Certainly that entire alphabet soup of travel industry terms, such as GIT, APEX, and Super APEX, should be avoided unless they are spelled out for the reader.

Standardize the itinerary presentation. If hotels are listed by name, list them in all cities in the itinerary, not just in some. Do not jump from "you" to "we" do such and such. And above all, avoid being too specific. It is all well and good to say "afternoon departure by Air France jet to Paris." But saying "We leave via Air France flight number 5 at 2:00 p.m. for Paris," could back you into a corner if, by the time the tour leaves, both the flight number and flight time have been changed.

## The Tour Price

Adequate space should be allowed for information concerning the tour price and a full itemization of what is included and what is not included in the price. Prices may be indicated from more than one city, and should be shown for both share room and single room basis. In some cases the triple room rate can be listed, as well as special family rates and children's rates.

The type of airfare on which the tour is priced, such as APEX, GIT, or ITX, should be specified, and the restrictions governing the particular fare noted. Indicate the minimum number of passengers on which the tour is priced, and stipulate the publication date on which the airfare and the foreign currency exchange rates are based. If the air fare is restricted to a specific air carrier, this should be so specified.

The brochure should have a paragraph that lists all services included in the tour price—airfare, hotels, meals, sightseeing, gratuities, and surface transportation. The more specific the better. For example, instead of just stating that meals are included, say "three meals a day, *table d'hôte* basis, in accordance with local custom in the country concerned." Specify if breakfasts are continental or full American style and if lunch and dinner are *à la carte* or *table d'hôte*.

Conversely, there should also be a paragraph listing services not included in the tour—things such as connecting airfare to the published gateway city; personal expenses such as liquors, wines, mineral waters, or laundry; and increases in airfares or currency exchange rates after date of publication. Also not included would be items such as passports and inoculations, travel insurance, services apart from the group, expenses due to flight delays, strikes, or other irregularities, meals not stipulated—in effect, any item not included in the tour price. This information gives the passengers an accurate way to budget for the out-of-pocket expenses they will incur. It also gives the tour brochure an aura of plain speaking.

## The Reservation Form

To facilitate booking each individual client, have a good reservation form in the brochure, thus getting all the information needed from each client at one time. This eliminates needless telephoning or corresponding back and forth with each tour participant. The reservation form may be one panel in the brochure itself, or, if space is in short supply, it could be a loose insert panel. Figure 6.5 is a sample reservation form.

The form should ask the basics: client's name and names of accompanying family members, home and business addresses, telephone numbers, and occupation. If accepting children, ask for their ages. There should also be a place where the client can indicate a choice of either a twin bedded or single room, smoking or nonsmoking section

RESERVATION

Rosemont Country Club
1985 European Highlights Tour

NAME (please indicate full name) _____

ADDRESS _____

CITY _____

STATE _____ ZIP CODE _____

TELEPHONE   Area Code _____ Number _____

ACCOMPANYING FAMILY MEMBERS (if children, state ages)
_____
_____

PROFESSION _____

PLEASE ARRANGE FOR MY AIRLINE TRANSPORTATION FROM
_____
airport nearest my home

I/WE WOULD LIKE THE FOLLOWING HOTEL ACCOMMODATIONS (check one)

__ Twin/share at basic tour price       __ Single room at supplement

WHEREIN POSSIBLE TO PREASSIGN SEATS ON AIRCRAFT, I/WE WISH TO BE SEATED IN (check one)

__ Non-smoking section       __ Smoking section

AT THE END OF THE TOUR, I/WE WISH TO (check one)

__ Return directly home with the group       __ Remain in Europe independently and
   from Rome September 16                        return on _____
                                                        specify date

I HEARD ABOUT THIS TRIP THROUGH (check one)

__ I am a member of the Rosemont Country Club and received direct-mail notification

__ Through a friend who is a member of the club

__ Through an ad (specify publication if possible) _____

__ Other, specify _____

PLEASE SEND INFORMATION ABOUT THIS TOUR TO THE FOLLOWING PERSON(S) WHO MAY BE INTERESTED (indicate name and mailing address)
_____
_____

THIS IS TO CERTIFY THAT I HAVE READ THE BROCHURE AND RESPONSIBILITY CLAUSE AND AGREE TO THE CONDITIONS OUTLINED THEREIN

_____
signature

DEPOSIT:   Make deposit check for $100 per person payable to "Rosemont Country Club"

MAIL TO:   Rosemont Country Club, 1234 Fifth Street, Anywhere, U.S.A.

**Figure 6.5** Sample reservation form.

of the aircraft (for preassigned seating), and decisions on any optional tours that may be offered within the basic tour package or as posttour optional features. When selling a cruise, be sure that space is provided for the client to indicate choice of cabin category and corresponding price. There may even be a place for first and second choice of cabin category in case the first choice cannot be confirmed.

Reserve a place for the client's signature and a spot at the bottom of the reservation form to indicate the amount of deposit that should accompany the reservation form, to whom it should be payable, and the exact address to which it should be mailed. If, by any chance, there is any extra space left on the reservation form, a good marketing technique is to ask the client for the name and address of any friend(s) who might also be interested in the tour or in being placed on the mailing list to receive information on future tours.

## The Responsibility Clause

All brochures should include a complete responsibility clause—a clause which may be written by the agency staff and then reviewed by the company attorney, or a clause which is prepared from scratch by the attorney. An example of a responsibility clause will be found in the sample itinerary in chapter 3.

Of particular importance is a statement allowing the agency to decline to accept a tour applicant or to drop a tour member if need be. (See chapter 11 for a discussion of why a tour manager might find it necessary to drop a member enroute.) A proper statement on this subject might be "The right is reserved to decline to accept or retain any person as a member of the tour at any time."

Another very important inclusion in the responsibility clause is one related to foreign currency fluctuation and fare changes. Since the tour will be costed many months in advance, there will undoubtedly be changes in airfares, hotel rates, motorcoach costs, and other pertinent components between the date on which the tour was costed and the date on which the tour actually departs. In some cases, suppliers may have agreed to honor the original quotes and not pass increases on to the tour operator once a price has been quoted and a brochure published.

In many cases, tour operators protect themselves by building in a financial margin to allow for such increases; they thus avoid having to advise tour members of a price increase later on. In other cases, particularly if suppliers' increases prove to be steep, the tour operator has no alternative but to pass the increase on to the tour members in the form of a surcharge. For this reason, a statement in the brochure such as the following is helpful: "The price of the tour is based on tariffs and exchange rates in effect at the time of printing the brochure and is subject to change in the event of any changes in tariffs and exchange rates."

It is suggested that the planner read a variety of responsibility clauses in a variety of tour brochures on the market today; it will become apparent that virtually no two are exactly alike—each one is slightly different as interpreted by each company's ownership and its legal advisors. One clause which is standard throughout, however, is the airline clause portion, a portion which must be printed verbatim and which will be verified by the tour's sponsoring air carrier before approval for the final publishing of the brochure.

## Last But Not Least

Remember to put the publishing date on the back of the brochure (actually the date on which the tour is priced, not the date that it comes off the press). And do not forget to obtain the itinerary number (IT number) from the sponsoring airline and to print it in the brochure; this is needed on international air to qualify the agency for the 3 percent additional commission (11 percent versus 8 percent). Airlines will sometimes insist on seeing the printer's proof of a brochure before assigning the IT number, and may perhaps even send the proof to their head office for approval, so be sure to allow sufficient time for this in the overall time frame.

The final product can act as a true showcase for a travel agency, and, if slick and professional in appearance, the additional sales that a good brochure provides should more than warrant the time and money expended on it. If the first brochure does not turn out perfectly, consider it a learning experience and make the next one even better. It is a good idea to run a supply of extra copies and use them as marketing tools when making sales presentations to other groups and potential new tour sources, to show the type of brochure that the agency is capable of producing.

When the brochure is finally off the press, be sure to check with the originating (sponsoring) air carrier as to any forms which may be required for approval of international inclusive air tours. In the past it has been necessary to complete an IATA form; at press time it is not known if this will still be necessary or if there will be a new procedure required either by the individual air carriers or the new Passenger Network Services Corporation.

# 7
# Marketing the Tour

The term *marketing* may conjure up the image of interviewers in shopping malls, new soap product samples left on the doorstep, or telephone surveys asking for preferences in television shows.

This image is partly true, since marketing does include research into demographics and buying habits. But marketing also includes many other components, such as direct mail, public relations, sales efforts, a cruise night or similar promotion, use of a well-known personality as tour leader, news releases to the press, and advertising. And advertising itself contains still more components: newspapers, magazines, radio, and on rare occasions perhaps television, billboards, and posters.

However, despite the seeming complexity of the subject, the process of marketing a tour need not be intimidating. It is not necessary to hire a $100-an-hour expert to market a tour properly. When all the Madison Avenue mystique is stripped away, *marketing a tour simply means getting the tour to market*. The combination of how the tour gets to market and what it costs to do so is, simply, the marketing plan.

## Developing a Marketing Plan

A *realistic* marketing plan and budget are essential, and should be developed *before* the tour is priced, not after. Special group tours are not included in an agency's overall annual promotional budget. That budget covers the usual institutional marketing, such as Yellow Pages advertising, newspaper advertising, newsletters, and so forth. A special separate promotional budget should be established for each tour the agency operates, and this budget can then be built into the tour's costing formula.

### THE MARKETING MIX

A good marketing plan uses a variety of components, not just one. The particular combination of components selected for a given tour is termed the *marketing mix*. The mix selected may vary from tour to tour. One tour might need a mix of direct mail to a club's membership and a cruise evening. Another tour might be marketed through paid advertising, a local personality, and news releases to the press to generate free publicity.

The selection of components will depend on the type of itinerary, the desired clientele, the best means of reaching that clientele, and the promotional budget than can realistically be incorporated into the tour costing. Figure 7.1 shows a sample budget, based on marketing plan decisions for a specific tour project.

### SELECTING A SPECIFIC MARKET SEGMENT

It is important to research the various promotional avenues carefully, and then choose those that will be most effective in generating interest in a particular travel product. The trick is to direct all promotional efforts to a specific market segment. A ski tour would best be promoted by advertising in ski magazines, mailings to ski clubs, and so forth. An expensive advertisement in the Sunday travel section of the *New York Times* would be wasted, because only a small percentage of readers would be skiers.

### DECIDING ON A PROMOTIONAL BUDGET

Not only is it necessary to select the promotional avenues that lead to the desired clientele but also to estimate the cost of acquiring clients for a tour. One can then decide whether the potential for profit on the tour warrants the promotional risk investment. If the profit is projected to be only $100 per client, the agency will probably not risk $80 per client on promotional expenses. On the other hand, if the per client profit is projected to be as high as $500, perhaps a promotional investment of $80 per client is justified.

The following discussion looks in more detail at various means of marketing.

(1) PROMOTIONAL EVENING, maximum 100 guests

    (a) Wine and cheese estimate (including paper plates, napkins, table decor, etc.) .................... $300.00

    (b) Films - no charge, complimentary from sponsoring airline. However, contingency for rental of film projector if necessary .................... 30.00

    (c) Door Prize, if not donated..................... 50.00

    (d) Room rental ................................... 100.00

    (e) Tips, associated with room rental, waiter etc... 15.00

    (f) Invitations and stamps for 200 to assure 100 in attendance ..................................... 60.00

    Estimated total budget for promotional evening ......     $555.00

(2) PAID ADVERTISING

    Three consecutive monthly ads in the Club's magazine, one quarter page, at $275 per issue x 3 .............     $825.00

(3) DIRECT MAIL to 2,000 member club list. Initial announcement mailing.

    (a) Postage at 11¢ bulk rate x 2,000 ............... $220.00

    (b) Printing cover letter from club president....... 85.00

    (c) Mailing house charges - folding, stuffing, sealing, sorting, taking to post office, etc........ 100.00

    Total estimate for initial announcement mailing......     $405.00

(4) TOUR BROCHURE, 3000 copies (2,000 to mail out, 1000 to keep for inquiries and miscellaneous purposes)....     $600.00

(5) SECOND FOLLOW-UP MAILING if necessary to boost sales

    (a) Postage at 11¢ bulk rate x 2,000................ $220.00

    (b) Reminder letter from club president............. 85.00

    (c) Mailing house charges ......................... 100.00

    (d) Enclosure flyer or perhaps an additional 2,000 brochures ..................................... 300.00

    Total estimate for follow-up mailing ................     $705.00

(6) CONTINGENCY FEE, for late "boost" if necessary ......     $100.00

GRAND TOTAL MARKETING PLAN AND BUDGET FOR THIS PROJECT....     $3,190.00

**Figure 7.1** Marketing plan budget. This is a sample only. Each tour's budget should be costed using specific quotes for that job from printers, mail houses, and so forth.

## Direct Mail

Direct mail, although an expensive method of marketing, certainly can bring results and may, in the long run, prove to be the most cost-effective. Agents always ask "What percentage of return can I expect?" The answers to that question depend on the validity of the mailing list, the tour product itself, its price, and the income level of those on the list. Probably of prime importance is how closely-knit the group on the mailing list is. A list of members of an upper-income private organization, solicited by letter from the organization's president for their officially sponsored tour, might draw as high as 5 percent. On the other hand, with a list purchased by the travel agency and solicited by a representative of the agency—an outsider—one might be lucky to draw 1 percent.

Assume that the agency has presold a trip to an organization—a church, tennis club, Chamber of Commerce, or professional group. The directors have been convinced that they should sponsor an official trip for their organization next year. They have accepted the proposed itinerary, the agency has booked it and now holds confirmed space with all hotels, airlines, and so forth.

The directors of the organization may already have made advance teaser announcements to their membership in publications or at meetings. But the first official announcement should be via direct mail to each family in the organization, to assure total coverage. It is best to have the mailing go out in the organization's envelope, rather than in the agency's envelope. The brochure describing the tour in detail should be customized to the organization, so that it appears to be their tour, not the agency's. Of course, the agency's name will appear in the brochure, but it should be played down, with full buildup given to the sponsoring organization. A letter of invitation from the organization's president should accompany the brochure and to facilitate reservations the brochure should include a reservation form to be completed and returned with the deposit.

If possible, the reservation should be returned to the sponsoring organization, which will then endorse the check and forward it to the agency with the reservation for handling. This procedure will keep most of the workload in the agency and out of the organization's office. At the same time, members feel more comfortable sending money to their own organization rather than to a travel agency with which they might not be familiar.

Assume that the agency is working with an organization that has

3,000 members. A direct-mail budget might look like the following sample.

SAMPLE DIRECT-MAIL BUDGET

| | |
|---|---|
| Envelopes, 3,000 including printing with club's return address and logo on them | $ 75.00 |
| Letters, 3,000, from the club's president announcing the trip, including printing and folding | 110.00 |
| Brochures, 3,000, size 9" x 16" (8 panels). Based on buying shells from the airlines at 5 cents each, plus printer's charges for typesetting, layout, and folding | 750.00 |
| Postage, at bulk rate of 11 cents each for 3,000 | 330.00 |

Mailing house charges

| | |
|---|---|
| Minimum setup charges | 12.50 |
| Affixing address labels at $8/M | 24.00 |
| Stuffing envelopes at $15/M | 45.00 |
| Sealing, metering, at $5.50/M | 16.50 |
| Tying and sacking at $8/M | 24.00 |
| Delivery to post office | 7.00 |
| Total mailing house estimated charges | 129.00 |
| Total direct-mail budget | 1,394.00 |

The estimates in this sample budget are based on the assumption that the club does not charge the agency for use of its membership list. If an outside list must be purchased, estimate approximately 5 cents a name for one-time use. Also, even if the club allows free use of their membership list, there still may be a charge for a printout of the address labels.

The above $1,394.00 total must be costed in to the tour as promotional expenses (see chapter 5, Costing and Pricing a Tour). Ultimately, these expenses will be paid for by the passengers themselves as part of their tour cost. Note that in the meantime these direct-mail costs are an upfront expense for the agency. If, for any reason, the tour should fail to operate, they are nonrecoverable expenses—to be looked at as a risk investment in the project.

A FEW HINTS FOR DIRECT-MAIL MARKETING

*Host club arrangement.* If the organization is not large, consider a host club arrangement. In this arrangement, one organization sponsors the tour, handles all the decisions and works with the agency but opens the trip to related clubs. Rotary clubs frequently do this. One club sponsors a trip, opening it to other clubs in the same Rotary district. Quite often, an organization may be overly optimistic about the numbers that it can generate from a small membership list, so it is wise to discuss this at the outset and perhaps cost in for direct mail to affiliated organizations at the time the tour budget is drawn up.

*Personalized envelope.* The more personalized the direct-mail approach, the better the results. If the list is small, a hand-addressed envelope with a first-class stamp instead of a metered envelope will ensure the recipient's opening it, because it will not appear to be junk mail. Of course, in dealing with large lists, this personal touch may not be feasible.

*Sole occupancy in the envelope.* A direct-mail piece will receive greater attention if the envelope is not stuffed with a multitude of pieces. On the other hand, it is possible to cut down the cost of the mailing by offering two nonconflicting tours in the same envelope and splitting the promotional costs of the mailing between the two tour projects.

*Plan for several mailings.* One mailing alone will not be enough. Most likely it will be necessary to do a followup mailing and perhaps even a third "last call." Be sure to budget accordingly. Once the tour is announced and has sold out, a second or third mailing can be eliminated if not needed, thus effecting a savings on promotional expenditures. But the reverse is not true. If just one announcement mailing has been budgeted, but it is later decided that the tour needs a boost, the project will be in financial difficulty. It is not necessary to let the organization know that a second mailing has been costed in to the project. Later, when the agency offers to make a second mailing, it can suddenly appear as a knight in shining armor, rescuing the project.

*Combine direct mail with other marketing methods.* Do not expect direct mail to succeed all by itself. It probably works best in conjunction with reminder advertising in the organization's publication, and with a sales organizer inside the organization working toward the complimentary trip.

*Check with a professional mailing house.* Consult carefully with the post office and a professional mailing house before beginning. It is important to discuss such things as bulk mail permits, zip code sorting, size and dimensions of mail pieces, standardized sizes for mechanical folding and stuffing machines, and other matters.

*Nonprofit postage?* Check to see if the organization sponsoring the tour has nonprofit status. If so, it will have a nonprofit mailing permit which they *may* elect to use for this project, thus keeping postage costs down. In this case, the brochure, cover letter, and envelope will have to comply with certain requirements to qualify for nonprofit mail, so this should be decided before the brochure is prepared.

## Using an Organizer or "Draw"

One of the most effective methods of forming a group is by using an organizer, or "draw," as it is sometimes called. This is the name whose affiliation with the project ensures that people will be drawn to the tour. It could be the minister leading his congregation to the Holy Land, a renowned writer or lecturer speaking to the group during the tour, the golf pro forming a group from his or her country club, or an outstanding business person promising to open import/export doors overseas. Another name for such a person is a "Pied Piper."

Use of a name draw can be a decided advantage in that this person can serve as a focal point around whom people will gather—that is, this person can provide built-in publicity. People who may not have thought of traveling in a group may be motivated to travel as part of this group for a number of reasons, such as the following:

- Respect for the leader.
- Desire to be a member of the "in group."
- Entrée to people and places overseas not generally available to the individual traveler or even to the average group.
- Assurance of travel companions of similar tastes and interests.

If used effectively, a name draw can mean that less publicity will be needed, or that the publicity that is needed will get further mileage. For example, a news release to the local newspaper using the name draw may have a better chance of being published, and the brochure that is printed with the famous name on the cover may have a better chance of being read (see Figure 7.2).

But for all the advantages a name draw can bring to the travel project there can also be some disadvantages, or at least some factors that should be considered.

**Figure 7.2** Name draw sample brochure.

## Things to Consider When Using a Name Draw

- Free trip(s). Usually such an individual will require a free trip (sometimes two, to include the spouse). Lesser-known individuals probably will be willing to receive one free trip for a given number of passengers booked—perhaps one with fifteen, the spouse with thirty, and a cash payment (also called an honorarium) with forty-five and above. On the other hand, certain well-known individuals may require a guarantee of the free trip or trips upfront, without sales volume prerequisites. In other words, conceivably an agency could be placed in a risk position, so that if the tour did not sell well, the complimentary trip(s) would still be required as agreed on in exchange for use of the draw person's name. In this event, the agency might have to pay out of pocket for complimentary air tickets, hotel rooms, and so forth if insufficient complimentaries were forthcoming from suppliers due to low sales figures.
- Some name draw persons may act as salespersons for the agency and actually work at helping to fill the tour. Others may simply lend their name to the project but expect the agency (or the tour's sponsoring club or church) to do all the work. They are, in this case, a "silent draw."
- A name draw person or organizer may be an excellent public relations person or salesperson, but may not have the personal qualities necessary to act as the real working tour manager. Such a case requires putting on a professional tour manager in addition to the draw person, and costing this person in as well. (See chapters 10 and 11.)
- The agency should take the responsibility of reminding the name draw or organizer to be sure that important deadlines are met. Someone from the agency will have to make sure the organizer is adhering to a strict schedule, if the trip is to be a success.

LETTER OF UNDERSTANDING

It is important to have a contract, or at least a letter of understanding (Figure 7.3), between the agency and the name draw person or organizer, clarifying areas of possible misunderstanding. This letter should mention the following.

- Complimentary trips—will they be upfront or as earned, for one or for two?

LSI TRAVEL AGENCY, INC.

June 23, 1984

Mrs. Elaine Whittaker
167 Rose Court
Kansas City, Missouri 64106

Dear Mrs. Whittaker:

This will reconfirm our discussion today regarding your participation in our July 11 cruise to the Baltic with Royal Cruise Line.

(1) The cruise described is RCL's Baltic Cruise July 11-25, 1985 as described on page 17 of their 1984 brochure.

(2) It is agreed that you will be entitled to one complimentary air/sea cruise round-trip from Kansas City with a minimum of 30 adult air/sea passengers joining this project and a second similar complimentary when the group reaches 45 adult air/sea passengers.

(3) The complimentary will consist of the same services as included in the cruise for other members of this group. Conversely, any services not included for other members of the group are not included for you.

(4) You will agree to give a minimum of four shipboard lectures exclusively for our group, subject matter and brief description of each to be made available to us no later than January 1, 1985. No honorarium will be paid for these lectures.

(5) You will agree to allow your name to be listed as group leader in all promotional materials published on this project.

(6) You will travel on air tickets accrued through volume bookings and issued by Royal Cruise Line. Travel will be via economy class air and choice of airline, flight schedule and other flight matters will be as designated by Royal Cruise Line.

(7) Complimentary cruise accommodations will be on a share-cabin basis and will be in a category which is an average of categories purchased by participants in this group. Final assignment of cabin will be at the discretion of Royal Cruise Line.

(8) You will agree to make available use of the special mailing list of the approximate 8,000 member "Lovers of Archaeology" organization with which you are affiliated.

(9) LSI Travel Agency, Inc. agrees to provide a professional tour manager for this project to handle all behind-the-scenes business details. No tour managing duties are to be expected of you while on the cruise.

(10) All expenses related to promotion and sales of this project shall be at the expense of LSI Travel Agency, Inc. No sales efforts are expected of you.

(11) You will agree to participate with us in one pre-trip promotional evening, the date of this event to be cleared with you first.

Signature: *Marty Sarley de Souto*    Signature: _____

**Figure 7.3** Letter of agreement with a "name draw" leader.

- Additional remuneration—will there be a salary, a speaker's fee, or honorarium?
- What does the complimentary trip consist of? What meals, what sightseeing, or shore excursions will be included? Will lodging be on a share basis or single-room basis?
- What expenses are not covered in the complimentary trip? Must the individual remain with the group throughout? What duties are expected of this person? (Many times agency personnel may lead a name draw to believe that the position involves nothing more than a little public relations. In actuality, once out on tour the organizer may find a great deal which needs doing such as reconfirming air tickets, assisting ill passengers, tracing lost passports, acting as host at parties, and so forth.)
- Will the agency have use of the organization's mailing list or a list of the organizer's personal following? Often an agency may wish to stipulate that the offer depends upon the draw person providing one-time access to a specific mailing list for promotion of the project. Granted, the mailing will cost money, but it might reach clients to whom the agency would not otherwise have access. A minister, for example, might agree to circulate a brochure not only to his own congregation but to affiliated congregations. A university alumni association might promise to mail to all alumni who were graduated within a given time period. A celebrity might give an agency a list of his or her personal "following."
- If bookings are coming in on this tour from more than one source, how will the source of each booking be identified? Will the organizer's initials be on the reservation form? Will a different color reservation form be assigned to different organizations? Will the agency rely on the passenger's word? (These details should be clear so that there is no infighting over a client by different organizers or outside salespeople.)
- Will free air fares be given from the home city or the gateway city?

## Promotional Evening

If the potential tour participants are in a reasonably close geographical area, a promotional evening could be an effective way to generate interest (and, it is hoped, enrollments) for the tour. On the other hand, if the tour is being sold nationwide or even statewide, it probably will not be possible to get sufficient attendance in one locale.

Assume, however, that the tour is being marketed locally and that 90 percent of the tour participants will come from the local community. In this case, a promotional evening can be quite effective without being unduly expensive. This gathering is not to be confused with a predeparture party or briefing. The purpose of a promotional evening is exactly that—to promote the tour. The success of such an evening is not measured by how many attended, how many glasses of champagne were consumed, or what a wonderful time was had by all. The success of the evening is measured by how many tour bookings it generated—either with enrollments that very night or shortly thereafter. So, it is important to be sure that invitations are issued to the following:

1. Those who already are enrolled in the tour. They will generate enthusiasm.
2. Friends of those enrolled in the tour. Why not ask each person already under deposit on the tour to bring a friend?
3. Those whom the agency representative and the tour organizer believe are "on the fence"—people who have called the agency to inquire about the trip or who have told the organizer that they are considering the trip, but who have not yet signed up.
4. Other potential travelers whom the agency and the organizer carefully cull from lists.

If this is a private club's tour, the promotional function will have to be open to all members of the club; it is not possible just to pick and choose which members to invite. However, double check to be sure that those in the above four categories are especially encouraged to come.

Of course, the function need not be held in the evening. If appealing to a senior citizens' group who might not wish to go out at night, or to a clientele that is not employed during the day, it may be more appropriate to schedule an afternoon function, perhaps a tea.

PREPLANNING

The first thing to be done is to establish the date of the promotional function, being sure that there is more than enough lead time to plan the function properly, get the invitations out, and be assured of a good turnout. Clear the date first to avoid conflicts with other functions the target group might be expected to attend. Then pick the location—it is a good idea to have a second choice of date available in case the chosen location is not available on the date selected.

After the date and the place are confirmed, be sure to reserve any films, speakers, or other programming that are planned. Get the participating airline or cruise line involved. Often, they will give financial help or will provide films or props. Group operators have known air and cruise lines to supply everything from engraved matchbooks to a Japanese torii gate.

CHECKLIST

As does any good host or hostess, it is wise to have a checklist to be sure that everything goes smoothly. Points to check include the following:

1. *Invitation RSVP control*—a system to keep track of how many are coming; how many have not answered the invitation and need followup; and how many have declined. Knowing the anticipated turnout makes it easier to plan for refreshments, seating, and other items. Be sure to allow for last-minute cancellations due to illness, bad weather, and so forth; invite more guests than might be needed.

2. *Refreshments* that are attractive and generous but do not overshadow the program itself. Emphasis should focus on program content and on building interest in the trip. Wine and cheese or coffee and tea with finger desserts are particularly appropriate.

3. *Equipment check* or trial run on such equipment as the PA system, movie projector, tape recorder, light-dimmer, draw draperies, and extension cords. There is nothing more embarrassing than having a hundred people sitting quietly waiting for the film to roll and having the projector break down.

4. *Miscellaneous details*—arrangements for greeting people at the door, handling coats, parking, and other seemingly extraneous details can help make the evening a success.

PROMOTIONAL EVENING FORMAT

A successful promotional program will not be overly long. It should incorporate a film or two of the area(s) to be visited—a film that is up to date and slick. Any film should be previewed before it is shown to assure that it is appropriate, in good condition, and will generate excitement. Slide shows, unless professionally done by an airline or cruise line with multiscreen projections, tend to appear homemade. Few people truly enjoy sitting through a slide show of someone else's trip.

Music is one of the greatest catalysts in the world. When promoting a trip to the Adriatic, a strolling Greek bouzouki player during refreshments would be appropriate. Or, if the evening is designed to promote a trip to Latin America, perhaps a local college would have a student salsa band or guitarist for hire. Plan for music that is appropriate to the destination; a Mexican mariachi band would not do much to promote a trip to Spain.

Handicrafts, posters, artifacts, and costumes can add to the color of the evening. Agents have been known to lead a Greek folk dance to promote a Greek Islands cruise, wear an alpaca poncho to promote a trip to Peru, show off their favorite Japanese wood-block prints, and even weave artificial cherry blossoms up an entire staircase for a Night in Japan.

And, if the guests' senses have been appealed to both visually and aurally, why not provide a taste treat as well? Many finger foods suggest foreign countries—miniature Italian pizzas, French petit fours, Chinese egg rolls, or Argentinian empanadas, to name a few.

After the film has been presented and refreshments have been served, allow a period for questions. Some agents plant one or two friends in the audience, prepared with a couple of good questions in case people are shy about starting the question-and-answer period. Everyone present should be given another copy of the tour brochure. The agency representative should plan to make a sales pitch that night, referring to the brochure, the reservation form therein, and stating that reservations are being accepted that evening. Some agents, at this point, state that the tour is already more than half-filled and there is room for only a limited number. If people do not have their checkbooks with them, the agent can suggest that they complete the reservation form and turn it in that evening, and ask them to forward the check in a day or two. Writing out something that night makes clients feel committed to taking the tour.

GIVEAWAYS

Giveaways or door prizes, although sometimes gimmicky, can be fun and can ensure that the audience will stay until the drawing. Records, picture books of a foreign country, or travel calendars are often appreciated, Gift certificates to a popular department store are welcome prizes, also. Of course, a free around-the-world trip could be raffled off, but the local rules on raffles, lotteries, and the like should be checked first. Sometimes suppliers will help out, depending on how rich they are feeling at the time. Perhaps local merchants would help with luggage, a travel diary, or a foreign cookbook. Ask! If not, buy one impressive door prize and cost it into the promotional budget for the tour.

WRAPUP

It is helpful to know exactly who was present at the promotional event. An elegant way to find out is to have each guest sign a guest book with name and address on arrival. At the end of the program remind the audience to sign on the way out in case they did not get to do so on the way in.

After the festivities are over, it is time to take stock—pay the bills, see how much the event finally cost and how many bookings resulted. It is also considerate to send thank-you notes to all those who helped, such as the guest speaker, the airline sales representative, the hotel banquet manager.

## Advertising

Undoubtably an agency will want to use advertising in some form for promotion of a tour product. Even if the tour is for a private organization, not requiring public solicitation of tour membership, it still may be necessary to advertise in the organization's newsletter or to augment the tour membership formed by a strong nucleus from the organization by advertising to outsiders from the general public.

In some cases, an agency may simply be putting together a tour on speculation, hoping to promote it in the community or within a certain profession. In this case, it will most surely be necessary to plan an advertising campaign.

## Advertising Agencies

If an agency plans on using nationwide advertising or has a fairly large advertising budget, it may be possible to consider using an advertising agency. Advertising agencies, like retail travel agencies, work on a commission basis. Their suppliers are the media they use—the newspapers, magazines, radio and television stations and so forth. These media usually pay them 15 percent.

So, if the media selected will pay the advertising agency a commission, it probably will not cost any more to work through an advertising agency than to go direct to the publication. On the other hand, if the media selected will not pay a commission to the advertising agency, the agency undoubtably will charge a service fee—a situation similar to a client asking to be booked into a pension or small hotel that does not pay a travel agent a commission. Usually newspapers do not pay commissions to advertising agencies for local advertising. Most magazines and radio and television stations do. If in doubt, ask!

Whether or not they receive a commission, advertising agencies will charge production costs for such things as typesetting, art, layout, and photos. Many agencies are full-service agencies, offering a complete range of services, including market research, public relations, advertisement preparation and placement, advertisement clipping service, and coordinated billing. This is similar to the full-service travel agency that sells everything from a two-day local bus tour to an around-the world cruise. Other advertising agencies are smaller operations, or agencies that elect to handle only specific services in a selective fashion. This is much like some travel agencies that elect to handle only certain cruise lines or tour operators whom they know are reputable, or to specialize in certain kinds of travel, such as commercial accounts, adventure trekking, and so forth.

Dealing with only one or two publications may be relatively simple to do. However, running advertisements in a wide spectrum of publications may become totally unwieldy. It requires juggling different deadline dates, varying advertisement sizes and dimensions, and billings, In such cases, it may be worthwhile to work through an advertising agency just to keep visits from advertisement salesmen, phone calls, and the work load within reason.

And just as it is important for the traveler to have a good relationship with a travel counselor, so it is important to have a good working relationship with the advertising agency selected. Shop around. Ask questions. Does the advertising agency really want the account? Is the account big enough to interest them? Can their copywriters write about travel? Have they handled any other travel accounts? Are their artists creative? Ask to see some of their work—particularly travel-related campaigns. Expensive four-color process slick catalogues with professional color photos will not show what an advertising agency can do on a small budget for a one-color 4" x 9" magazine advertisement.

Many travel agencies find that their advertising account is not large enough to warrant an advertising agency, meaning that they have to learn to do it themselves. This requires learning how to work with a typesetter and a freelance commercial artist, probably writing the headlines and copy, and selecting media on a trial-and-error basis.

Perhaps one might well start with newspaper advertisements and then graduate to magazines (and perhaps radio occasionally as skills improve). Here are some of the advantages and disadvantages of the different media.

## Newspapers

Newspapers are one of the most effective media, because newspapers are heavily read by the public and the cost of advertising in them is relatively low compared to the costs in magazines, radio, and television. Newspaper rates are based on circulation, so the more readers the paper has, the higher the rates. Do not overlook the small weekly papers, however, many of which are much less expensive than the dailies, and may even reach a targeted local market more effectively than the higher-circulation dailies. It is fairly easy to schedule advertisements in newspapers because of frequency of publication and short lead time (advertisements do not have to be scheduled months in advance). However, newspapers are read by all—rich and poor alike, tour prospects and not—so a tour advertisement may be wasted on armchair travelers.

## Magazines

If a magazine is directed to a specific market segment, that is, photographers, single working women under age thirty-five, the male bon vivant, or any other specific type of reader, it will be more beneficial to direct advertising to this specific clientele rather than to the general public. Special-interest magazines of this nature, instead of general-circulation magazines, are the trend nowadays. Magazines reach more affluent readers than do newspapers, and they stay around the house longer than the daily newspaper, so an advertisement might be read several times and by several different people. However, magazines require a longer lead time than newspapers, requiring that advertisers place the order for space and then submit the advertisement several months in advance to meet the magazine's publication schedule.

## Radio and Television

Just as some magazines specialize in certain markets, radio stations appeal to specific audiences—those who enjoy country and western music, soul, rock, the classics, and so forth. Radio stations will be happy to provide details on who is listening when. Drive time during commuting hours usually is most expensive. Radio advertisements do not need to be just a straight message. They can combine music and sound effects along with the message. But it is important that the message be short (usually thirty-second spots) and easy to remember. Most listeners are not just sitting with pencil and paper in hand poised waiting to write down a telephone number; it is necessary to repeat it over and over, slowly, so that they can retain it in mind long enough to get a pencil.

Television is rarely used for tour promotion by the small-to-medium-sized travel agency or tour operator. Owing to high costs and the need to produce a truly professional advertising spot, it is not recommended.

### Some Hints for Using Media Effectively

*Continuity.* One advertisement, in one issue of a magazine or newspaper, will not bring the desired results. Plan and budget for a series of advertisements to improve the chances of success. Many readers do not clip the coupon and send in for the brochure the first time they see the advertisement, but by the second or third week they begin to assume that a company must be solid if it can continue advertising week after week. A minimum of three advertisements will be needed. Stay with the same style of advertisement (same typeface, same artistic appearance), even if the copy changes each week. Readers will begin to recognize the style when they see it.

Also note that publications give a better rate if a series of advertisements is reserved in advance—they have a one-time rate, three-time rate, and so forth. Figure 7.4 shows some small ads that follow the following guidelines:

*Focus.* An advertisement cannot tell the entire story of the tour. It should focus around the major points, both visually and in words. Think of different approaches; then emphasize one. When planning an advertisement, ask: Are we selling price? Elegance? Unusual itinerary? A sun break from rotten winter weather? A learning experience? Camaraderie? In selecting the approach, remember that the ultimate purpose of the advertisement is not to sell the tour. It is to get the reader to call or write in for the brochure.

*Simplicity.* The best advertisement is probably the simplest. An advertisement can be clever and different in order to stand out from others around it, but it need not be complicated or overly elaborate. An advertisement that incorporates one piece of dominant art with good headlines and a small amount of body copy probably works best.

*Borders.* An advertisement does not appear alone. It usually appears on a page surrounded by articles and other advertisements competing for the reader's attention. Something should set an ad off from surrounding clutter—a border, dotted lines, or art forming a natural barrier indicating where one advertisement ends and the next one begins.

*White space.* There is nothing more valuable than white space—that is, empty, uncluttered, perfectly blank space. Often, the more elegant the ad, the more empty it is. Since advertising space is expensive, there is a tendency to fill it. But an advertisement that is too full, too busy, simply confuses the reader. Also, white space can act as a buffer, forming an undeclared barrier around the advertisement, onto which neighboring copy cannot encroach.

*Think double duty.* Often an advertisement can be used later. It can be blown up and reprinted as a flyer that can be used as a reminder insert in a mailing. When paying for original art or graphics, encourage the artist to produce a design that can also be used for the cover of the tour brochure, for another advertisement, and for invitations to promotional evenings.

COUPONS

A reply coupon included in an advertisement serves two purpose. First, it gives the reader something physical to cut out and send in, requesting information on the tour (thus providing the interested reader's name and address for further followup). Second, it helps an agent to track which publications are bringing results and how much these results are costing the agency, or what is termed *acquisition costs.* Reply coupons should be coded. For example, the code CPD71185 might be used for an advertisement in the July 11, 1985 issue of the *Cleveland Plain Dealer.* The same advertisement on the same date in the *San Francisco Chronicle* could be coded SFC71185. These codes, typeset on the advertisement itself, provide a record of the number of responses each advertisement generates. If an advertisement costing $300 brings 100 inquiries, it is costing $3 per inquiry, or what is called a $3 per inquiry acquisition cost. By running exactly the same advertisement—same size, same tour product—in different publications, and by tracking the number of inquiries that result from each, it can easily be determined which publications are most effective.

**Figure 7.4** Samples of ads showing (a) interesting border and simulating a border; (b) effective headline; (c) developing an art theme for brochure cover and ad; (d) advertising several tours under one theme; (e) good small ad with dominant headline, effective art, and small amount of copy.

MARKETING THE TOUR 135

When first reserving advertisement space with a publication, indicate if the advertisement will have a coupon. This will help prevent two coupons being printed back to back. Ask for an *outside position*—that is, the outside edge of the page. It is much easier to cut out a coupon if it is not in the center of the page. The coupon should also be large and clear enough to permit the reader to write on it easily. See Figure 7.5 for a sample coupon.

CO-OP ADVERTISING

The possibility of cooperative (co-op) advertising should not be overlooked. This is advertising in which the costs are shared with a supplier. Sometimes several stores in one city suddenly seem to be advertising Wrangler Jeans instead of Levi's, or Martex towels instead of Cannon, in a given week. It may be because the jeans company or towel company had offered to share the cost of the advertising campaign with the department stores that particular week. A travel agency can look to its travel suppliers for similar help.

If an agency is selling a cruise or an existing tour package as is, the supplier should have advertising slicks for that particular product available. The agency can them simply drop in its own name and address. In many cases, the supplier will share the cost of the advertisement with the agency upon receipt of proof that the advertisement actually ran. This proof can be a sample tear sheet from the publication and invoice. Check first with the supplier to make sure this arrangement is acceptable. In other cases, if the supplier already has agreed to pay the agency an override commission, it may be assumed that the override is paid to cover promotional expenditures of this nature and, therefore, the supplier may not be willing to spend additional monies on co-op advertisements.

When a tour package is put together from scratch, the availability of co-op advertising funds is a strictly negotiable item between the agency and the sponsoring airline or other suppliers (see chapter 4 regarding negotiations with suppliers) and would be considered part of the total negotiated package. If planning to use a supplier's advertisement slicks do note they may not be really appropriate for a custom-designed tour product. Also the supplier's slicks may project the image of the supplier and its product rather than the agency's image.

## Press Releases

In the past, getting one's name in the paper was a sure route to social ruin. Top families paid to keep their names out of the press. Today, as

# Travel with Friends

... the new friends you'll make as a member of the Mariner Club, a club for those who enjoy cruising.

**NO FEE TO JOIN ★ BONUSES**
**SPECIAL PARTIES ★ SHORE EVENTS**

———— *Sampling of Cruises:* ————

★ **New England/Eastern Canada**  ★ **Amazon, Caribbean**
Sept. 22. *Royal Viking Sky*        Jan. 4. *Stella Solaris*
★ **Asia Discovery**                ★ **World Cruise**
Oct. 25. *Pearl of Scandinavia*     Jan. 6. *Rotterdam*

## The Mariner Club
### New Members Welcome!

The Mariner Club is the original Matson Lines and Pacific Far East Line Past-Passengers Club founded in 1961.

To: The Mariner Club
c/o Golden Bear Travel
P.O. Box 3926 • San Francisco, CA 94119

Please send me information on the Mariner Club and a copy of a current Calendar of Cruises.

Name _____
Address _____
Town _____ State _____ Zip _____

(SFC 4/16/85)

**Figure 7.5** Ad coupon. Note the coding (circled).

cafe society and the jet set have replaced the old society, at least in the public eye, people are more and more assured that they are somebody if their name appears in print. Many pay to see that it does. The public wants to read who vacationed where, and what new farflung corner of the world is in fashion today. Many enjoy traveling vicariously through the society pages, or through a relatively new phenomenon—the travel section of the newspaper or the travel columns of leading magazines.

And, although a tour may not make the pages of *Vogue* the first time around, perhaps it is possible to get a mention in the hometown newspaper or in a specialty magazine. The average retail travel agency that may be large enough to have a tour department, still cannot afford to retain a full-scale public relations company or professional press person. Once again, it is a matter of the do-it-yourself approach, learning how to get the tour into the press.

The usual vehicle for placing an article in the press is what is termed a press release or sometimes a news release. This is a short, punchy article that is sent to various editors. (See Figure 7.6 for an example of a press release.) It should be sent to a specific editor (Travel Editor, Theater Editor, or whatever). Many theater tours may be better promoted in the Sunday theater section than in the travel section, for example. If it is possible to get the name of the editor and address this individual personally, so much the better.

PRESS RELEASE FORMAT

The usual format is to type the release double-spaced, on plain white bond paper with the agency name, address, and telephone contact in the upper lefthand corner. This lets the recipient know immediately who sent it and how to reach that person quickly and easily for further information or an interview. The release should be dated and should also indicate when the news may be released. Note the term *news;* it should be worded carefully so that it *is* news. If it is the same old tour repeated every year, a new angle should be stressed. A publication needs a news "peg" on which to hang the article, a reason to justify the article. It cannot appear that they are just giving away free advertising in the form of an article.

If possible, keep the release to one page. The essentials should be in the first paragraph—where the tour goes, dates, highlights, name of leader if a known name, and any unique angle. Remember, the editor is inundated with similar press releases for many tours every week. So anything unusual about this tour which might catch the editor's eye should be mentioned early in the release. Is the tour sponsored by a local college for academic credit? Does it feature behind-the-scenes visits to private homes? Perhaps the tour is sponsored by a local museum and raises money for the museum. Whatever the local, unusual angle, stress it. Most important, the news should be told in a straightforward, simple manner. A release is not an appropriate place to write poetic descriptions of the scenery. Accuracy and credibility are important. If the tour stays at first-class hotels, say so; do not inflate them to deluxe. If the tour is open to the public and if there is still space available, say so. Many readers assume that a private-sounding tour is just that, private. At the end of the release, put the journalistic sign-off sign: -30-. Then, check the release for errors, mispellings, and misunderstandings. Let it stand for a day or two and then reread it. Does it still sound as good as it did when you wrote it? Are all those extra words necessary, or can you tighten it up a bit?

FROM:
LSI Travel Agency, Inc.
1234 Fifth Avenue
Anytown, U.S.A.

March 1, 1985

For Immediate Release

TO:
Sunday Travel Editor
Your local newspaper
Address

FALL TOUR TO EUROPE SCHEDULED
BY ROSEMONT COUNTRY CLUB

An exciting eleven-day trip to Europe will depart on September 6, sponsored by the Rosemont Country Club.

The itinerary includes Amsterdam, Paris and Rome. Highlights include a cruise along Amsterdam's canals, a full-day excursion to the Hague and Delft to see the world-famous blue Delft-ware china, and an evening at the Lido Night Club in Paris. Other features are a personally-escorted tour of the Louvre, an afternoon at the Vatican Museum and Sistine Chapel while in Rome, and a full-day Sunday excursion with country lunch to the Villa d'Este outside of Rome.

The trip is via Trans World Airlines and is operated by LSI Travel Agency, Inc. of Anytown, U.S.A. It is fully escorted and includes deluxe hotels, air fare, full program of sightseeing and social events, many meals, taxes, tips, and all tour services.

Although planned by the Rosemont Country Club for its members and their friends, other interested members of the community are welcome to join the tour. To obtain full details including a day by day itinerary and prices, contact LSI Travel Agency, Inc. at 1234 Fifth Avenue, Anywhere, U.S.A. or call toll-free: 800-123-4567.

**Figure 7.6** Sample press release.

## PHOTOS

Sometimes a photo may be included with the press release. The newspaper may not have room to run both the article and the photo, but the photo may at least draw the editor's attention to the release. And if the photo and the release are good enough, the editor just might make room for them. Of course, it can be costly to send photos if releases are sent simultaneously to a large number of publications. Photos should be black-and-white glossies, not color, and preferably 8" x 10" size. They should be well focused and not too dark, since newsprint paper stock tends to absorb ink and darken photos. Be sure that the photo carries a caption and, if necessary, a credit line recognizing the photographer or source of the photo. Subject matter can be a destination scene of an area the tour will visit or it can be several of the group organizers together packing a suitcase or discussing the trip (they should not look too posed). Be sure to obtain written permission from those in the photo before using it.

The press release and accompanying photo should go out some months before tour departure, since the newspaper may not find a place for it until later and since it should appear early enough to bring in some sales. The release will not do much good if it appears five weeks before tour departure when unsold air and hotel space had to be released forty-five days prior.

Do not be disappointed if the paper does not use the release. They are not obligated to do so. Advertising is paid space and, therefore, guarantees that a paid advertisement will appear. But a press release is not paid space. If it is published, it is simply free publicity, a bonus, but not something to be counted on. The editor may choose to use it or not, to rewrite it or to chop it, as more important competing news or a large advertisement comes along. An article will have a better chance of being published if it is news, if it has a local angle (a local organization sponsoring it or a local name escorting it), and a local price. The price out of New York is not really relevant to a tourist in Des Moines.

PRESS RELEASE DO'S AND DON'TS

Do continue to send releases to publications even if they do not publish them at first. *Don't* threaten to withdraw advertising if they will not run a story. *Do* try to develop a rapport with the editor if possible. And *don't* forget the rural or residential weeklies, where there may be a better chance for publication than in a big-city daily newspaper and where news or feature articles are often needed. And *do* remember to be considerate. Even the most callous big-city editor appreciates a gracious "thank you."

MARKETING THE TOUR 141

# SPRING HAS ALMOST SPRUNG WITHOUT YOU!

**SEE HOLLAND AT TULIP TIME WITH THE MARINERS**

Cruise the scenic Holland Waterways aboard the M.S. Amicitia
Then visit Belgium's historic cities
Optional - continue on to the British Isles aboard the Royal Viking Sky
25 Days • April 26 - May 20.

If our earlier brochure missed you or if you'd still like to reserve a place, call us toll free:
SAN FRANCISCO/BAY AREA (415) 258-9800 • ELSEWHERE IN CALIFORNIA (800) 451-8572 • OUTSIDE CALIFORNIA (800) 551-1000

**Figure 7.7**  Sample followup flyer.

# 8
# Client Handling

Once promotional material on the tour is out, the first thing that may happen is that prospective clients will write or call for information. Someone will have to answer those questions; so the week that promotion breaks is not the week for the person or persons responsible to be on vacation. Staff should be carefully briefed in advance on the tour so that they can sound knowledgeable (and gracious) when those phones start ringing or those letters come in. This will be the client's first contact with the agency, so be ready to make it a favorable first impression.

**Inquiries**

It is best to be prepared with a standard letter to answer those who ask for a brochure (see Figure 8.1). This letter accompanies the brochure because it is impersonal to send a brochure alone in an envelope. This letter can be preprinted if a large volume of inquiries is anticipated, or it can be typed on a memory typewriter, personalizing each letter. The letter should convey personal warmth and friendliness and the closing should urge some action. Keep a record of the names and addresses of those who inquire, so that a followup letter can be sent to those who do not enroll. (Figure 8.2 is a sample followup letter.)

Many group operators offer a client an option date if it appears that there is real interest. To do this, offer to hold a firm place on the tour for a certain limited period—usually ten days or so—by which date the

LSI TRAVEL AGENCY, INC.

Date

DEAR FRIEND (or personalize)

We are so pleased to know of your interest in our tour program.

Enclosed is the brochure you requested, giving full details and including a day-by-day itinerary that will give you an idea of the many exciting activities planned.

Please refer particularly to the paragraph entitled "Tour Price Includes." You will note our price is virtually all-inclusive -- air fare, top hotels, many meals, a full program of sightseeing and social activities, baggage handling, even tips -- thus enabling you to plan ahead and budget accordingly, knowing you won't have lots of unexpected expenses along the way.

Most of our tours do fill up well in advance, so if you are serious about joining us, we would urge that you submit your reservation quickly to assure you of a place. We like to keep our groups to a fairly small, friendly size, so once our space is sold, we close out the tour rather than trying to secure additional reservations.

If you have questions before enrolling, do feel free to call us collect at 312-626-8060.

Cordially,

Marty Sarbey de Souto

Marty Sarbey de Souto, CTC
Group Manager

MS/s
enclosure

**Figure 8.1**   Inquiry reply letter.

client must submit the required deposit and registration form to formalize and enroll (Figure 8.3 is a sample of such a letter). Never count in the booking totals people who have said that they are coming but who have not yet sent in a reservation form and deposit. Without a deposit they cannot be considered firm bookings.

LSI TRAVEL AGENCY, INC.

Date

DEAR FRIEND (or personalize)

We recall that earlier you inquired about our tour program. (Or, you can individualize it to the fall tour to Europe with the Rosemont Country Club). To date, we have not heard from you further and we wonder if you are still hoping to travel with us.

This is simply a courtesy note to let you know that the tour space is selling rapidly and that if you are still considering going, we must hear from you quickly. Enclosed is a duplicate copy of the tour brochure in case you may no longer have the one sent you earlier.

Would you be kind enough to give us a call or drop a line and let us know of your plans? If you have questions not answered in the brochure, feel free to call and chat with us.

Awaiting word ...

Sincerely,

Marty Sarbey de Souto, CTC
Group Manager

MS/s
enclosure

**Figure 8.2** Inquiry followup letter.

## Reservations and Deposits

As bookings start coming in they should be acknowledged immediately. The client will want to know if the reservation and deposit have been received and whether or not space is confirmed. Try to make it a rule to acknowledge all bookings the same day they come in. The acknowledgment need not be a lengthy and complicated letter. It can even be a preprinted thank-you card of some sort (Figure 8.4). But promptness is important.

If the agency is selling a cruise and cannot immediately confirm the category of space that the client requests, that thank-you should simply acknowledge the booking but do not use the word "confirm." That way,

LSI TRAVEL AGENCY, INC.

March 1, 1985

Mrs. Merle Davis
2433 Beaver Place
Briston, IN 46507

Dear Mrs. Davis:

It was nice chatting with you today and we are looking forward to having you and Mr. Davis join us on the European Highlights Tour sponsored by Rosemont Country Club.

To reconfirm our telephone conversation, we are holding two places for you under option for ten days, that is until 5:00 p.m. March 10. We will need to receive the reservation form from the brochure along with a $400 deposit by then in order to secure these reservations.

If you have any more questions, do feel free to give me a call. In the meantime, I'll be on the lookout for your reservation in the mail.

Sincerely,

Marty Sarbey de Souto, CTC
Group Manager

MS/s
cc: Mrs. Charles Goodwin-Rosemont Country Club

**Figure 8.3** Option offer.

if clients request category "E" on the ship (an outside twin), and only an "F" (inside twin category) can be confirmed they cannot later quote the letter to say that the request had been "confirmed."

If a client is enrolling in the tour through a club or organization which, in turn, is forwarding the booking to the agency, have an acknowledgment letter preprinted on the club's letterhead for it to send to the applicant when it receives the reservation (see Figure 8.5). This letter should advise the applicant that the reservation form and check have been received and have been forwarded to LSI Travel Agency, Inc., the official business agent for the project. The clients should also be assured that they will be hearing directly from LSI Travel.

*Thank You*

for joining our

A detailed record of your charges and payments is being kept and an itemized accounting of your membership will be sent to you before the last payment is due.

Your cancelled checks will serve as receipts for payments made.

Sincerely,

**Figure 8.4** Standardized acknowledgment card.

## Information Bulletins

Between the time when members join the tour and when they depart on the trip, they should receive a minimum of three major mailings and information bulletins. The first one goes out right after they enroll, perhaps along with their welcome or acknowledgment letter (Figure 8.6). This first bulletin should be the most complete. The second one goes out with the members' bill at invoice time; that is a short update bulletin. The third major mailing is the departure bulletin, which goes out with the final documents a couple of weeks before departure. These information bulletins are pieces that will have to be written from scratch and then photocopied or printed. These bulletins serve five basic purposes.

1. Information bulletins give the tour members a feeling of confidence, of well-being, because they show that the agency has anticipated many of their questions as they prepare for the trip.

ROSEMONT COUNTRY CLUB

DEAR FRIENDS: (or personalize to individual names)

This will acknowledge receipt of your application and deposit for membership in our exciting tour to Europe this fall. We are pleased that you have decided to come along!

As you may know, we are working in cooperation with LSI Travel Agency here in town. As travel professionals, they are handling all the business details of the program for us. Therefore, your reservation request has been given to them, and very shortly you should be hearing from the tour manager in their office in charge of our trip.

You will also be receiving a great deal of background information that should help you in your pretrip planning and that should answer a number of questions one always has before such a trip ... information on things like passports, luggage, appropriate clothes for the various functions we'll be attending, and so forth.

We at the Rosemont Country Club know it's going to be a wonderful vacation. We look forward to traveling with you.

Sincerely,

*Marian Goodwin*

Mrs. Charles Goodwin
President

MG/mfs

**Figure 8.5**  Sponsoring club's acknowledgment letter.

2. Information bulletins answer many questions that could not be covered adequately in a tour brochure. For example, in the brochure it may be possible to have one short paragraph on clothing, packing, and wardrobe selection. However, it is not possible to give a complete list of wardrobe suggestions in a brochure, nor would it really be appropriate there. The main purpose of the brochure is to sell and to move the reader to enroll in the tour. The bulletins have room for more information; that is their purpose.
3. Information bulletins standardize information, ensuring that all group members receive exactly the same answers.
4. Information bulletins reduce the number of letters and phone calls to the agency office, allowing the staff more time to deal

LSI TRAVEL AGENCY, INC.

Date

Mr. and Mrs. Elliott Wing
2433 Brown Derby Road
Rosemont, IL. 60018

Dear Mr. and Mrs. Wing:

We have been advised by the Rosemont Country Club that you are applying for participation in their tour to Europe this fall. As I believe they may already have advised you, we are the agency working with them in handling all the business details of the trip. Therefore, we wanted to get in touch with you right away to say "Welcome Aboard" and to let you know that your space on the tour is definitely confirmed.

To assist you in your pre-trip planning, we are enclosing an information bulletin that should answer a number of questions that may occur to you. Please read it carefully and if there are any things of concern to you, feel free to call us collect.

If you do not already have a passport, or if your present one has expired, may we urge you to begin passport proceedings right away. The U.S. Passport Office gets terribly backlogged during the summer months, so it is urgent that you not delay. Full instructions on how to apply for a passport are enclosed.

You probably will not be hearing from us again until late in June, when we will be in touch with you with any new tour developments. At that time we will be sending your itemized bill for balance of payment, which, as indicated in the brochure, is due July 6. You might wish to flag that date on your personal calendar so you plan and budget accordingly.

One last word -- the tour is filling rapidly, so if you know others in the Club who are planning on going or if you have friends who would like to join you, do tell them to send in their reservations quickly while space remains.

With all best wishes, and again Welcome!

Cordially,

*Marty Sarbey de Souto*

Marty Sarbey de Souto, CTC
Group Manager

MS/s
enclosures
cc: Mrs. Charles Goodwin-Rosemont Country Club

**Figure 8.6** Agency's acknowledgment letter.

with operational problems, volume of bookings, and the true management of the tour. Of course, personal contact with tour members should not be eliminated, but rather the time spent with them should be quality time, not time spent in showing them how to fill out a visa form.
5. These written bulletins form a strong legal basis. The client who later says, "I didn't know I had to cancel by July 1 to avoid a penalty" can be told, "Sir, you were told, in writing, not only in the original brochure on this project, but you were reminded again in our first information bulletin."

LEARNING TO PREPARE BULLETINS

Probably one of the most difficult transitions that a travel counselor goes through in converting from individual client handling to group handling is learning to convert from the spoken word to the written one, from personal counseling across the desk or by telephone to mass counseling via written publications such as brochures or bulletins.

When first starting in the group business, the tendency is to think of local groups, to encourage the participants to feel free to call at the office, and perhaps to have a group gathering at which they receive verbal instructions.

As an agency expands its group business, however, this method quickly outlives its usefulness, particularly if business depends on group volume. It soon seems more practical to turn to suppliers for prepublished pamphlets and instructions—to cruise lines, for example. But, although some of that information is helpful, much of it is not pertinent to the group and, in fact, may even give information conflicting with that which the agency wants the tour members to receive. For example, a cruise line's preprinted literature may instruct passengers to fill out a dining room seating request form and return it directly to the cruise line. However, the agency may have selected late sitting for the entire group, and arranged with the cruise line to have the group seated together at tables of eight. These cruise line instructions would only confuse tour members. In fact, one problem to be faced in putting a group on an existing travel package such as a cruise or another company's tour is eliminating information that is not pertinent to the group.

As the agency handles more and more groups, it is likely eventually to handle statewide or even nationwide groups rather than local ones. At this point it is essential to master the art of client handling by mail—information bulletins, letters, departure instructions, and so forth, with the only verbal contact being a WATS telephone line when clients need special help on an individual matter. By this stage, the agency should be preparing and printing its own tour information bulletins and not depending on other sources.

FIRST INFORMATION BULLETIN

The first information bulletin will be quite lengthy, and will take a good deal of time to prepare. It should cover the numerous subjects about which the tour members are going to be anxious, such as passports, inoculations, visas or tourist cards, rooming arrangements, airport security check, cameras and film, travel insurance, and seating on motorcoaches or airplanes. Other subjects to cover are cancellations and refund policy, smoking/nonsmoking, airfare restrictions, tipping, use of credit cards, and spending money. First bulletins are also concerned with foreign currency, appropriate clothing, luggage and packing, care of valuables, customs, and duty-free shops. If the trip is a cruise, the first bulletin would include information on optional shore excursions, bon voyage parties, and special social events on board. Tour participants also appreciate background reading recommendations, information on shopping enroute, and advice on how to handle special diet restrictions or certain health limitations. Let us look at some of this information in detail.

*Passports.* If a passport is needed on the trip the bulletin should let the tour member know that immediately. This is particularly important today, with lengthy delays at most United States passport offices. If visas must be secured, bear in mind that they cannot be obtained until after receiving the passenger's *valid and signed passport*. If there is a deadline date for receiving the passport, be sure to advise clients of that deadline date *at once* and urge them to begin passport proceedings *immediately*. Often, older people have trouble getting a birth certificate; the courthouse burned down, they have to obtain an affidavit of birth instead, and so forth—all of which further delays the proceedings. Try to avoid losing a tour participant at the last minute for lack of a passport! To expedite matters, include passport application forms and a separate "how-to" instruction sheet with details on number and size of photos, required acceptable identification, and cost.

*Inoculations.* Advise clients as to which inoculations are required and urge them to see their physician. Advise them also of inoculations that are recommended but not required, again referring them to their own physician.

*Visas/tourist cards.* The passport represents permission from one's *own* country to travel, while visas or tourist cards represent permission from other nations to visit them. It is important to check each country on the group's itinerary carefully to verify if a tourist visa or tourist card is needed (either in addition to or instead of a passport) and then to formally advise each passenger of what must be done. The first information bulletin is an ideal place to do this.

If visas or tourist cards are required for any of the countries on the itinerary, it will be necessary to obtain a supply of visa or tourist card applications from the particular consulate(s) concerned, or perhaps to work through a visa service that will handle this for a fee. A visa service will charge the consular fee for issuing a visa, if any, as well as a service fee and registered mail charges. (Be sure these total charges are budgeted into the tour costs at the outset.)

The agency will have to give tour members detailed written instructions on how to complete the forms and what type of photos are needed. If tour members know this in advance, they can obtain visa photos at the same time that they obtain their passport photos. To avoid confusion in filling out the visa or tourist card applications, many tour operators fill them out for their passengers, simply instructing the passengers to sign by the "X."

*Rooming arrangements.* Although the tour brochure probably stipulates that accommodations are twin or single basis, this bulletin is an excellent place to elaborate on such things as class of hotels, because many inexperienced travelers do not understand what is meant by hotel terminology such as first class, deluxe, five-star and so forth. Many Americans who assume that first class in Europe is the same as first class at home become angry upon finding that the accommodations are much simpler than what they thought they were to get.

This first information bulletin is also the place to discuss single room supplements and share-room with strangers. It is helpful to include a sentence to the effect that "Paying a single-room supplement ensures privacy but does not necessarily guarantee superior accommodations," since many knowledgeable tour operators know that single rooms often are the worst rooms in the house, located under stairways, next to elevator shafts, and in other undesirable locations.

This bulletin should also state the company's policy on sharing a room. Will the agent/tour operator team up roommates? If there is a "leftover" at the end with no potential roommate, will this person be forced to pay the single-room supplement or will the agency absorb that cost? Tour participants are entitled to know the company policy, particularly since, in some cases, people traveling alone may withdraw from the tour if they have to pay the differential for forced single-room occupancy. Conversely, some clients will refuse to enroll on the trip unless they *can* be guranteed single room occupancy. In either case, it is wise to include a statement that the agency cannot assume responsibility for the compatibility of share-room arrangements and that if individuals move out of a shared room midtour, such additional charges are at their own expense.

*Airport security.* Passengers should be advised that even as part of a tour group they still will have to go through individual airport security check (whether by metal-detection device or by hand search) and should be reminded not to carry penknives or other things that can set off the metal detectors and delay the entire group.

*Cameras and film.* It is best to alert people to the cost and scarcity of film overseas. Let them know that they should carry an adequate supply of film with them, and not depend on buying it enroute. Holding up an entire tour bus while one passenger goes out in search of film is not fair to the other passengers. This first bulletin is also the appropriate place to remind passengers that a small camera is allowed as carry-on luggage but that large cameras, cases, flash equipment, tripods, and so forth will be weighed in and/or counted as part of their tour luggage allowance. Either here or in the advice concerning airport security remind them not to let film go through the x-ray equipment, even with a shield on it; they should hand-carry it and pass it around the x-ray equipment. Many tour members, who have returned home with film totally ruined, have blamed the tour manager or the agency for not issuing a warning.

*Travel insurance.* It is probably best to send detailed information and application forms for travel insurance in a later mailing. However, this first information bulletin can allude to the fact that full information on this subject will be coming later, so that passengers do not worry and start asking for it or buy it elsewhere.

*Airplane and motorcoach seating.* Passengers should be reminded that the agency needs to know if they wish to be seated in the smoking or nonsmoking section of the aircraft, so that when it comes time to request preseating assignments from the airline, the group can be appropriately divided. This is also an opportunity to advise that even if their preference is known, there is no guarantee that the airlines will comply—that there are some airlines, some countries, where this division is not followed as rigorously as it might be in the United States.

Motorcoach seating is another subject to be brought up—perhaps gently at first, then reinforced later by the tour manager at the tour briefing once the tour is under way. The agency should establish a policy on whether smoking will or will not be allowed on the coach; for a large group, have one bus for smokers; for a smaller group, perhaps limit smoking to rear seats only. Many tour companies simply state that there will be no smoking at all in the coaches but that there will be occasional stops for rest rooms, smoking, camera buffs, and so forth.

It will be helpful to mention now that motorcoach seats will be rotated. This pretour warning (also reinforced later by the tour manager at the briefing) will help when it comes to dealing with the difficult tour passenger who may wish to establish squatter's rights on the front seat for the entire trip. Another very helpful suggestion is that anyone who suffers from motion sickness be prepared with a supply of Dramamine or something similar.

*Cancellations and refunds.* Although the tour brochure should give specific details on cancellation dates, penalties, and refund policy, this first information bulletin is the place to reiterate those details. If nothing else, the bulletin should remind passengers to refer to the company's policy as stated in the brochure. One might use a statement such as, "While we certainly hope you will be able to travel with us as planned, sometimes illness or family emergency or unexpected events can force one to cancel travel plans. Therefore, we urge you to reread the Cancellation/Refunds clause in your brochure to be absolutely sure you understand it and are clear as to how late you may cancel without any penalty. If you have questions, please ask now."

*Tipping.* It is appropriate in this first information bulletin to reiterate what tips are included so that the passengers may budget accordingly. Be specific. Which of the following are or are not covered: airport porters, hotel bellboys from the motorcoach into the hotel lobby and from hotel lobby into the passenger's hotel room, dining room waiters, *maitre d'*, room maids, bus drivers, local guides, tour manager. For cruises additional tips have to be considered. Which of the following are or are not covered: room steward, dining room waiters, *maitre d'*, wine steward. Where tips are not included, what are some guidelines for the appropriate amount: 15 percent, so much per day, or so much per person?

*Credit cards.* Credit cards are so widely used in the United States that many tour members assume that their cards will be readily accepted everywhere overseas. No matter how wealthy the clients may be, they often fail to bring sufficient funds in travelers checks with them, planning to rely entirely on credit cards. This assumption is a mistake—a mistake that, unfortunately, the credit card companies do little to remedy, since they want to convey the impression that their card is accepted at the far corners of the globe. Often this is true; more often it is not. For example, even some cruise lines do not accept credit cards for enroute passengers, although many will accept a personal check. A large number of the better hotels and restaurants will accept them, but small out-of-the-way country inns, trattorias or small-town shopkeepers will not. Many tour managers have had to spend the better part of a day in a city overseas trying to get a check cashed for a tour passenger, or assisting the passenger in cabling home for funds.

*Spending money.* At the time a client buys the tour, he or she may be overwhelmed with everything that is included in the tour price. It sounds so all-inclusive. And many of the more deluxe, quality tours are just that—virtually all-inclusive. However, some of the moderate-priced tours (and certainly the no-frills, stripped package type of tour) cannot claim to be all-inclusive. The passengers will have to pay a number of expenses out of pocket as the tour moves along. It is only fair that they be prepared, so that they have a rough idea of what to budget.

It probably is not advisable to recommend a dollar amount, since there may be a great difference in spending habits among tour members. But it is legitimate to remind them of what is not covered, so that they can mentally calculate how much extra money to take. Items to mention might be cocktails, wines, souvenirs, shopping, postcards and stamps, some tips, baggage overweight, meals not in the tour, optional tours or shore excursions not included in the basic prepaid trip, laundry, telephone, illness and other emergencies, snacks and room service.

*Foreign currency.* Tour members seem to worry unnecessarily about purchasing foreign currency, not realizing that on a prepurchased group tour most of their major expenses are already prepaid and that expenditures overseas will be primarily for incidental expenses not covered by the tour. This situation is in contrast to the independent traveler who, indeed, needs to have available a sizable amount of funds.

Therefore, the principal things that the information bulletin should tell tour participants about foreign currency are: (1) that the agency does not recommend carrying large amounts of cash, in any currency; (2) that the agency urges them to carry all funds in travelers checks; (3) that if they do wish to exchange fairly large amounts of currency, they will get a better rate at a bank than from a hotel cashier (however, point out that often it is not convenient to break away from planned tour activities during local banking hours, and they may spend more on a taxi to and from the bank than they lose exchanging with the hotel cashier); (4) that if they are going to be in any country for a fairly lengthy period, they might consider buying travelers checks at home directly in the currency needed: English pounds, Swiss francs, or whatever. Such travelers checks usually can be purchased at many American Express offices, foreign banks in the larger cities in the United States, or through exchange houses. If dealing through a branch bank or small-town bank, it is best to do this well in advance, because such banks are not yet geared to handling foreign currency quickly (if at all).

*Baggage.* Passengers should be advised about what kind of luggage and how much to take. Usually, hard-sided luggage is recommended instead of the new popular soft-sided lightweight luggage, because thieves can easily slash soft luggage. On tours, baggage receives heavy use—in and out of hotels, on and off luggage trucks, in and out of airports; in short, it takes a beating. Passengers should realize this and perhaps not take their very best matched Gucci luggage this time. Of course, specific tours may have specific needs—particularly adventure tours, which may require backpacks, duffle bags, or other equipment. Special arrangements can be made with the airlines on ski tours to allow one suitcase and one set of skis instead of two suitcases. A similar arrangement is popular for golf tours; that is to accommodate a bag for golf clubs in lieu of one suitcase.

The agency may also wish to limit passengers to one or two suitcases, depending on the length of the trip and on whether the tour is costed on handling and tipping for two suitcases per person or one. Regardless of costing and regardless of airline regulations, certain limitations are necessary in certain areas of the world. For example, a trip such as the Chilean Lakes crossing from Puerto Montt, Chile, which includes numerous boats and buses enroute to Bariloche, Argentina, would be an exercise in madness if a tour manager were expected to safely shepherd forty passengers, each with two bags through to the end. And getting eighty bags off the bullet train in Japan during a 60-second station stop is not exactly easy. Most boats in the Galápagos Islands restrict each passenger to one fairly small suitcase. In this situation, it is better for passengers to bring two small suitcases rather than one large one, so that they may take one with them on the boat, leaving the other at the hotel.

Those who travel frequently within the United States but infrequently internationally are under the impression that two suitcases, regardless of weight, are the rule. However, on many flights and in many countries the old 44-pound limit (20 kilos) still holds, particularly for smaller airlines flying within a given country.

Also, those who travel frequently on business in the United States may be accustomed to traveling with garment bags, which are not suitable for touring. Probably the best kind of bag, in addition to being hard-sided and sturdy, is the kind with dividers and pockets so that the passenger can devise a system for finding things. It is one thing to pack solidly for a single destination and then unpack on arrival (or pack for a cruise and then unpack totally once you are aboard). It is quite another to live out of a suitcase during a series of one-night stands.

*Luggage tags.* One of the things the agency will want to send to the tour members along with final documents will be luggage tags. Tell the tour members that these will be coming with their final documents. It is also a good idea to suggest that they put their name and address somewhere inside each suitcase in case the outer luggage tag wears off.

*Packing suggestions.* Although many tour members are experienced travelers and have learned a number of tricks of travel for packing, undoubtably the novices in the group will appreciate hints. Remind them to pack around one basic color, leaving things that cannot be worn with that color at home. Warn them to use plastic bottles for all liquids, and to plan clothes for multi-use (a raincoat that can double as a bathrobe, separates that can be mixed and matched, and sandals that can be used as slippers). Warn them about the perils of air conditioning on planes and in hotels (and subsequent traveler's bronchitis), of the practicality of drip-dry fabrics (except in the tropics, where they are too warm because they do not breathe), and the need for good walking shoes (broken in, not new). Suggest a travel alarm (to ensure their being on time for morning departures).

People usually want to be dressed appropriately, so they will appreciate being advised about where formal wear, or at least coat and tie, is expected. Local customs that would affect clothing are important to mention. For example, in Japan, where one takes shoes off and puts them on a dozen times a day entering and leaving temples and shrines, passengers like to wear slip-on rather than tie shoes.

Discuss electric plugs and converters and the use of hair dryers and electric shavers. And certainly, if there are any special functions requiring certain attire, such as a costume party aboard ship, or a formal reception with business colleagues, passengers would like to know in advance. The agency might even wish to make up a suggested wardrobe checklist for men and one for women. And for certain countries, passengers might be advised to take along some small token gifts to give out to local friends they might make enroute—perhaps things typical of their home state or city.

Those who plan to carry a prescription drug should be warned to carry it in the original bottle with the pharmacy's label on it, and to carry all medicines with them—not packed in checked luggage. There is nothing more frightening for a tour manager than to have a tour member announce that her blood pressure medicine, which she must take within the next four hours, is packed in a lost suitcase.

*Care of valuables.* Passengers should be urged to be prudent while traveling—women to carry a purse that zips closed and men to carry their wallets inside their jacket, not in a rear pocket readily accessible to a pickpocket. Also remind them that good jewelry, cameras, travelers checks, tickets, and passports must be handcarried and watched, never packed in their checked luggage. Tour participants sometimes see a trip as a festive occasion, perhaps as a chance to show off new clothes and good jewelry, so they often need to be urged to leave expensive furs and valuable jewelry at home. Simply tell them not to take anything on this trip that they cannot afford to lose. The tour manager should reinforce all this later enroute, but it is also best to tell tour members before they start planning their wardrobe, so that they can shop and pack accordingly.

*Shopping on tour.* Advise passengers what some of the good buys are in the country that they will be visiting, so they can plan ahead. This is a good time to let them know that the agency is not pushing shopping stops and cannot assume responsibility for bad buys that they might make nor assist in tracing lost shipments. One of the problems that plagues tour operators is that some passengers will write several months after a tour is completed complaining that the cuckoo clock they bought at that cute little shop the tour manager took them to in the Black Forest broke down, or the tile coffee table they had shipped from the factory in Mexico has not arrived—asking that someone from the agency follow up the next time he or she happens to be there. A suitable statement to include in this first information bulletin would be, "We urge you to be cautious and discriminating in your purchases. We regret that we cannot be responsible for any shopping activities and are unable to intervene on your behalf in the event that merchandise does not live up to your expectations or if merchandise that you may ask to be shipped home does not arrive."

*Health problems.* It is important to obtain information on any health difficulties that passengers have that could be a problem enroute. The tour manager will need to know about passengers who have potentially dangerous conditions, such as high blood pressure, heart disease, or diabetes. In addition, if the tour visits areas of high altitudes, it might be wise to require that tour members with a history of heart disease or high blood pressure obtain a physician's written permission to travel. The first information bulletin provides the opportunity to discuss this matter and to impress passengers with the importance of revealing pertinent medical information. It is difficult for the tour manager who discovers at 11,000 feet that a tour member has a heart problem, or only finds out at the airport that a tour member is in a wheelchair.

*Suggested background reading.* Some tour members like suggestions for pretour reading about the countries and cultures that they will visit. It should never be implied that this is required reading, but merely suggested as enjoyable reading. The author once had a gentleman cancel from a tour, saying that he was frightened by the reading list and that he had joined the tour thinking it would be a vacation, not a study tour.

In making suggestions, perhaps give no more than three or four possibilities. One might be an overview of a country, one something on history, perhaps another on the arts and crafts, or another something for light reading. Consult with the local library or university for suggestions.

*Airfare restrictions.* If the tour is traveling on a special airfare, tour participants should know what kind of fare it is and what the restrictions are. Although this may have been mentioned briefly in the brochure, the first bulletin is the place to give further information. For example, if the tour is traveling on the Group Inclusive Tour (GIT) airfare, a statement might be "Passengers are advised that this tour is based on a special 14/35-day Group Inclusive Tour airfare, which requires a minimum of 15 passengers and that passengers travel together as a group on all international flight segments of the trip."

*United States Customs.* Discuss duty-free airport shops and mention the $400 per person limit on duty-free items that United States residents may bring back. Also alert passengers to the fact that items shipped and not accompanying them will be subject to duty. Discuss written versus oral customs declarations and the $50 gifts that may be sent free of duty. The agency may wish to obtain supplies of the United States government publication, "Know Before You Go," to include in the mailing.

STANDARDIZING BULLETINS

The preceding pages show that the material to be presented in this first information bulletin is quite comprehensive. Writing it and presenting it in a professional manner can be very time-consuming. In fact, it may take several days to prepare this information bulletin the first time.

As the agency develops more and more tours per year, bulletin preparation can become quite a chore and it will become obvious that much of it is repetitious. Large tour companies solve this by writing different standardized bulletins for different programs—one for their South Pacific tours, one for the European tours, and so forth.

Another solution for small to medium-size agencies is to write one standardized bulletin that is suitable for all tours anywhere in the world, augmenting it with supplemental short bulletins pertinent to a specific area or to a specific subject. For example, discussions of clothing and wardrobe checklists would be standardized, with no comments about the tropics or skindiving or ski clothes or winter rains. Any discussion of special wardrobe needs other than those listed in the standardized bulletin can be covered in a supplemental bulletin. Similarly, information on visas for specific countries, flight schedules, names of tour managers, time of year, and climate would be deleted or generalized in this standardized bulletin.

In fact, if the agency is operating a large number of tours per year, this lengthy first information bulletin might be typeset and printed instead of photocopied. It can be done nicely in pamphlet form, perhaps with some attractive or humorous illustrations, and then used for a number of years—supplemented each time by a short bulletin that touches on subjects pertinent only to the particular tour in question at that time. Before investing in printing such a pamphlet, however, it might be a good idea to use just the photocopied one for a year or two, to live with it and be sure that it really is working as anticipated.

This first information bulletin has one additional function. It can also be an effective sales piece. If a client is undecided, or is asking a great number of detailed questions before joining a tour, a good sales counselor can volunteer, "Mr. Jones, I have an information bulletin we normally don't send out until someone has joined our tour. But it sounds as though you're really seriously interested in traveling with us and I think if I sent it to you now ahead of time it might answer a lot of your questions."

TOUR QUESTIONNAIRE

A considerable amount of information will be needed concerning each passenger as the agency begins final preparation of tour lists, documents, and materials for the tour manager. Probably the simplest way to obtain all this information is to develop a tour questionnaire (Figure 8.7) that can be enclosed with the first information bulletin; each passenger must fill this out and return it with the final payment or earlier. Like the information bulletin, this questionnaire may be standardized to work for all tours. The following is a list of needed information:

1. Name of tour on which member is enrolled.
2. Legal listing of member's name (to match name as listed on passport—not nicknames).
3. Home address, telephone area code and number.
4. Business name, address, and business area code and telephone number.
5. Citizenship (important to know if there are people in the group traveling on foreign passports; visa and immigration policies vary for them).
6. Passport number, date and place of issue.
7. Birthplace, (city, state, country).
8. Birth date (including year and thus age).
9. Emergency contact—name, address, telephone number, and relationship to tour member.
10. Any health or diet history—particularly diabetes, heart disease, high blood pressure, difficulty in walking, respiratory problems.
11. Smoker or nonsmoker.
12. Any special interests.

PREPACKING ENVELOPES

Once all the materials are prepared for this first mailing, it expedites things to prepack them into large envelopes ready to mail as bookings come in by adding the acknowledgment letter and putting a label on the envelope. If it is a party of two, the agent will need only one confirmation bulletin and welcome letter but two passport application

CLIENT HANDLING                                                    161

TOUR QUESTIONNAIRE
(one per person required, not one per family)
                                  Mr.
                                  Mrs. _____
Last Name _____ Ms.    First Name

Home Address _____ City _____ State _____ Zip Code

Name of Business _____ Business Address _____ City _____ State _____ Zip Code

Home Phone (____) _____ Business Phone (____) _____
         Area Code   Number                      Area Code   Number

Birth Date _____ Birth Place _____
           Month   Day    Year                     City         State      Country

Present Nationality _____ Former Nationality, if any _____

If a naturalized citizen, date and place of naturalization _____

Passport Number _____ Date of Issue _____ Place of Issue _____

Occupation/Position _____

Special interests? _____
_____

Do you smoke?  ___ Yes  ___ No

In case of emergency during the trip, whom do you wish us to contact?

Name _____ Relationship _____

Address _____ City _____ State _____ Zip Code

Home Phone (____) _____ Business Phone (____) _____
         Area Code   Number                      Area Code   Number

Please indicate how you wish your name badge to read (we usually show your first and
last name)
_____

                         Confidential Information
                            For Tour Manager

Do you require special medical attention or diet?       ___ Yes      ___ No

Heart Problems? ___ Yes ___ No; Respiratory ailments? ___ Yes ___ No; Diabetes? ___ Yes ___ No

Difficulty walking long distances and/or climbing stairs? ___ Yes ___ No

Further details on above health _____
_____

              Use reverse side if you need additional room

**Figure 8.7**  Passenger tour questionnaire.

forms, two tour questionnaires, and so forth. Therefore, it is handy to prepack envelopes ready for parties of one and parties of two. Also, remember to put one master set in the file for later reference to show what was sent to everybody and as a sample for the tour manager.

INTERIM MAILINGS BETWEEN FIRST BULLETIN AND BILLING

Some tour companies believe that three mailings (welcome mailing, billing mailing, and final document mailing) are more than adequate and, in fact, are trying to find ways to cut down on these. Other tour companies believe that it is important to keep in touch with the tour members so that they will not lose interest. These operators send out what they call "Keep the Interest" mailings (additional mailings in between the three basic ones), to ensure that the customer remains excited about the trip.

Sometimes this can be a postcard mailed from a city that the client will be visiting on tour. Sometimes it is a little booklet or news item. Perhaps these "Keep the Interest" mailings are most valid if there is a long timespan between the date that the client enrolls in the tour and the date that the bill is mailed out. For example, if a client enrolls in January for a late September tour and would not hear from the agency between January, when the booking is acknowledged, and July when the agency invoices, it might be effective to design a mailing piece to go out around April or May.

## Billing

Approximately two weeks before final payment is due in the agency office, it is time to send out final bills. If the brochure states that final payment is due 90 days before departure, it will be necessary to bill by 104 days before departure, to ensure that all payments are in on time. If the brochure states that final payment is due 60 days prior, bills should go out 75 days prior. A master control calendar should be flagged accordingly, and it is also helpful to flag the week before as a reminder, should it be necessary to bring in temporary help to prepare the bills.

It is important to send out bills sufficiently early for two major reasons:

1. If tour members are going to cancel, most likely they will do so when final payment is due. It is best to find this out early—not to receive these cancellations as a late surprise.

2. An agency needs turnaround time—the time between when all payments are received in the office and when it is time to pay suppliers—cruise lines, hotels, and others. Always leave a sufficient time gap; never set the final payment date from passengers as the same date on which suppliers must be paid.

BILLING FORMAT

There are many different ways of billing passengers for a group project. If the group is relatively small, it is possible to type individual invoices for each family (Figure 8.8). If the group is quite large, more sophisticated methods such as computer billings are available. Some agencies simply bill by photocopying the client's master control card. Whatever the method selected, remember that the bill must be *understandable from the client's point of view*. Although the agency may know that the airfare has gone up $140 since the brochure was printed, the client may not. The agency may understand what a YLAP airfare is, but the customer probably does not. In addition, of course, more complicated tours will require more detailed bills to cover such items as single-room supplements, convention fees, pre-or posttour independent travel arrangements, and so forth.

Whether the initial deposit was sent directly to the agency or to the sponsoring club, it is best for final billing to be from the agency directly to the client. By now the client should know that the agency is handling the club's trip and will feel comfortable paying the bill directly.

ACCOMPANIMENTS TO THE BILL

Sending a bill out by itself seems cold and impersonal. Although the bill must not be lost in a sea of information stuffed into the envelope, a short cover letter (Figure 8.9) and a second brief, information bulletin are appropriate accompaniments.

The tone of the cover letter should be warm and friendly, exciting the passengers about the trip but at the same time gently reminding them that payment is due shortly.

The second information bulletin could touch on new tour developments—something upbeat. For example, the news that a particular celebrity is going to meet with the group while in Rome, or that a restaurant where the group will be dining has just won a Michelin star rating, or that the exchange rate between the French franc and the dollar has improved, and that therefore the dollar will go further when travelers are shopping in Paris.

LSI TRAVEL AGENCY, INC.

June 21, 1985

Mr. and Mrs. Merle Davis
2433 Beaver Place
Briston, IN 46507

For Rosemont Country Club European Highlights
Tour Sept. 6-16, 1985. Basic tour at $2985
per person x 2 persons ...................... $5,970.00

Increase in air fare since publication date
of brochure ... $140 per person x 2 (see
enclosed Information Bulletin #2 for
details) ........................................ 280.00

Optional Purchases
   Half-day Paris Gastronomique tour Sept. 11,
   Mrs. Davis only at $24 x 1 ................ 24.00

   Airport Inn Sept. 5, confirmed at $68 for
   two plus 6% tax ........................... 72.08

Total Charges .............................. $6,346.08

Less deposit on account ............................. $400.00

Balance Due and Payable ......................................... $5,946.08

PAYMENT DUE NOW BUT NO LATER THAN JULY 6
PLEASE MAKE CHECK PAYABLE TO LSI TRAVEL AGENCY, INC.
LAST DATE TO MAKE ANY CHANGES -- JULY 1

Tour Accounting Code #576

**Figure 8.8**    Sample simple invoice.

This bulletin also should give any update information, even if negative—that certain visas are now required or cholera inoculations suggested because of an outbreak. This also is the time to advise passengers if the airfare has increased since publication of the brochure, how much the increase is, and how the agency plans to protect them against any future possible increases if they pay quickly so that their air tickets can be issued immediately.

    It is a nice touch to include some giveaways, such as a map, a book, or some background reading. The State Department publishes excel-

LSI TRAVEL AGENCY, INC.

June 21, 1985

DEAR FRIENDS:

September and departure day for the Rosemont Country Club tour to Europe may seem like a long way off! But it's closer than you think. As mentioned in the tour brochure, final payment is due 60 days before departure, so I'm afraid payment date is upon us shortly.

Therefore, enclosed is an itemization of your charges. Please review them carefully. Payment is due in our office by July 6. A stamped self-addressed envelope is enclosed for your convenience.

We are including some supplemental information bringing up you to date on a few new developments. Also enclosed is full information and an application form for optional travel insurance -- medical, baggage, and trip cancellation. We urge you to give it your serious consideration, particularly the trip cancellation coverage due to the heavy cancellation penalty that goes into effect 60 days before departure.

May we also point out that July 1 is the last date you may make any changes in your travel plans or request additional pre-trip or post-trip arrangements.

This is going to be an exciting trip for all of us and as departure time draws near you may have questions on matters we have not covered in our information bulletins. If so, do feel free to call and chat with us.

Sincerely,

Marty Sarbey de Souto, CTC
Group Manager

MS/s
cc: Mrs. Charles Goodwin-Rosemont Country Club
Enclosures: Information Bulletin No. 2
 Invoice
 Return Mail Envelope
 Insurance Information Bulletin
 Insurance Application Form

P.S. Reminder. Anyone who has not yet turned in his or her tour questionnaire, please do so quickly. We need the information therein to finalize your tour arrangements, preregister our group at all the hotels, and so forth.

**Figure 8.9** Sample invoice cover letter.

lent pamphlets entitled "Background Notes" on each country; they can be ordered from the Bureau of Public Affairs. They give information on the country's history, population, economy, agriculture, educational system, and so forth. Also try other organizations such as the United Nations, the Organization of American States, and the Pan American

Union or perhaps magazines such as *National Geographic.* Although government tourist offices and airlines of the countries concerned may be helpful, sometimes their materials are mere pretty pictures and sales pieces, rather than solid background information. Do not overlook novels or popular nonfiction such as Michener's *Iberia,* de Gramont's *The French—Portrait of a People,* or Magner's *Men of Mexico.* Of course, giveaways such as this should have been costed-in to the tour price from the outset and should have been ordered sufficiently early to arrive on time for inclusion in the billing mailing.

TRAVEL INSURANCE

One of the things that an agency most surely will wish to offer is personal travel insurance. Both the Travelers and Mutual of Omaha offer it and there is the ASTA-backed Travel Guard, as well; and there may be others on the market in the future. The information and application form for this optional insurance coverage can be included in the billing mailing or, if preferred, it can be a separate mailing.

Usually such insurance packages are divided into three parts: (1) medical/accident coverage; (2) baggage and personnel effects coverage; (3) cancellation or trip interruption coverage. Emphasize how important it is for tour members to *consider* this insurance; on the other hand, do not oversell and *insist* they purchase something that they do not really need. Often it is best to suggest that they check what they already have in the way of insurance and then augment it. For example, if their personal medical insurance covers them for claims incurred overseas, perhaps they do not need the supplemental medical coverage. But if their present medical coverage does not protect them while traveling overseas (as is the case with Medicare), undoubtedly they will appreciate having this brought to their attention.

Many tour passengers erroneously assume that since the agency is handling baggage throughout the tour, it is legally responsible for loss or damage to luggage or personal effects. This is not the case, and it is important that the client be reminded of this—first in the brochure and second in the information bulletins that follow. A suggested statement to appear in the second information bulletin might be:

"As stated in the brochure describing the tour project, 'LSI Travel Agency, Inc. shall not be responsible for loss, theft of, or damage to baggage or belongings, and we highly recommend that you double check your personal insurance and/or purchase the optional baggage insurance offered. Valuables such as jewelry, cameras, travelers checks, tickets, passports, and so forth always should be hand-carried, never checked in your luggage.' This is simply a courtesy reminder of this matter so that you now may enroll in the appropriate insurance coverage for your baggage and personal effects if you so desire. A descriptive bulletin and application form are enclosed for your convenience."

It is also a good idea to advise tour members what the Warsaw Convention insurance coverage is under the contract of their air ticket. Liability for loss, delay, or damage to baggage is limited unless a higher value is declared in advance and additional charges are paid. For most international travel (including domestic portions of international journeys) the liability limit is approximately $9.07 per pound for checked baggage and $400 per passenger for unchecked baggage. For travel wholly between United States points federal rules require any limit on an airline's baggage liability to be at least $1,250 per passenger. Tour members should be reminded that these provisions cover baggage only while in care of the airline. Warsaw Convention protection does not cover luggage if it is lost in a hotel or baggage truck enroute to the airport, and so forth.

RETURN-MAIL ENVELOPE

It is helpful to enclose a stamped, self-addressed return-mail envelope in the billing mailing. This expedites payment, and for the cost of a first-class stamp, appears gracious.

## Cancellations

It is important to be prepared for cancellations. Although it is hard to predict numbers, probably an estimate of from 17 percent to 20 percent would be accurate. If the tour has a high percentage of couples, cancellations may be more, since if a partner becomes ill and has to cancel, the spouse usually cancels as well. If the tour is a short, inexpensive tour with a small deposit—under $100—cancellations may be higher than if there is a fairly heavy deposit of $400 to $500 per person. Usually if clients have had to pay a large deposit, they have thought about the trip carefully at that time, whereas if they had to deposit only $50 or so, they may have enrolled on impulse without really thinking it through.

The brochure should have an explicit cancellation clause outlining cancellation dates, refund policies, and penalties, and specifying that cancellations must be in writing (to protect the agency against clients who cannot really make up their mind whether they are officially cancelling or not, or couples who cannot come to an agreement).

Once the agency has received a written cancellation notice, the cancellation should be processed immediately and the refund made as quickly as possible. Of course, if there is any possibility of salvaging the booking it might be advisable to call the client first to express regrets about the cancellation and to see if there is anything that can be done to retain the client. It is not a good idea to try to hang on to a client by delaying the refund; this will incur nothing but ill will. An immediate refund with a short accompanying note of regret will do wonders to establish the agency's reputation as a serious tour operator to be considered in the future. If it is not possible to get the refund into the mail by the end of that same week, or if the agency, in turn, has to apply to someone else for the money (for example, to a cruise line), at least process the refund request and acknowledge the cancellation in writing the same week that it is received (Figure 8.10), explaining the circumstances and advising the client that refund will follow.

## Waiting Lists

One way to protect against cancellations is to maintain a waiting list of people ready and eager to go the minute an opening occurs. Do not offer to put people's names on the waiting list without a deposit. If the tour is sold out and people call or write in for space, add a paragraph to the usual sales letter advising them:

"At present, the tour is fully booked. However, since we always receive a certain number of cancellations due to illness or last-minute emergencies, we will be happy to put your name on our waiting list and advise you as openings develop. To establish your waiting list priority, kindly complete the reservation form in the brochure and return it along with your deposit in the amount of $000.00 as indicated on the reservation form. Of course, if for any reason we ultimately cannot accommodate you on the trip, your money will be totally refundable. We regret that we cannot accept waitlist applications without a deposit."

It is also a good idea to service the waiting list passengers just as one does the confirmed passengers, sending them information bulletins, visa applications, and so forth. It keeps their spirits up and makes them feel that their chances of getting on the trip are good.

Of course, as "D" Day (for departure) draws near, it is only fair to these people to give them an honest assessment of the situation. If all final payments have been received from all passengers, the chances of

LSI TRAVEL AGENCY, INC.

June 30, 1984

Mrs. Louis Seidman
10035 Gardenside Drive
Waite Hill, Ohio 44094

Dear Mrs. Seidman:

We were sorry to receive your note advising us that Mr. Seidman will have to go into the hospital for surgery and that you, therefore, must cancel your participation in our European Highlights Tour for the Rosemont Country Club this fall. We have a nice group making the trip and you two will be missed!

Here's hoping that Mr. Seidman recuperates quickly and that perhaps you can make the trip with us next year instead, as this is an annual tour and we will be offering it again in 1986 around the same time of year.

There will not be any cancellation fee since your cancellation was received prior to the 60-day cut-off date. Your refund is being processed and you should be receiving a check from our accounting department in about ten days.

With all best wishes...

Cordially,

Marty Sarbey de Souto, CTC
Group Manager

P.S. We're enclosing a calendar of our future tours ... for Mr. Seidman's bedtime reading while he's recuperating!

**Figure 8.10**  Cancellation acknowledgment letter.

there being many cancellations are fairly slim. At that point, the few cancellations there might be would be bona fide emergencies—illness, death in the family, and so forth. On the other hand, before final payment date there probably will be a number of cancellations—those who overplanned, underbudgeted, were not really sure in the first place, have had business reversals, have court dates. So the biggest drop in passengers will be around final payment date—90 days prior, 60 days prior, or whatever date is specified in the tour brochure as final payment date. Plan accordingly!

## Acknowledging Final Payments

Once billings are mailed, anticipate that final payments will come in fairly quickly and be prepared to handle them. Also be prepared to follow up those few who do not pay on time. If they do not pay on time, it may mean they are cancelling, and the agency should be concerned.

The agency may wish to acknowledge final payments as they come in with a thank-you letter, assuring tour members that their file is in order and advising them when their final documents will be mailed. This is also an excellent time to review the clients' files and remind them if anything is missing, such as their tour questionnaire, passport data, decision on whether they want to take insurance, any decisions on pretour or posttour optional tours, or any decisions on domestic flight connections to and from the gateway airport. In short, if there is any piece of information missing from the file, the time to handle it is *now*, not discover it later while preparing the final documents.

## Flight Bags

Some agencies like to give out complimentary flight bags—either airline bags that they purchase from the air carrier or their own tour company bags. They believe that passengers appreciate receiving them and that they serve as free advertising for the tour company. In some instances, organizations that repeatedly do tours have their own flight bags. A number of university alumni groups do this; in fact, some have developed their travel program to a science, traveling with their own flight bags, T-shirts, pretrip bulletins, and other items.

If the agency elects to send flight bags, they can be mailed separately—perhaps right after final payment is received. A major problem with flight bags is storing, packing, and shipping—all of which can be unwieldy and timeconsuming. Be sure to budget for flight bags in the tour costing if planning to purchase them.

## Final Documents

Three to four weeks prior to departure, package the departure materials to be sure that they reach tour members at least two weeks before departure. Nothing is more surely the sign of a careless tour operator than participants receiving departure documents just before departure. And nothing is more likely to upset participants and start them out on the tour on the wrong foot than not getting their documents in time.

After all, so far they have paid out several thousand dollars, but have nothing to show for it. The participants want time to receive everything, read it over carefully, savor it, and be sure that they understand it.

Therefore, it will be necessary to work backward, planning far enough ahead to have everything that is needed on hand and ready to mail out so as *to reach the tour members no less than two weeks before they leave home.* Allow extra time for holiday mail delays, if necessary. This means, in turn, that items that come to the agency from elsewhere (tickets from a cruise line, vouchers from a wholesale tour operator, and so forth) must be ordered sufficiently early. Plenty of time must be allowed to check each air ticket, each cruise ticket, each voucher to be sure that it is issued correctly and at the rate charged to the customer, and with the customer's name spelled properly. If there is some error, the items must be returned to the supplier for exchange. If the agency and the supplier are in the same town, errors may be corrected quickly. But if the agency is in Iowa and has purchased the ground arrangements through a wholesaler in New York, extra time must be allowed. An agency must plan ahead and insist that suppliers do likewise.

The following is a checklist of final documents and other items the agency might send out to clients.

1. Passport billfold or decorative document envelope of some sort to hold all final materials (do not just throw them loose into a mailing envelope).
2. Air tickets in appropriate airline ticket jacket, with individual flight itinerary tucked inside the jacket.
3. Cruise ticket in appropriate cruise line ticket jacket.
4. Departure bulletin giving final instructions.
5. Lapel name badge to be worn on the day of departure (and perhaps throughout the tour) so that the tour manager and others can identify the group members.
6. Baggage tags—one per suitcase to be checked in or handled by tour bellmen and porters (do not include agency baggage tags for hand-carried luggage; they confuse the porters and might cause them to pick it up by mistake.)
7. Supply of mailing instructions (Figure 8.11) to leave with friends, family, and office colleagues, showing hotel names and addresses and emergency cable contacts where tour members may be reached while traveling.

INSTRUCTIONS FOR ADDRESSING MAIL TO PARTICIPANTS
OF ROSEMONT COUNTRY CLUB TOUR OF EUROPE 1985

This list is furnished you to give to your family, friends, and business contacts who may wish to correspond with you while you are on tour.

| ARRIVAL DATE | DEPARTURE DATE | HOTEL AND ADDRESS | EMERGENCY CABLE |
|---|---|---|---|
| September 7 | September 10 | Hotel Krasnapolsky<br>Dam 9, 1012 JS<br>Amsterdam<br>The Netherlands | KRASNAPOLSKY |
| September 10 | September 13 | Hotel Meurice<br>228 Rue de Rivoli<br>Paris 1$^{er}$<br>France | MEURISOTEL |
| September 13 | September 16 | Hotel Ambasciatori<br>70 Via Veneto<br>00187 Rome, Italy | HOTELAMB |

Please allow at least one week transit time to all places and be sure that you have sufficient postage on all letters. The cost of airmail to all of the above destinations is forty cents PER HALF OUNCE, and the cost of an airgram letter is thirty cents (airgram forms may be obtained at any United States Post Office). We suggest that you address your envelope as follows:

                                                          40¢ per half-ounce

Your return address

        Mr. and Mrs. (Participant's Name)
        Rosemont Country Club Group
        Ambasciatori Hotel
        70 Via Veneto
        00187 Rome, Italy

Please hold for group
arrival September 16                                                     AIR MAIL

**Figure 8.11** Mailing instructions.

8. List of tour participants—including their home addresses at the agency's discretion.
9. Map of departure airport, indicating meeting place. Not mandatory, but helpful.
10. Vouchers, if necessary, for basic tour package. Also vouchers for any independent pretour or posttour services, such as airport hotels and so forth.

11. Insurance policy, if purchased by the passenger, with instructions to take the number of the policy on the trip but to leave the policy itself at home in a safe place.
12. Passport, if precollected for obtaining visas, with visas stamped therein.
13. Miscellaneous items, if desired or if not sent earlier, such as phrase books, currency exchange charts, and so forth.
14. Bon Voyage cover letter (Figure 8.12) attached to the front of all this material.

It is important to send final documents via certified mail (since air tickets are negotiable) or, if passports are enclosed, to send via registered mail with return receipt requested. Accurate records of certified or registered number, date mailed, and exact address on the mailing label should be kept. This will help the agency and the post office in tracking a lost envelope in case a customer calls in to say that final documents have not been received.

**Contents of Departure Bulletin**

The departure bulletin should be short and to the point, giving the passengers the essentials of what they need to know to get packed and onto the plane. Points to cover in this bulletin should include the following:

- Where and when to meet—specify airline, flight number, departure time, airport check-in place and time, whether to check in as an independent traveler at the airport or look for someone special.
- Tour manager—name of manager and exactly when and where the manager will be greeting the passengers.
- Baggage tags—how to fill out baggage tags and the importance of having them on the bags so that the tour porters will handle them correctly.
- Baggage check-in—instructions on what airport passengers should check baggage to, whether to interline luggage through to the final destination or just check it to a certain point and reclaim it; the importance of holding the luggage stubs and turning them over to the tour manager later.
- Name badge—the importance of wearing it on departure day so that the tour manager can identify people.

LSI TRAVEL AGENCY, INC.

August 20, 1985

DEAR FRIENDS:

Very shortly you will be leaving on our exciting Rosemont Country Club European Highlights Tour. Enclosed are all necessary final materials for the trip. Please review all items enclosed to make sure they correspond to the check list below  If anything has been omitted inadvertently, call us right away -- do not wait. You should find the following:

(1) Your air tickets, in the airline ticket jacket, with a typed flight schedule inside.

(2) Departure instruction bulletin - important.

(3) Name badge.

(4) Baggage tags (see departure bulletin for instructions on use).

(5) Supply of mailing instructions (to leave with family and friends).

(6) List of tour participants

(7) Vouchers for any independent pretour or posttour hotel reservations or other services you may have asked us to arrange for you.

(8) Your insurance policy (if you have purchased this optional coverage).

(9) Miscellaneous items -- currency converter, phrase booklet and so forth.

Your tour manager, Mrs. Margaret Kimberly, will meet you at the TWA check-in counter at O'Hare International Airport when you arrive the afternoon of September 6; please be on the lookout for her.

We know that you must be very busy getting ready for the trip, but please take the time now to read the enclosed departure bulletin carefully. It should answer most questions you may have, but if not, feel free to call us. May we also remind you that your passport is valuable and the enclosed air tickets are negotiable, so please put them all in a safe place.

Bon Voyage!

Cordially,

Marty Sarbey de Souto, CTC
Group Manager

Enclosures

**Figure 8.12** Sample passenger Bon Voyage letter.

- Last minute reminders—to be sure that they have passport, tourist cards or visas, air tickets, cruise ticket, travelers checks, and any medication with them, not packed in checked luggage or left at home.
- Emergency instructions—what to do if there is a last minute emergency, if they miss their plane, and so forth—around-the-clock telephone contact, particularly if on a weekend or when the agency office is closed.

With this much information and attention prior to departure, a participant should leave on tour in a favorable mood, anticipating the tour with excitement, convinced that the agency has done a good job so far and that the trip will live up to expectations. Now it is up to the tour manager to take the trip to the next stop along the road to success.

# 9

# In-house Operations and Dealing with Suppliers

The single most important mark of a professional tour operation is the operations department behind it. Promotional material may be beautiful. Sales may be fantastic. But if the operations department does not come through with the product that the client expects, all other efforts have been useless. Both the client and the suppliers have every right to expect reasonable efficiency, a feeling that the agency is in control. And this control can come only through organization, by attention to the most minute details.

But how does an agency achieve this control? What contributes to the assurance that important dates will not slip by, that deposits will not be overlooked, that promises will be kept and deadlines met? When a large number of tours must be juggled at once, each with its own set of dates, how does agency staff avoid sleepless nights spent worrying whether anything important has been overlooked or whether some deadline has been missed?

## Calendaring

The secret to the control of any travel project is calendaring—keeping a meticulous *visual* calendar of what must be done on each tour or cruise project. Many large tour companies keep such a calendar on the wall and plot the progress of a tour for everyone to see. Others keep a desk calendar and enter each duty on the appropriate date. Whichever method is selected, the trick is to write the information on the calendar and then adhere to the schedule by planning ahead and, when necessary, by hiring temporary, part-time help to keep work on schedule. Many professional tour operators not only calendar the exact date that a given task is to be done, but also calendar a reminder the week before. For example, if June 20 is the date to invoice tour passengers for final payment, they will put on their calendar for June 13: "Bills out June 20. Hire typist." This way they are a week ahead of the problem, instead of a week behind trying to catch up.

TYPICAL DATES TO CALENDAR

In entering important dates on the calendar, the usual procedure is to work *backward* from departure date. For example, if September 6 were tour departure date, the following might be entered:

| | |
|---|---|
| August 6 | 30-day review and finalization |
| July 6 | 60-day review |
| | Final payment due from clients |
| June 20 | Billing date (in order to get payment in by July 6) |
| June 6 | 90-day review |

If hotels have given specific dates by which time reports or deposits must be made, these dates should be entered as well. If there are any cancellation penalty dates—dates by which clients lose their money or dates by which the agency might lose deposits to cruise lines or hotels—these dates should also be entered, perhaps in big red letters.

Certain promotional dates should also be included on the calendar. These would include advertising deadlines, date to submit press releases, date for a promotional evening (including such things as date to mail invitations, catering deadline, and so forth), date to do a "last call" follow-up mailing to fill remaining spaces on the tour. *In short, the year should be plotted on paper from tour conception to departure.* Of course, as an agency calendars for many tours, the calendar will reflect many different stages of many different tours all in the same week, or perhaps even on the same day. June 20 may be the date to send out bills for the Europe tour leaving on September 6, but it also may be the date to do the 30-day finalization wrapup on a July 30 Orient tour. And if one can graphically see this pileup occuring on June 20, something can be done about it by bringing in extra help or by doing some of the work in advance during a relatively slack period.

## Review Dates

One of the most important factors in an agency's growth as a successful tour operator is its credibility and professionalism, not only as percieved by clients but *as seen from within the travel industry.* It will be crucial to an agency's continued success as a group operator that a good reputation be built with suppliers.

Suppliers are quick to judge. They watch to see how an agency measures up in its professional behavior and dealings with them. If suppliers constantly have to contact the agency to see how the tour is doing (and if the agency is not prepared to give them the answers they need when they call), they will have doubts about that agency's success and productivity.

There probably will be five important times to contact overseas hotels, reception ground operators, airlines, and other major suppliers:

1. When first booking—asking for space confirmation and rates.
2. When brochures come off the press—sending them a courtesy copy and inviting them to check it over to pick up any discrepancies (many an error has been caught this way!).
3. The ninety-day review—that is, ninety days before tour departure, just a note letting everyone know how the tour is selling, mostly for public relations purposes. If it is obvious that all the space held is not going to be filled, it is considered more ethical to drop some of it ninety days before departure rather than closer to departure date, when perhaps it is too late for the suppliers to sell it elsewhere. (See Figure 9.1 for sample 90-day review.)
4. The sixty-day review—that is, sixty days before tour departure, giving everyone a realistic look at numbers, cutting back on space that probably will not be filled in the next thirty days. (If sixty days is also the date by which the clients had to make final payment, there should be a fairly accurate picture of booking numbers by this time.) However, the agency might still want to retain a few unsold places in order to accept late bookings within the next thirty days. (See Figure 9.2 for sample 60-day review.)
5. The thirty-day review—that is, thirty days before tour departure, giving a final report. At thirty days, the agency cancels all unsold space and finalizes with suppliers, submitting rooming lists, flight manifests, and all other necessary final information. (See Figure 9.3 for a checklist of things to be done at 30-day review time.)

LSI TRAVEL AGENCY, INC.

June 6, 1985

Mr. Hans Van der Hooten
Sales Manager
Hotel Krasnapolsky
Dam 9, 1012 JS
Amsterdam
The Netherlands

                RE:    Rosemont Country Club
                      European Highlights Tour
                      Arriving: Sept. 7, 1985
                      90-day review

Dear Hans:

As you know, you are holding 14 twins and 4 singles for us on the above-mentioned tour group.

This is just a courtesy report to advise you that the tour seems to be selling well and to ask you to continue to hold all space. We will be reporting to you again at 60-day review time, at which time we will be able to give you a further booking picture.

You may be interested in the attached photocopy of our advertisement on this tour, which is currently running every Sunday in the travel section of our local newspaper. We are also enclosing a sample copy of the tour brochure which we published and mailed to 2,000 members of the Rosemont Country Club.

Thank you for your continued cooperation. We look forward to having our group at your property next September.

                                        Sincerely,

                                        Marty Sarbey de Souto, CTC
                                        Group Manager

MS/s
enclosures: 2

**Figure 9.1**    90-day review letter to hotel.

The above is a rule of thumb. In some cases, one might skip the 90-day review. In domestic tours, it is possible that many hotels do not require final rooming lists until fifteen days before arrival, not thirty, giving the agency a little more leeway. Conversely, when working with cruise lines, it is usually necessary to finalize much earlier and release unsold cabins considerably earlier, depending on the cruise line and

LSI TRAVEL AGENCY, INC.

July 6, 1985

Mr. Hans Van der Hooten
Sales Manager
Hotel Krasnapolsky
Dam 9, 1012 JS
Amsterdam
The Netherlands

                RE:   Rosemont Country Club
                     European Highlights Tour
                     Arriving: Sept. 7, 1985
                     60-day review

Dear Hans:

You are currently holding 14 twins and 4 singles for us on the above-mentioned tour group. We have currently sold 8 twins and 2 singles for a total of 10 rooms (18 persons) in our group so far. Unfortunately, a few of the participants found it necessary to cancel.

We are continuing our advertising and other promotional efforts for the next 30 days, so we are hopeful to be able to sell up to a maximum of 28 persons. Therefore, kindly:

        Continue to hold:    13 twins, 2 singles
        Cancel now:          1 twin,  2 singles

We will finalize with you 30 days prior to the group's arrival. At that time we will send final rooming list, prepayment, and other last-minute details. In the meantime, if you have any questions, feel free to contact us.

                                  Sincerely,

                                  Marty/Sarbey de Souto, CTC
                                  Group Manager

MS/s

**Figure 9.2**    60-day review letter to hotel.

CHECKLIST  30-DAY TOUR FINALIZATION*

___  Make final master tour roster, showing names, addresses, passport data, hotel rooming status and roommates, flight assignments, and any optional tours.

___  Finalize all air with controlling airline. Send final flight manifests showing breakdown smoking/nonsmoking passengers, friends traveling together, any special in-flight meal requirements. Request any special handling at departure airport. Release any unsold air.

___  Finalize with all hotels, sending final tour roster which shows rooming breakdown. Prepay or send sizeable deposit. Release any unsold rooms.

___  Finalize with all reception operators, sending final tour roster, verifying arrival/departure flights. Prepay or send sizeable deposit. Recap services expected, advise name of tour manager, and outline any special requests. Release any unsold space.

___  If cruise is involved, finalize with cruiseline*, recapping total numbers, cabin assignments, meal sitting, any special requests such as parties, meeting rooms, presold shore excursions, and who is using the cruise-line's group air blocks.

___  Request all complimentaries formally in writing, even if agreed to previously. Specify names and itineraries of those who are to utilize the complimentary tickets or accommodations.

___  Prepare departure materials for clients, to include final itinerary, air tickets and flight schedule, list of tour participants, departure instruction bulletin, mailing lists, voucher(s) for ground services if needed, cruise tickets, baggage tags, name badge, and any special materials (such as special convention materials, for example).

___  Prepare tour manager's materials and set date to meet with tour manager for final briefing.

* Finalization on most tours is at thirty days prior to departure. However, where a cruise or convention is involved, it may very well be required as early as ninety days prior. Be sure to double-check the requirements of each particular tour in question.

**Figure 9.3**  Checklist—30 day finalization.

on the popularity of the particular sailing. But the 90-day, 60-day, 30-day reviews are fairly standard in the industry and should be used as a base plan, adjusting as necessary around the constraints of specific suppliers. Obviously, with Carnival in Rio or Christmas in Hawaii, suppliers are going to hold a much tighter rein than they would on a Caribbean tour in a slack season.

Although these five contacts with each supplier for each tour may sound like an overwhelming amount of correspondence, a great deal of it can be standardized by developing *modified form letters* or standardized letters with fill-in blanks. For protection, these five contacts should be made by letter or telex—in writing—not verbally.

However the agency makes these frequent contacts with suppliers, whether by letter, telex, or form postcard, the important point is that it *take the initiative, both in plotting these dates into its calendar and in contacting the suppliers* rather than waiting until the suppliers contact the agency. After working with a given airline or hotel on several tours, an agency will earn a reputation for taking the initiative and for automatically contacting suppliers with a progress report. The airline or hotel will begin to feel at ease working with such an agency and will respect it.

## Control Forms for Operations

Many times it is necessary to make quick decisions—whether to continue to promote a tour or cancel it, whether to release certain flights or retain them, whether to run more advertising or not. But these management decisions are not made in a vacuum. They are made on the basis of information on the current status of the travel project. And how is that information acquired? With the proper tools—tools that in this case are office forms developed to help keep track of all essential information.

One such form might be a weekly office booking report, showing how many new bookings were received on each tour that week, how many cancellations, and the current net standing. (See Figure 9.4 for a sample weekly booking report.) Another typical form might be a control sheet for hotel space on a tour, showing at a glance how many twins or singles have been sold, how many rooms remain unsold, and how many share-rooms are open for roommates. Similar forms can be developed to show how many passengers are on which flights, or how many are signed up for an optional tour, or who is a smoker and who is a nonsmoker.

These forms can be as simple or as complicated as desired, depending on how large a tour is anticipated and how many variables there are. It is not too difficult to keep track of a one-week Hawaiian tour for thirty people, all staying at the same hotels, all flying out of a Los Angeles gateway on the same flight, and having the option of returning with the basic group at the end of the tour or of staying on for a two-day Kauai option.

It is quite another feat to know the status at any given moment if handling a meeting for 120 passengers divided into three busloads, going to three different Waikiki hotels, originating in a choice of three West Coast gateways (Seattle, San Francisco, or Los Angeles), and

# IN-HOUSE OPERATIONS AND DEALING WITH SUPPLIERS 183

WEEKLY BOOKING REPORT

WEEK ENDING  December 2, 1984
TOTAL BOOKINGS THIS WEEK ...... 72
TOTAL CANCELLATIONS THIS WEEK.. -12
NET GAIN THIS WEEK............. +60

| Project | Accounting Code Number | Dates | Under Deposit Last Week | New Bookings This Week | Cancelled This Week | Net Status As of Today | Total Space Held | Space Open For Sale |
|---|---|---|---|---|---|---|---|---|
| Europe Rotary Tour 1 | 805 | Feb.08–Feb.28 | 31 | 8 | 2 | 37 | 80 | 43 |
| Europe Rotary Tour 2 | 806 | Feb.25–Mar.17 | 18 | 8 | 1 | 25 | 40 | 15 |
| Roundhill Country Club Hawaii Golf Tour | 901 | Feb.28–Mar.08 | 121 | 12 | 3 | 130 | 160 | 30 |
| Mississippi Cruise | 917 | Apr.09–Apr.16 | 13 | 8 | 0 | 21 | 32 | 11 |
| Aspen Spring Ski Week | 933 | Apr.16–Apr.23 | 81 | 11 | 4 | 88 | 100 | 12 |
| Omaha Garden Club Japan Spring Tour | 937 | Apr.17–May 05 | 14 | 4 | 0 | 18 | 32 | 14 |
| Pearl Cruises China | 942 | Jun 04–Jun 20 | 24 | 4 | 2 | 26 | 40 | 14 |
| Alaska – Westours Tour/Cruise | 948 | Jul 07–Jul 21 | 13 | 2 | 0 | 15 | 32 | 17 |
| Rosemont Country Club European Highlights | 956 | Sep.06–Sep.16 | 0 | 11 | 0 | 11 | 32 | 21 |
| Stella Solaris Xmas– New Years Cruise | 972 | Dec.17–Jan.04 | 0 | 4 | 0 | 4 | 40 | 36 |
| University Xmas in Oaxaca Tour | 979 | Dec.21–Jan.06 | 0 | 0 | 0 | 0 | 40 | 40 |
| TOTALS | | | 315 | 72 | 12 | 375 | 628 | 253 |

**Figure 9.4**  Weekly booking report.

having a choice of four post-meeting optional tours from which to choose.

One simple method for a fairly small tour is to keep one master control sheet (see Figure 9.5) and add each client's name to the sheet as he or she joins the tour. Put a check mark in various columns under different headings next to the client's name—for example, under gateway city selected, under special optional tours selected, and so forth. Instead of everything on one master control sheet, another system involves a separate control sheet or index card for each variable—one card for the San Francisco/Honolulu flight, another for the Los Angeles/Honolulu flight, and so on. In this case, it is necessary to enter each client's name on each of these pertinent cross-reference cards.

These methods show at a glance what is selling and what is not. If an agency anticipates thirty passengers, it may have initially booked fifteen seats out of Los Angeles and fifteen out of San Francisco. But if a disproportionate number of passengers are signing up for the Los Angeles flight, the agency can adjust the flight request, perhaps asking the airline to change to twenty seats from Los Angeles and only ten from San Francisco. This early change is better than waiting until the 60-day or 30-day review later. The agency does not want to be surprised suddenly to find that the Los Angeles flight is oversold and the San Francisco one undersold.

A master control also permits keeping track of totals to be sure that no one has been lost. If the booking sheet indicates that bookings have been received from twenty-four participants, but there are records of only fourteen on the Los Angeles flight and nine on the San Francisco flight, somebody is missing. Perhaps somebody has not been listed on the flight. Here again, with a small group of thirty, it is possible to locate the missing name and balance fairly quickly. But with large groups, hours can be spent searching for the lost participant, whose name was inadvertently omitted from the flight.

**Client Records**

Not only is it necessary to keep track of what each tour member is doing and to enter the name on the proper operational records so that suppliers are kept accurately informed, it is also necessary to know what each tour member is doing so that staff can sound knowledgeable about the file when he or she calls. In addition to operational control records, therefore, it will also be necessary to maintain some sort of individual tour member control record. A variety of systems can be

TOUR NAME AND DEPARTURE DATE: ROSEMONT COUNTRY CLUB.  SEPTEMBER 6, 1985

| NO. | NAME | SHARE | SNGL. | OTHER | BLOCK AIR ORD | BLOCK AIR JFK | OPTIONAL GASTRONOMIQUE TOUR | COMMENTS |
|---|---|---|---|---|---|---|---|---|
| 1. | DAVIS, Mr. Merle | X | | | | X | | Prefer king-size bed if available |
| 2. | DAVIS, Mrs. Annie | X | | | | X | X | See above |
| 3. | GOODWIN, Mr. Charles | X | | | X | | | |
| 4. | GOODWIN, Mrs. Marian | X | | | X | | X | VIP. Club President |
| 5. | WILSON, Mr. Craig | | X | | | | | |
| 6. | HOLMES, Mrs. Winifred | X | | | | X | X | Willing to share |
| 7. | SELDMAN, Mr. Louis | X | | | | X | X | Cancelled 6/24/85 |
| 8. | SELDMAN, Mrs. Helen | X | | | | X | X | Cancelled 6/24/85 |
| 9. | KNOWLES, Mr. George | | | X | X | | X | Party of 4. Two adjoining twins, or suite arrangement OK. |
| 10. | KNOWLES, Mrs. Nancy | | | X | X | | X | |
| 11. | KNOWLES, Miss Melanie (18) | | | X | X | | X | |
| 12. | KNOWLES, Miss Jane (16) | | | X | X | | X | |
| 13. | PICKETT, Mr. James | X | | | X | | | Leg injury. Aisle, bulkhead |
| 14. | PICKETT, Mrs. Elaine | X | | | X | | X | |
| 15. | NEFF, Mr. Charles | X | | | X | | | |
| 16. | NEFF, Mrs. Ruth | X | | | X | | X | |
| 17. | MARTIN, Miss Adele | X | | | X | | X | Shares with Roswell |

**Figure 9.5** Master tour control sheet. Note that names are entered in order in which they booked, and that cancellations are not erased or renumbered.

devised, ranging from rather sophisticated computer programming for large convention or incentive groups, right down to a homemade shoebox file system for small, simple groups.

Whatever system is ultimately used, the idea is to have a synthesis of each tour member's travel plans readily available and visible. If clients call and want to know how much they owe or want to know if they are registered for a certain optional tour or if their final payment has been received, it should not be necessary to read through an entire file to locate the answer. Files are for storage only—a good place to keep the participant's letters to the agency, copies of the agency's reply letters, copies of invoices or reminder notes to the file following telephone conversations. But the file is not the place to locate quick answers or to have a quick visual grasp of that individual's trip.

Instead, a one-sheet or one-card recap should be available separately. Some agencies have the front cover of the tour member's file printed with such a chart. Other agencies keep a card index and complete a master client control card for each new member as booked. These cards are then kept alphabetically in a card box for each tour, readily accessible to the tour counselor when calls come in. These cards are never taken out of the box; they are not filed in the client file.

Unless an agency already does a lot of group business, it probably will not have such a system and will have to design one. The usual cards that the agency may be using for commercial accounts or for individual air reservations probably are not suitable. The card should have a place to list each participant's name, home address, business address, telephone number, age, passport data, and birth data. It should show what services each member of the party is purchasing—basic tour, optional tours, single-room supplement, and individual purchases such as airfare to the gateway city, insurance and so forth. It should have a place for financial history, showing deposits received, charges, and balance due. (See Figure 9.6.)

## Handling of Monies

As deposits and subsequent monies come in, they should be deposited and acknowledged. To ensure accurate profit-and-loss figures on completion of each tour, *be sure to assign an accounting code number to each tour project.* Subsequently, all payments coming in on that tour should be credited by the agency accountant to that specific tour. Any checks that are issued for expenses against the tour should also carry that accounting number.

# IN-HOUSE OPERATIONS AND DEALING WITH SUPPLIERS 187

**Figure 9.6** Client control card system.

If the agency is just beginning in group business, a meeting with the agency accountant is recommended. At this meeting the accounting codes can be discussed, so that there is a thorough understanding of the agency's goal, which is to have an accurate, *separate financial picture of each tour or cruise project.* Achieving this goal may require that some changes be made in the accounting system or that the accountant may have to do additional work so that the agency can obtain these figures quickly and easily.

## Tracking Inquiries

In addition to keeping track of bookings and participants' records, it is a good idea also to keep track of bookings that do *not* come in. The agency staff should keep a record of every inquiry coming in concerning a tour. If the inquiry converts into a booking, the original inquiry can be pulled out and filed with the client file. With such a system, all inquiries remaining in the inquiry file will be from people who did not book and thus need followup. Inquiries that come in by letter are easy to keep track of; the agency has the letter in the file. However, inquiries that come in verbally, either by telephone or in person, are not as easily controlled. Often sales counselors receiving the initial phone inquiry are rushed; they may jot down only the bare essentials. They may send out a brochure and do nothing else.

To assist sales counselors taking these calls, it is helpful to develop a small card, leaving supplies on each counselor's desk to be completed each time a query comes in. The card should have a place for the date of the call, the caller's full name, address, telephone, and the source (how he or she heard of the tour). Knowing the source is helpful in knowing which advertisements or promotional efforts are bringing results and which are not. (See Figure 9.7 for a sample inquiry record card.)

## Finalizing with Suppliers

THE AIRLINES

Normally, at thirty days before departure, the agency should make its final report to the airlines involved in the tour, giving them passengers' names and final details. This is done with the originating (controlling) air carrier, who in turn, passes the information downline to other airlines involved in the onward air space. It is not necessary to contact

```
                        INQUIRY RECORD
DATE OF INQUIRY _____

TOUR BROCHURE _____

NAME _____

ADDRESS _____

CITY _____

STATE _____ ZIP CODE _____ PHONE _____

SOURCE OF INQUIRY _____

DATE BROCHURE SENT _____
```

**Figure 9.7**  Inquiry record card.

every air carrier on the group's itinerary. Although it may be easier to finalize by telephone at first, ultimately this should be done *in writing* by submitting a flight manifest and a cover letter.

*Flight manifest.* The flight manifest should be numbered for the total count of passengers. Anyone in the group who uses a seat gets a number. An infant, carried on the parent's lap and not assigned an individual seat, is listed by name on the manifest but on the same line next to the parent's name. An older child occupying a seat is listed on a separate line and with a corresponding number. Remember, the airlines are counting seats, not couples, families, or hotel rooming units. For a domestic tour, last name and first initial may be all that the airline requires. For an international tour, the usual procedure is to list the full, legal name exactly as it appears on the passenger's passport (or other legal document that he or she is carrying as proof of citizenship). If a man goes by the name of "Buzz" Jones but his real, legal name is Mortimer Alfred Jones on his passport, list him as: Jones, Mr. Mortimer Alfred. The manifest should be divided into smokers and nonsmokers, to help the airlines and the tour manager in seat assignment.

If the group is traveling together as a unit from beginning to end, only one flight manifest is necessary. If, however, members are dropping in and out of the group tour flights, so that the name list is not standard for each flight on the itinerary, separate manifests will be needed for each flight leg where the list varies. The tour manager's name should be at the bottom, listed as the manager for easy identification by the airline. Be sure to photocopy a supply of extra lists for the tour manager so that a separate one is available for checkin at the airport on each flight sector, and for presenting to the airlines for flight reconfirmation overseas at each stop. (See Figure 9.8 for a sample flight manifest.)

*Cover letter to controlling airline.* The flight manifest should be submitted to the controlling airline with a cover letter (Figure 9.9). The cover letter might touch on the following:

- Formal release of unsold flight space. (An agency may wish to ask for permission to retain a few unsold seats, referring to them as "no-name" seats for late sales, if it honestly believes that there is the potential for late sales.)
- Recap of total number of smoking and nonsmoking seats needed and grand total.
- Indication as to how seating reservations should be handled.
- Any special group requests or reminder of things promised to the agency earlier, such as use of VIP departure lounge, a special group check-in lane, and special group baggage marking.
- Any special individual requests that certain passengers may have made, such as diet meals or seating with extra legroom.
- Name of the tour manager and contact prior to flight time.

THE HOTELS

Normally, at thirty days before departure, a final report is made to each hotel involved in the itinerary if hotels have been booked directly. If hotel accommodations were booked by a wholesaler or by an overseas reception ground operator, there is no need to contact the hotels directly, but the wholesaler or overseas reception ground operator must be given the same information that would have been sent directly to the hotels. This procedure should be done *in writing,* with a rooming list and with a cover letter, just as with the airlines.

*Rooming list (confidential tour roster).* Whereas the flight manifest was listed alphabetically by name, one name to a line (since airlines

LSI TRAVEL AGENCY, INC.

Rosemont Country Club
European Highlights Tour 1985
Flight Manifest

NON-SMOKING (Total 20)

1.  DAVIS, Mr. Merle (Ex JFK)
2.  DAVIS, Mrs. Annie (Ex JFK)
3.  HOLMES, Mrs. Winifred (Ex JFK)
4.  KIMBERLY, Mr. Eugene
5.  KIMBERLY, Mrs. Margaret (Tour Manager)
6.  KNOWLES, Mr. George
7.  KNOWLES, Mrs. Nancy
8.  KNOWLES, Miss Melanie (18)
9.  KNOWLES, Miss Jane (16)
10. LEVINSON, Mr. John
11. LEVINSON, Mrs. Martha
12. MARTIN, Miss Adele
13. OSBORNE, Mrs. Joan (Ex JFK)
14. PICKETT, Mr. James (Requests bulkhead, aisle seat due to leg injury)
15. PICKETT, Mrs. Elaine
16. ROSWELL, Miss Betsy
17. SMYTHE, Mrs. Jennifer
18. SMYTHE, Miss Connie
19. WING, Mr. Elliott
20. WING, Mrs. Frances

SMOKING (Total 8)

1. GOODWIN, Mr. Charles
2. GOODWIN, Mrs. Marian
3. LANDAU, Mrs. Louise
4. LANDAU, Miss Karen
5. LEWIS, Miss Angie
6. NEFF, Mr. Charles
7. NEFF, Mrs. Ruth (Requests salt-free meal)
8. WILSON, Mr. Craig

**Figure 9.8** Flight manifest.

count seats), the rooming list should be prepared by rooms. One method is to list twin-bedded rooms first, then singles, and last triples or suites or other special rooming arrangements. At the bottom should be a recap, indicating totals—total number of twins, singles, and triples being used, grand total number of rooms, and grand total number of people.

Some tour companies prefer to have the rooming lists be just that—rooming lists only—and then backup information such as passengers'

LSI TRAVEL AGENCY, INC.

August 6, 1985

Mr. Jeffrey Whelan
Trans World Airlines

RE: Rosemont Country Club
European Highlights Tour
Departing Sept. 6, 1985
30-day finalization

Dear Jeffrey:

We are now ready to finalize the above-mentioned tour. There are a total of 28 in the group (27+1), per the attached passenger manifest. Since you are holding 32 seats, you may now release any unsold space. Note that of the 28, 24 board at ORD and we pick up four at JFK for a total of 28 out of JFK.

May we remind you that TWA earlier offered use of the VIP departure lounge at O'Hare and a special group check-in lane. We will appreciate your reconfirming that these two requests are in order.

The tour manager's name is Mrs. Margaret Kimberly. I will be mailing the formal request for her ticket in a day or two. She will check with your counter two hours prior to flight time out of ORD and will be present to assist as our passengers arrive. They will be carrying their own tickets and will be checking in for this initial flight individually.

Please arrange to have the group seated as a block and to have the seats pre-assigned with boarding passes ready to expedite matters. We have indicated on the attached flight manifest smokers/nonsmokers for seat assignment purposes. Also please note that there are two special client requests for seating and special meals on the attached manifest. Please assign Mrs. Kimberly to an aisle nonsmoking seat.

Many thanks for all your help, Jeffrey, in seeing this tour through to fruition. You've been great to work with!

Cordially,

Marty Sarbey de Souto, CTC
Group Manager

MS/s
enclosure: flight manifest

**Figure 9.9** 30-day finalization with airline.

passport numbers, addresses, and so forth on a separate sheet. Others prefer to put everything on one master tour roster that is broken down by rooming arrangements but also lists all the backup information on the same sheet. (See Figure 9.10 for a sample final roster.)

Under this arrangement, items that should appear on this tour roster sheet would be the following:

- Each passenger's full, legal name, shown with his or her roommate (therefore, the list may not be alphabetical).
- Each passenger's home address (if a passenger charges something to the hotel room and for some reason checks out without paying for it, the hotel can write to the passenger directly to collect, rather than using the agency as middleman).
- Each passenger's passport data—number of passport, date of issue, place of issue. This information often is required of the hotel by local police or immigration authorities.
- Each passenger's full birth place and full birth date. Here again, this is often information that the hotel must have on its records if requested by local law enforcement authorities.
- Options—a column for pretour or posttour optional tours that passengers may have elected to take or not to take—and a total at the bottom showing how many are on each optional tour.
- Smoking/nonsmoking column. Although this information is not necessary for the hotel, it should appear on the master tour roster for other purposes: the airline's information, the tour manager's information in assigning smoking or nonsmoking motorcoaches and so forth.
- Air ticket numbers (should one be lost, this information helps the tour manager in reporting the loss quickly).
- Comments—a special column to indicate such things as passengers traveling with friends, or a passenger who may have difficulty in walking.

Remember, this list is *confidential;* it is used by the agency and the tour manager with hotels and other suppliers only. It is *not* given out to the passengers. Many passengers are sensitive about their ages and other personal data and do not want this information distributed to the other tour members.

One of the principal purposes of this detailed list is so that the hotels may *preregister* the members of the group. If the hotel has done its

FINAL ROSTER — ROSEMONT COUNTRY CLUB EUROPEAN HIGHLIGHTS TOUR

| NO. | NAME | ADDRESS | BIRTHDATE AND PLACE | PASSPORT NO. EXPIRATION | BLOCK AIR ORD | BLOCK AIR JFK | GASTR. OPTION | COMMENTS |
|---|---|---|---|---|---|---|---|---|
| 1. | DAVIS, Mr. Merle | 2433 Beaver Pl Briston, IN 46507 | 9/06/31 Plains, GA | D62386938 7/15/93 | | X | | |
| 2. | DAVIS, Mrs. Annie | Same as above | 4/15/33 Reno, NV | D62386937 7/15/93 | | X | X | |
| 3. | GOODWIN, Mr. Charles | 625 Oak View Dr. Rosemont, IL 60018 | 2/06/28 Buffalo, NY | B2395849 9/03/94 | X | | | |
| 4. | GOODWIN, Mrs. Marian | Same as above | 4/16/32 Akron, OH | J23975927 6/02/93 | X | | X | President of Rosemont Country Club |
| 5. | HOLMES, Mrs. Winifred | 4600 W.Whitesbridge Erie, PA 16502 | 6/20/19 Erie, PA | C54769392 8/16/94 | | X | X | |
| 6. | OSBORNE, Mrs. Joan | 1591 Palmetto Lane Kokomo, IN 46901 | 10/09/21 Erie, PA | C29358939 4/30/93 | | X | X | |
| 7. | KIMBERLY, Mr. Eugene | % LSI Travel Agency 1234 5th Avenue Anytown, U.S.A. | 10/06/21 New York, NY | B29396029 5/16/93 | X | | | |
| 8. | KIMBERLY, Mrs.Margaret | Same as above | 7/08/24 Boise, ID | B6923809 6/03/93 | X | | X | Tour Manager |
| 9. | KNOWLES, Mr. George | 12 Eton Place Joliet, IL 60432 | 9/30/41 Joliet, IL | B69939292 9/15/94 | X | | | Family of four. Two adjoining twins or suite arrangement |
| 10. | KNOWLES, Mrs. Nancy | Same as above | 5/16/45 Chicago, IL | B69939291 9/15/94 | X | | X | |
| 11. | KNOWLES, Miss Melanie | Same as above | 2/24/67 Joliet, IL | B69939293 9/15/94 | X | | X | |
| 12. | KNOWLES, Miss Jane | Same as above | 9/01/69 Joliet, IL | B69939294 9/15/94 | X | | X | |
| 13. | LANDAU, Mrs. Louise | 3201 Longwalk Dr. Rosemont, IL 60018 | 7/13/33 Bisbee, AZ | C5939299 10/02/93 | X | | X | |
| 14. | LANDAU, Miss Karen | Same as above | 3/06/57 Rosemont, Il | C9223902 11/16/93 | X | | X | |

Continued ............

**Figure 9.10** Final roster.

| | | | | | | |
|---|---|---|---|---|---|---|
| 15. | LEVINSON, Mr. John | 2617 Le Conte Av. Rosemont, IL 60018 | 10/05/22 Miami, FL | B29935983 7/16/93 | X | |
| 16. | LEVINSON, Mrs. Martha | Same as above | 12/02/24 Chicago, IL | B29935984 7/16/93 | X | X |
| 17. | MARTIN, Miss Adele | 2093 Cedar Ave Indianapolis, IN 46901 | 1/13/18 Roswell, NM | D39295083 11/04/94 | X | | Share strangers |
| 18. | ROSWELL, Miss Betsy | Route 1, Box E Granville, IL 61326 | 11/19/22 Chicago, IL | B39602397 12/03/93 | X | X |
| 19. | NEFF, Mr. Charles | 5909 Gloucester Pl Park Ridge, IL 60068 | 5/23/21 Ames, IA | B39672093 1/06/94 | X | |
| 20. | NEFF, Mrs. Ruth | Same as above | 9/22/25 Chicago, IL | B39672094 1/06/94 | X | X | Salt-free menu |
| 21. | PICKETT, Mr. James | 379 Lyman Circle Des Plaines, IL 60016 | 10/16/22 Dallas, TX | B39270963 7/15/93 | X | | Requests aisle/bulkhead seat due leg injury |
| 22. | PICKETT, Mrs. Elaine | Same as above | 12/02/25 Dallas, TX | B39270965 7/15/93 | X | X |
| 23. | SMYTHE, Mrs. Jennifer | 1168 Parkside Drive McHenry, IL 60050 | 6/12/41 Raleigh, NC | C39276092 9/03/94 | X | |
| 24. | SMYTHE, Miss Connie | Same as above | 12/02/64 McHenry, IL | C39276093 9/03/94 | X | X |
| 25. | WING, Mr. Elliott | 2433 Brown Derby Rd. Rosemont, IL 60018 | 11/16/52 St.Louis, MO | C36923792 10/13/94 | X | |
| 26. | WING, Mrs. Frances | Same as above | 6/17/55 St.Louis, MO | C36923793 10/13/94 | X | X |
| | | | | | 24 | 4 |

| | | | | | | |
|---|---|---|---|---|---|---|
| 27. | LEWIS, Miss Angie | 617 Broadmore.Apt.A Oak Park, IL 60303 | 6/19/21 Atlanta, GA | B3926709 11/03/93 | X | X | Requested single; paid supplement |
| 28. | WILSON, Mr.Craig | 1501 15th Ave. Evanston, IL 60204 | 12/01/29 Evanston, IL | B5920762 12/03/94 | X | X | Forced single |
| | | | | | | 18 |

RECAP
13 TWINS, 2 SINGLES = 15 ROOMS = 28 PERSONS
BLOCK AIR ORD: 24
BLOCK AIR JFK: 4
OPTIONAL PARIS GASTRONOMIQUE TOUR: 17+1

homework, when the group checks in, rooms should be preassigned, with keys laid out for passengers to pick up, after which they can go to their rooms. In some cases, particularly if the group is arriving early in the morning when all rooms are not cleaned or available, this may not be possible. But 90 percent of the time submitting a detailed list such as this enables an efficient hotel to work ahead, so that when the group arrives, the passengers simply sign the hotel registration card and do not have to fill it out with name, address, passport data, and so forth. If the desk clerk does ask them to do so, the tour manager can tactfully mention that the hotel already has been given this information by mail on the final tour roster.

*Cover letter to hotels.* When the tour roster is sent to each hotel, a cover letter recapping arrangements should accompany it. (See Figure 9.11.) Some of the things that this cover letter might touch on are as follows:

- Recap of arrival date, flight number, and approximate time. Name of reception ground operator in that city transferring the group in from the airport to the hotel (so the hotel has a local contact to find out what has happened to a group if they do not arrive on time).
- Recap of departure date and approximate time. (The departure flight may be late in the day, which would mean that passengers have to check out of their hotel at the hotel's regularly posted checkout time and then wait in the lobby with their luggage until time to transfer to the airport.) Never assume that rooms may be kept past checkout time. Always ask. If the hotel is not heavily booked, they may permit it. On the other hand, if the hotel is booked solid, it probably will not be possible unless the agency offers to pay a day rate—if there is one—or the extra night—an item that should be thought of when costing the tour, not later! Some deluxe operators do cost in for the extra night, particularly if the departure flight is leaving in the middle of the might, as often is the case in tours to India.)
- Résumé of total rooms to be used—twins, singles, and triples.
- Release of any unsold rooms, or request to retain one or two no-name rooms for late sale.
- Recap of any special arrangements. This would include meals, special dinner parties or receptions, rooms set aside for briefings and meetings, special dining room hours, and extra bellboys on duty at arrival and departure times.

LSI TRAVEL AGENCY, INC.

August 6, 1985

Mr. Hans Van der Hooten
Sales Manager
Hotel Krasnapolsky
Dam 9, 1012 JS
Amsterdam
The Netherlands

RE: Rosemont Country Club
European Highlights Tour
Arriving September 7, 1985
30-day review

Dear Hans:

We now wish to finalize the above-mentioned tour with you. We have sold a total of 28 (27+1), so our final needs are:

    13 twins
    2 singles

Full details of rooming arrangements are on the attached roster.

The group arrives September 7 via TW 814 at 07:05 from New York and departs September 10 for Paris via morning train. We wish to hold a briefing at 5:00 p.m. on September 7 followed by a cocktail party/welcome dinner. Kindly reserve a small room suitable, and send us suggested menu and prices including tax, tip, and domestic liquor/wines.

Enclosed is our check #0217 in the amount of $0000, with breakdown of charges on the check. This is per your original quote, including daily accommodations, 4% tax and 15% service to hotel personnel. It is understood that meals are not included in the rate. The welcome party will be paid by our tour manager upon checkout. Any other charges are to be billed to the individual folios of the passengers concerned.

Mrs. Margaret Kimberly is the tour manager in charge. Should there be any questions, please feel free to query her.

Cordially,

Marty Sarbey de Souto, CTC
Group Manager

Enclosures: Check #0217
Roster of Members

**Figure 9.11**  30-day finalization with hotel.

- Recap of finances and payment, showing rates for each type of room, totals, complimentary rooms, taxes, and deposits. This can appear in the cover letter itself, on a separate calculation sheet, or on the check if there is room. Normally the agency will prepay at thirty days prior, less any early deposits that may have been made. However, some tour operators arrange to have the tour manager pay by company check as the tour moves along. Some volume operators work from a *float*—a large, rotating fund left on deposit with a given hotel. Others, who may have preestablished credit, arrange to have the hotel bill the agency later. This decision is between the agency and each individual hotel, depending on a number of factors.
- Name of the tour manager and an indication to the hotel as to what his or her role is; for example, instructions as to what may be charged to the master account and what the tour manager or the individual passengers must pay for directly at the time. Putting this in writing helps to limit the agency's financial liability if there is a problem in this regard later. Some companies permit their tour managers to charge almost anything to the master account; others restrict them severely.

All of the above information can be synthesized in a cover letter and sent to each hotel with the rooming list (tour roster) and payment. If the hotel space was booked initially through a hotel chain office in the United States, such as Sheraton, Westin, Hilton or other, the considerate agency will copy that office in as a courtesy. Then the chain office knows that the agency has complied with the hotel in finalizing. However, the actual letter, list, and check should go directly to the hotel property, either to the attention of the sales manager or the front-office manager. The original should not be sent to the hotel booking office in the United States unless they have specifically instructed that this be done. (If submitting these lists at sixty days, then at thirty days, and perhaps updated corrected lists even later, learn to color-code. The first list could be done on green photocopy paper, the next list on yellow, and so forth. This way, when the tour manager checks in at the hotel, it is easy to spot if desk clerks are working with the most recent lists or if they need to be handed an updated one.)

RECEPTION GROUND OPERATORS OVERSEAS

At thirty days before departure, the agency should finalize with each reception ground operator handling the tour enroute. See Figure 9.12

IN-HOUSE OPERATIONS AND DEALING WITH SUPPLIERS     199

```
                    LSI TRAVEL AGENCY, INC.

                                           August 6, 1985

Mr. Jean Claude Murat
President
Treasure Tours
15 rue de l'Arcade
Paris 75008, France

             RE:  Rosemont Country Club "European Highlights Tour"
                  Arriving Paris Sept. 10, 1985

Dear Mr. Murat:

We are now ready to finalize the above-mentioned tour.  Final totals are 27 paying
passengers plus the tour manager (27+1) for the basic tour, and 17+1 for the
optional half-day Gastronomique Tour Sept. 11.  A copy of the group roster is
enclosed.  Also enclosed is our check No. 6372 in the amount of $0000 in prepayment
for services, as itemized on the check.

There have been no changes in arrival or departure.  The group will still arrive
Sept. 10 via the train which leaves Amsterdam at 09:15 arriving Paris 13:00, and
will depart Sept. 13 via AF 630 for Rome.

Mrs. Margaret Kimberly is the tour manager in charge.  She will be paying entrance
fees at the Louvre and at Versailles directly, as well as gratuities on behalf of
the group to the local guide, the bus drivers, and the hotel porters.

We have finalized with the Hotel Meurice directly.  However, we would appreciate
your double-checking with them that all is in order.  Should you find that by
doing the city tour enroute from the rail station to the hotel there may be a
problem with late arrival at the hotel, I would suggest you pull the room keys
earlier in the day and distribute them in the coach.

Should there be any questions, let us know.  Trusting that all is in order and
that everything will go smoothly.

                                           Cordially,

                                           Marty Sarbey de Souto, CTC
                                           Group Manager

MS/s
enclosure: Check No. 6372
           Final tour roster
```

**Figure 9.12**   30-day finalization letter to reception operator.

for a suggested 30-day finalization letter to a reception ground operator. (If the land tour was booked through a wholesaler in the United States, this step is not necessary; the agency finalizes with the wholesaler, who in turn notifies its overseas branches or representatives.)

If these operators are to act for the agency and do a good job, it will be necessary to give them full information, as follows:

- Several copies of the final tour roster, showing all necessary data, such as rooming arrangements, passengers' names, addresses, birth data, passport data, optional tours, and comments.
- Résumé of total passengers, total rooms, total on optional tours.
- Verification of arrival and departure flights, and a request that the local reception ground operator call the departing airline in their city at this time to verify that the group is, indeed, holding reservations, and to verify departure time. Many a group has left home with signed and sworn confirmations of onward flights, only to be bumped or to have a local airline employee inform them that there was no local record of the booking. This can be avoided by having the flight checked locally a month ahead of time.
- Name of tour manager and any necessary explanation as to this individual's financial limits, and other matters.
- Recap of services the agency expects the reception ground operator to provide.
- If reception ground operators are handling the hotels, each operator should be reminded to tell the hotels everything that the agency normally would have told them directly—information about preregistering the group, meal arrangements, parties, briefing rooms, arrival and departure times, request for adequate baggage assistance at those appropriate times.
- Any special requests; for example, a particular guide, a specific restaurant, a reminder regarding a tour participant with a health problem.
- Recap of finances and payment, showing breakdown of rates, complimentaries, and credit for any deposits already paid on account. This can be done in the cover letter, on a separate calculations sheet, or on the check itself if there is room. If the agency has established credit with these companies, perhaps it may be possible to have the tour manager pay by company check as the tour moves along, or to verify and initial the bill and have it sent to the agency office for payment. Never assume, however, that this arrangement will be satisfactory; always ask. The tour world is full of stories of embarrassed tour managers who were forced to pay by their own personal credit card before leaving.

The primary advantage of not paying in advance (other than cash flow) is that there is no risk of overpaying in case of a late cancellation or when some passengers do not show up for certain tour activities. In these cases, the reception ground operator owes the agency money, and must send the agency a refund check or, as often happens, issue a credit memo and retain the monies toward a future tour. This occurs particularly if local currency restrictions or exchange problems make it not worthwhile to refund relatively small amounts.

CRUISE LINES

If there is a cruise within the tour, or if the entire project is a cruise, the agency will want to finalize with the cruise line just as it did with the reception ground operator, sending a tour roster and cover recap letter.

*The cruise roster.* The final roster for a cruise has much the same information on it as a tour roster for a tour: passengers' full name, home address, passport data, and birth data. However, a cruise roster has some special requirements all its own.

- Cabin numbers, listed next to passengers' names.
- Purchased shore excursions, if any.
- Dining room seating (early or late seating) if group was given a choice.
- Flights on which passengers are flying, if the cruise line is handling the air as part of an air/sea cruise.

Sometimes the cruise line keeps its records by number, and each passenger is assigned a booking number when the booking is recorded. When this is the case, adding those booking numbers to the list assists the cruise line in locating the booking.

*Cover letter.* The cover letter that accompanies a cruise roster should recap all arrangements and previous discussions or promises. (See Figure 9.13.) For example:

- Total number on the cruise, on each flight, on prepurchased shore excursions, at meal sittings—recap of figures on the accompanying roster.
- Name of tour manager and reminder of his or her cabin arrangements, if not reserved previously. Formal request to send tour manager's cruise ticket.
- Special requests on behalf of group—meeting room for a briefing, welcome party, special use of the theater for seminars or lectures, observance of any birthdays or anniversaries, wine, tour of the bridge or the ship's galley.

LSI TRAVEL AGENCY, INC.

April 11, 1985

Ms. Jane Jones
Royal Cruise Line
One Embarcadero
San Francisco, CA. 94111

RE: 90-day finalization
"Lovers of Archaeology" Group
Baltic Cruise July 11, 1985
Royal Odyssey

Dear Jane:

Enclosed is our check #0000 in the amount of $0000 representing final payment for the above group. Please see breakdown attachment to the check for details.

Also enclosed is our final roster. Totals are as follows:

|   |   |
|---|---|
| Total passengers: | 40+1 |
| Meal sittings: | Early sitting 16, late sitting 25 |
| Options: | Pre-cruise London package 16 |
| Your block air: | ORD 31; JFK 10 |

By way of wrap-up, please implement the following points which we discussed previously:

(1) Mrs. Elaine Whittaker of the "Lovers of Archaeology" organization is our name draw and guest speaker. We would appreciate her receiving VIP handling. She is currently holding cabin C-15; if you can upgrade her, great! Do note she is not the tour manager; we have Mrs. Sandy Johnson aboard for this purpose.

(2) RCL is to host a welcome party on board. We would prefer this the second night out, if possible. Kindly request now and Sandy will reconfirm this after boarding.

(3) Note from the attached list that we have several special requests ... one diabetic and one salt-free diet. Kindly alert the dining room.

(4) Do recall that Mrs. Whittaker will be giving two lectures during the days at sea and you indicated that you would make meeting room space available to the group for this purpose. Please now advise us time and place so we may notify her accordingly.

We are now returning all unsold space, as required by RCL. This is with the understanding that we may continue to promote for late sales on a space-available basis only. Important -- since many of these people live in rural areas out of state, we will be mailing final documents June 11, so must receive tickets well in advance of that deadline.

Sincerely,

Marty Sarbey de Souto

Marty Sarbey de Souto, CTC
Group Manager

MS/s
enclosures

**Figure 9.13** Finalization letter to cruise line.

- Special requests on behalf of individuals—any with particular health problems or walking difficulties, special menu requests (if possible).
- Reminder of any item still outstanding such as a passenger still waitlisted.

APPLYING FOR TOUR MANAGER'S TICKET

When using an airfare that permits a complimentary air ticket, the agency must formally apply to the airline for this ticket. It does not just automatically arrive at the agency office. This application is made, in writing, on company letterhead and must contain specific wording. (See Figure 9.14.) Accompanying the letter of application must be the flight manifests (here is where the manifests that were prepared earlier can also come in handy).

Note that the letter must indicate exactly how many passengers are accompanying the manager on *each* leg. Also note that when it comes to issuing tour manager tickets, the airlines are concerned with how many *adult* fares are accompanying him or her, so two children's half fares count as one full fare, even if the children occupy two seats. If the tour includes children, it is a good idea always to indicate the age of each child next to the name on the airline manifest.

The air complimentary policy of a particular tour should be thoroughly understood *before* the tour is priced. It is no longer safe to assume that a ticket is received free for every fifteen passengers. This is still true with some fares to some areas of the world. However, on many fares to many areas there are absolutely no complimentary air tickets anymore, and the tour manager's airfare must be costed-in to the tour as a fixed expense, so that each tour participant is, in effect, paying part of it.

Those fares that do allow for a complimentary may be 15 + 1 free, 25 + 1 1/2 free, 30 + 2 free, and so forth. Note that some stop there with a limit of two free for 30, so that even if a group continued growing to 100 or so, the tour would still be limited to two complimentaries. On the other hand, other fares may allow the agency to continue to accrue complimentaries to infinity; for example, 30 + 2, 40 + 2 1/2, 45 + 3, 60 + 4, and so forth. *Be sure to ask from the outset* and get a commitment. If the limit is two complimentaries per group, it may be more advantageous to book the trip as two separate groups from the beginning, even though the two groups just happen to be traveling together on the same flights.

LSI TRAVEL AGENCY, INC.

August 6, 1985

Trans World Airlines

RE: Rosemont Country Club
European Highlights Tour
Departing Sept. 6, 1985

Gentlemen:

In accordance with existing IATA Regulations and terms of the tariff rules, we hereby request Tour Conductor transportation as follows:

    Name of Tour Conductors:  Mr. Eugene Kimberly
                                       Mrs. Margaret Kimberly
    Title of Advertised Tour: Rosemont Country Club "European Highlights Tour 1985"
    IT Number: TW1CHI385
    Type of Journey: Roundtrip

| From/To | Carrier | Flight No. | Date | No.Pax | Rebate |
|---|---|---|---|---|---|
| ORD/JFK | TW | 746Y | Sept. 06 | 22 | One at 100%; one full-fare |
| JFK/AMS | TW | 814Y | Sept. 06 | 26 | One at 100%; one at 50% |
| AMS/CDG | --- | --- | Surface | --- | --- |
| CDG/FCO | AF | 630Y | Sept. 13 | 26 | One at 100%; one at 50% |
| FCO/JFK | TW | 845Y | Sept. 16 | 26 | One at 100%; one at 50% |
| JFK/ORD | TW | 757Y | Sept. 16 | 26 | One at 100%; one full-fare |

Attached is a list of the names of members of the group and two copies of the promotional material used for this tour which has been distributed to the interested public.

In consideration of the granting of this Tour Conductor transportation, we agree that it will in no way be used to rebate any part of the cost to any or all individual members of this tour.

We confirm that the conditions attached to the fare paid by the passengers in the group do not prohibit the application of the tour conductor rebate.

We understand that in no case shall a tour conductor's reduced rate ticket, issued by a Member to a tour conductor, be sold to the tour conductor, directly or indirectly, at more than its face value, nor shall such ticket be resold.

We certify that the above application is true and correct in every respect, and all arrangements will have been paid for in full prior to commencement of travel.

Sincerely,

*Marty Sarbey de Souto*

Marty Sarbey de Souto, CTC
Group Manager

MS/s
enclosure: Passenger Manifest

**Figure 9.14**     Tour manager's ticket request.

## Ready to Go

When all of the above tasks have been completed, the tour is virtually ready to go. It now remains for the agency to make copies of the above materials for the tour manager and get ready to brief that very important individual who will be responsible for the success of the tour henceforth.

# 10

# Tour Manager Preparation and Dispatch

After the pretrip arrangements for the tour are completed, dealings with all suppliers are finalized, and final documents have been sent out to the passengers, one last thing must be done before the group leaves. The tour manager must be briefed and given all necessary materials for the trip. But first, let us look at this person, this manager who will determine the success or failure of the tour project. Has the tour manager been selected carefully? Do both agency and tour manager know what is expected? (For more indepth coverage of tour escorting, see chapter 11 and also *Handbook of Professional Tour Management,* by Robert T. Reilly, Merton House Travel and Tourism Publishers, Inc.)

**Tour Managers**

Managers come with all sorts of titles: tour escort, tour leader, tour organizer, courier, tour guide, and the current term, tour manager. What do these terms have in common? What is the role associated with each title?

The term *tour manager* is the important one for our purposes. It means the person who actually leads the group from point to point, usually from the gateway city. In some cases, however, the group may fly as a group, but unaccompanied (or as individuals on different flights from different gateways), convening overseas and meeting the tour manager there at a prearranged assembly point.

*Tour manager* is the current term in Europe, and this nomenclature now is being recognized in the United States, together with the new, upgraded title of *tour leader* or *director*. However, in many offices, the term tour manager still refers to the individual in the tour office handling the tour *inside,* not out in the field. Perhaps in the future this confusion of terms will be clarified; in this text, we will use *tour manager* to mean the person who handles the group enroute.

This individual, no matter what title is bestowed on him or her, is not to be confused with a guide. The tour manager is not a local city guide, and is not expected to know the year that every cathedral was built nor to speak the local language of each country visited. Those details are left to local city guides receiving the tour at each stop. However, the tour manager does provide continuity and carry-through from one city to the next, one country to the next, and acts as overall coordinator as the tour moves along.

### Who Is this Manager?

The tour manager may be a member of the agency's staff. He or she may be the organizer (the person who sold and recruited the group). Or perhaps it could be an outside professional manager, whose salary, as a professional, has been costed in to the trip.

Whoever it is, it is important to select this person carefully, since the failure or success of the trip may well depend on its tour manager. It is amazing how many companies will spend tremendous amounts of time, money, and energy on a tour, only to send it out with a totally inexperienced, unqualified individual, telling the person not to worry—that he or she does not have to do anything except to act as social director!

### Qualities to Look for in a Manager

Choosing someone to act as tour manager is an important act, one that requires both logic and commonsense. The person responsible for this choice cannot give the job to a friend, or to the office manager who has not been on a trip in a long time, or to a former Spanish professor because he or she speaks the language well. Most agents know individuals who are marvelous friends and colleagues, but who have made terrible tour managers. The author has a friend who teaches Spanish, who spends every summer in Spain, and who has been wanting for some years to be selected as a tour manager. However, she is totally disorganized. What is worse, she hates groups! Obviously this person would be totally inappropriate as a tour manager.

Although choosing the right person is always difficult, there are a few guidelines—qualities to look for in a tour manager.

- *Outgoing personality*—someone who is not shy, is able to mix socially, to speak in public, to approach strangers—the qualities often most prevalent in a good sales recruiter or tour organizer.
- *Common sense*—someone who can handle emergencies well, deal with enroute problems sensibly, and think quickly. Often maturity is an advantage here; an older person, just by virtue of having lived longer and having dealt with life's problems, may be better qualified than a young person. Age, however, is no automatic guarantee of common sense!
- *Organization*—the kind of person who can plan ahead and always be prepared for the next day's activities. Tour managers who cannot get themselves to a plane on time will never be able to get forty people there on time. The organized person is one who has pulled all the flight coupons prior to flight check-in, who has secured the right amount of change for departure bellboy tips and has it ready in an envelope, who is down in the lobby early on departure day checking on the bell captain to be sure that baggage gets down on time, and so forth. This attribute of organization is often the area where many sales recruiters and tour organizers are lacking. It is important to analyze the organizer, and if it appears that he or she is a real sales dynamo, a public relations person who may, however, be weak on details and organization, use this individual for what he or she is best at—sales and public relations—but put on a real, behind-the-scenes working manager as well. An organizer can act as host/hostess while the working manager handles the business details of the tour—baggage, air tickets, tipping. If each is properly briefed from the outset on the other's role, the two can work together effectively and smoothly as a team.
- *Empathy*—the kind of person who truly cares about other people, truly *likes* people, not in the backslapping, salesperson way but in a selfless, caring, human way. This is the manager who gets up at 2:00 a.m. to tend a sick tour member, the manager who goes

out of the way to take a passenger shopping or help him or her place an international phone call home. Tour managing means intimate contact with a group of individuals for an extended period. The tour manager becomes emotionally involved in the members' lives by force of circumstance since they may view him or her as a confidant in whom they entrust their hopes, aspirations, and tragedies. (As a tour manager, the author has had to tell a couple that their son had been killed in Vietnam. She has been go-between in some ontour romances and has been invited to the wedding later. She has encountered tour passengers with severe emotional, sexual, and psychological problems.) Although the person chosen as tour manager need not be a registered psychologist, he or she must have a humane, empathetic quality necessary to handle such situations.

- *Extreme tact*—the ability to handle people, to work well with others. These others are not just the tour participants; they are also the local guides, bus drivers, waiters, customs officials, reception ground operators, and local hosts overseas—people of various nationalities, educational levels, ethnic backgrounds, and motivations.
- *Even-tempered personality*—the kind of person who does not fluster easily, does not lose his or her temper easily. This is not to say that a tour manager never shows anger, but, when he or she does, it should be done cooly for effect, not just because the manager has lost control.
- *Commitment*—the person who does not have a nine-to-five mentality, who understands that tour managing is not an eight-hour day job, who is willing to invest extra time, energy, and personal involvement as needed. The manager who deposits the group at the hotel and says, "I'll see you all tomorrow at 9:00 a.m." will never be successful. Although everyone needs a night off now and then, it should be understood that one of the tour management functions is to fill in those time gaps when the group is not accompanied by a local sightseeing guide: the Dutch-treat dinners, the shopping expeditions, the free time. Therefore, if the manager wants to take this trip as a way to visit friends overseas or do research or business or for some reason other than dedicating time, attention, and energies to the group, he or she is the wrong person.
- *Leadership qualities*—probably this is the prime thing to look for— that nebulous, charismatic quality of leadership. It is always a

plus to find someone who has had experience in a leadership position, be it as president of the local Parent-Teachers Association or officer of a private club. A true leader is more qualified to be a tour manager than the person who may know the country and speak the language fluently but who cannot lead the way out of a paper bag!

- *Balanced personality*—the person with a sense of fun and a serious side, part intellectual, part social. After all, a trip is not all one thing or another, not all historical lectures, not all a big party. If it were, it would not be a success. The operator who puts together and carries out a balanced itinerary, one with some learning, (cathedrals, museums); some fun, (dining around, partying); some relaxation, (beaches, sports), seems to have the best prospects for success. So it would seem with tour managers also. If they emphasize socializing and ignore intellectual depth, they may fail. Conversely, if they see the trip as one vast classroom from which they may teach their specialty with no light touch or fun, they will lose their passengers.
- *Good health*—simplistic though it may sound, it is important that the tour manager be in good health at the outset and maintain it through the trip. As a manager, one is under stress with less sleep and less time for oneself and one's own needs than at home. A manager often finds it difficult to stay on a restricted diet or to remember to take medication or to rest when overtired.
- *Control and firmness*—the person who can keep a tight rein on a group, not letting his or her leadership be eroded by passengers or local guides. It is a fine line, this ability to be firm without becoming a dictator. Many people assume that teachers or ex-military men make good tour managers. This is not always the case, since many times they tend to treat their tour members like children rather than equals.

## The Importance of Experience

PREVIOUS TRAVEL TO THE COUNTRY

Those who need to select a tour manager often ask how important it is for that individual to have visited a country before. It certainly helps! But it is in no way a requirement. If one has to choose between someone who knows a certain country but who does not have leadership ability versus a born leader who has never visited that country before, the person with the leadership ability is probably the better choice.

LANGUAGE ABILITY

Similarly, one might ask how important it is for the tour manager to speak the language of the country or countries to be visited. If one speaks foreign languages, so much the better. The author speaks Spanish fluently. She probably does a better job as a tour manager in a Spanish-speaking country than if she did not. However, many of her colleagues without this language skill have led tours to Spanish-speaking areas quite successfully. Similarly, the author has led tours to Germany, Japan, and other countries where her vocabulary is limited to "Good Morning" and "Where is the bathroom?" Language ability alone is not a reason to select someone as tour manager.

However, in incoming tourism the tour manager must be *totally* fluent in the language of the incoming group, preferably a native speaker, because the members of the group are totally dependent on this person for translation, for an understanding of what is happening day to day. In outgoing tourism, however, there are English-speaking local guides overseas in addition to one's own English-speaking tour manager traveling with the group.

## Job Description

The previous discussion has made it clear that the role of tour manager is a complex one. It could be described as six professions in one:

- *Housemother (father) figure*—the person everyone in the group looks up to.
- *Business manager*—handling the day-to-day business of running the tour: checking in for flights, locating lost baggage, reconfirming onward reservations, tipping, handling hotel check-ins and check-outs, perhaps paying bills enroute, checking that buses and guides are on time and itineraries fulfilled as promised.
- *Social director*—setting up special meals and parties, observing birthdays and anniversaries, acting as host or hostess, introducing people, acting as a social catalyst.
- *Psychologist*—serving as a shoulder to cry on, a good listener.
- *Internationalist*—tying the countries together, comparing the country just left with the next one on the horizon, explaining

cultures and customs different from those to which the passengers are accustomed.
- *Teacher*—pointing out new things, giving clients an educational experience, however subliminal it may be, in addition to a good time.

**When to Select the Tour Manager**

Most decisions on leadership should be made *before* the tour is priced. The actual individual need not be selected by name at that time, but it is necessary to select the *category* of person. That is, if a professional, salaried leader will be used, this person's trip, salary, and expenses must be costed-in to the tour before the tour price is established and the brochure printed. It is not necessary to make a commitment to using a certain manager until it is definite that the tour has materialized, say sixty days in advance. The danger is to work in reverse; that is, to assume that the manager will be someone from the staff already on salary or an organizer who just wants a free trip and no salary—only to find out later that the organizer does not have the qualifications to perform as a real working tour manager, or that the staff person suddenly cannot get away, has left the company, or is eight-and-a-half-months pregnant.

**Agreement with the Tour Manager**

Regardless of who the tour manager is, it is wise to have an understanding with this individual. Some of the things to agree upon are:
- *Salary*—if any. If so, how much (per day? per trip?). And when is it paid? (Some managers are paid part in advance and part on completion of the tour; others are paid totally on completion.)
- *Free trip*—from what city? What is included in the free trip? All meals? Tips? Dutch-treat events if accompanying the group? Extra spending money for taxis, phone, baggage insurance, laundry, miscellaneous? Single room or share? Be specific!
- *Responsibilities*—is this tour manager totally in charge? Or will there be an assistant or overseas leader traveling with the group as well? Will the group be large or small? Will the person be a titular tour manager, or a real working one?

- *Gratuities*—can the manager expect to receive additional remuneration through tips or not? Is tipping encouraged, discouraged, forbidden by the company?
- *No-go date*—by what date would the prospective tour manager be told if the tour is being cancelled? It is not fair to have a manager hold certain dates and then be dumped at the end.

See Figure 10.1 for a sample contract for this important person.

## Getting Ready for the Briefing

Shortly before departure, the tour manager should be asked to come in for a pretrip briefing. This should be done early enough so that he or she may review all materials, read the files, and then ask questions on things not fully understood. No manager can do a good job if he or she receives departure materials the day of departure at the airport or in a mad rush the night before. The manager needs to feel well informed, totally in control, and self-confident.

## Materials for the Briefing

To prepare for the briefing session, make sure that the following items are ready (a checklist such as that shown in Figure 10.2 is helpful):

- *Supply of flight manifests*—if everyone is traveling together at all times on all flights, one master list will do (but give the tour manager plenty of photocopies so that he or she has a clean list to present at the airline check-in counter for each separate flight sector). If people are joining and leaving the group block air space at various points, separate flight manifests may be needed for each sector. It is helpful to have the list divided into smoking and nonsmoking sublists.
- *Supply of master rooming lists/tour rosters*—at least two for each city to be visited plus some extras.
- *Master group flight itinerary*—one copy. Should show airline, flight number, airport (not just city), estimated time of departure and arrival (ETD/ETA), and meal service for each flight sector. The tour manager should know the name of the controlling airline and that airline's record locator number for the tour, if any. This helps the manager in the field, if, when reconfirming onward air reservations, a carrier says that it has no record of the group's reser-

TRAVEL AGENCY/TOUR ESCORT AGREEMENT

Agreement made this _30th_ day of _November_, 198_4_, by and between LSI Travel Agency, Inc., an Illinois coporation with principal office at _1234 Fifth Avenue, Anytown, U.S.A._, (hereinafter referred to as "LSI") and Roberta Miller (hereinafter referred to as "Roberta");

Whereas, LSI is engaged in the travel agency and tour operator business; and

Whereas, LSI desires to engage Roberta to assist as a tour conductor;

Now, therefore, in consideration of the mutual benefits to them accruing, the parties hereto agree as follows:

1. LSI engages the services of Roberta to escort vacation groups.

2. Roberta shall be paid a fee of Eighty Dollars ($80.00) for each day of service including day of departure and arrival.

3. LSI will reimburse Roberta for all costs incurred in her duties, including, but not limited to, meals, baggage insurance, accommodations, laundry, telephone calls, cables or wires, and tips.

4. LSI will advance One Hundred Dollars ($100.00) per program for out-of-pocket expenses, which will be deducted from the expense report which must be submitted within thirty (30) days from the completion of the trip.

5. Roberta is an independent contractor and agrees that she is not to be covered by any employment compensation, workmen's compensation, or other health insurance, which LSI may provide for its employees. Roberta is not to participate in any pension or profit-sharing plan, nor will there be any payroll deductions for state or local wage tax, social security tax, unemployment compensation tax, or federal withholding tax. All fees will be reported on IRS 1099 MISC. form for federal income tax purposes.

6. Roberta shall be entitled to twenty-five (25) percent of her estimated fee prior to departure with the balance to be paid within fourteen (14) days subsequent to the completion of the trip.

7. LSI reserves the right to cancel this agreement for any specific tour without penalty up to four (4) weeks prior to departure. Any cancellations within four (4) weeks of departure will result in Roberta receiving her entire fee but no reimbursement for expenses.

8. This agreement may be terminated by either party hereto at any time upon ten (10) days written notice to the other party.

9. This agreement contains the entire understanding of the parties and supercedes all previous verbal and written agreements. There are no other agreements, representations or warranties not set forth herein.

In witness whereof, the parties hereto, intending to be legally bound thereby, hereunto set their respective hands and seals the day and year first written above.

LSI Travel Agency, Inc.

By_____

_____        _____
Witness                    President

_____        _____
Witness                    Roberta Miller

**Figure 10.1** Contract with tour manager. (Reproduced by permission of Jeffrey R. Miller.)

### CHECKLIST FOR TOUR MANAGER

___ Supply of flight manifests
___ Supply of master rooming lists/tour rosters
___ Master group itinerary
___ Photocopies of passengers' pretour/posttour air reservations
___ Photocopies of passengers' individual tour questionnaire forms
___ Supply of extra baggage tags
___ Supply of tour brochures
___ Sample set of all materials sent to passengers
___ Method of payment to suppliers: vouchers, travelers checks, or whatever
___ Supplies--rubber bands, tape, clips, marking pens, envelopes
___ Forms--expense report forms, tour report forms.
___ Names of all suppliers--their addresses, phone numbers, names of key persons
___ Copies of pertinent correspondence with suppliers
___ Tour manager's own personal travel documents--air ticket, valid passport, visas, pretour and posttour hotel accommodations

**Figure 10.2** Checklist of things to take.

vations. It is then possible to refer the overseas airline personnel to the controlling air carrier which originated the booking.

- *Individual air reservations*—photocopies of tour members' pretour and posttour air reservations, so that the tour manager knows how each passenger is arriving at the assembly point and, also, how each is continuing on after the tour terminates.
- *Tour questionnaires*—a photocopy of each of those personal questionnaires that the passengers sent in to the office, indicating their health problems, special diet requirements, personal interests, emergency contacts, and so forth.
- *Baggage tags*—supply of extra baggage tags, the same style and color as those distributed to passengers with their final documents. These are to be used to replace passengers' tags that fall off with wear and tear as the tour progresses or as samples to give to porters and bellboys to identify the group's baggage.
- *Sample set of passenger materials*—one complete set of everything that the passengers have received so far, from the tour brochure and initial offer right down through the information bulletins and

departure materials. The tour manager should know everything that the passengers were told so that he or she can continue in the same vein and not contradict something that they were told previously.

- *Method of payment to suppliers*—be it vouchers, company checkbook, travelers checks, or whatever mode used for payment. If the tour is completely prepaid, the tour manager should carry copies of checks or proof of payment. Even so, he or she may need to carry monies for emergencies, tips, and other items. Perhaps some foreign currency should be considered also—at least for the first overseas arrival in the event that the greeter does not show up at the airport and the tour manager is forced to move the group to the hotel in taxis.

- *Care package of supplies*—a small envelope of rubber bands, Scotch tape, paper clips, black marking pens, and expense report forms.

- *Tour manager's own documents*—air ticket, pretour or posttour hotel vouchers, baggage insurance policy, baggage tags, name badge.

- *Information on suppliers*—photocopies of pertinent correspondence with each supplier, particularly the original commitment letters and the agency's finalization wrapup letter. The manager should have the name, address, telephone number, and key person contact for each hotel and for each reception ground operator along the line. If the tour manager is a member of the agency staff or someone who leads tours for the agency frequently, a relationship of trust probably has been established and the agency will not mind this individual having copies of confidential correspondence with suppliers, particularly information on the net prices that are being charged. On the other hand, if the manager is a sales organizer representing the client (the club, church, or organization for whom the trip has been arranged), the agency may not wish that individual to have access to confidential information and prices. Use discretion. However, the more information the manager has, the better job he or she can do overseas if a problem arises. If the hotel tries to put the group into rooms overlooking the garbage cans and the agency was guaranteed ocean-front rooms, the tour manager cannot do as good a job getting what was promised as if he or she has in hand a letter signed by the hotel's sales manager guaranteeing ocean-front rooms.

**Briefing the Tour Manager**

When the manager arrives for the pretour briefing, all of the materials discussed above should be ready for review. After he or she has read through everything and made notes on questions of concern, a discussion clarifying certain philosophies is essential. This is the time to discuss how to handle certain kinds of situations in line with company policy. Obviously, every circumstance that could possibly arise cannot be anticipated and covered in this discussion. (That is why common sense is an important qualification for a tour manager.) Yet, philosophies do vary from agency to agency, from tour to tour within a given agency, and even from individual to individual within the agency. Therefore, it is not fair to expect the tour manager to second-guess someone else's wishes. Points of policy that might be helpful to discuss are:

- *How bills are to be paid*—does the tour manager pay enroute? Is everything prepaid and, if not, specifically what has not been paid? Has the tour manager been given more than adequate funds to meet these needs? If he or she is merely to sign bills, should the bills be analyzed and compared with the original quote given the company? Or is the tour manager merely to verify that the services were provided and the number of passengers present at each activity.

- *How is the tour manager to handle emergencies*—how should he or she handle death of a passenger, severe illness, political upheaval? Most professional tour managers have had experience in this regard, but a tour organizer or even a member of the staff who is not an experienced tour manager might not know company policy, what expenses are authorized, or what legal procedures should be followed.

- *Airfare*—what kind of airfare is being used? If the group members' air tickets are issued using a special fare, such as a Group Inclusive Tour (GIT) fare, an Advance Purchase Excursion (APEX), a Group Affinity, or other restricted fare, the tour manager should know the rules and regulations covering that fare. He or she may need to know whether there can be a change of air carriers, whether an ill passenger can travel apart from the group and catch up later, whether a passenger can change homeward travel plans without incurring an extra charge, and so forth. This will help the tour manager deal with passengers' questions; he or she will not

be at the mercy of a local airline clerk's interpretation of a fare generated in the United States.
- *Changing arrangements*—to what extent, if any, is the tour manager authorized to make changes in the published itinerary as the tour goes along? (Remember—the tour brochure is a legal/moral commitment to the passenger.)
- *Lost or damaged luggage*—how should the manager deal with this thorny problem, other than try to locate the missing luggage and try to get the airlines to assist the passenger? Is the manager authorized to spend any money on the passenger?
- *Celebrations and entertaining*—should the manager celebrate group members' anniversaries, birthdays, and other festivities? Should anyone be entertained enroute? If so, is this expense budgeted?
- *Emergency expenses beyond the budget*—in case of an emergency causing the group to be rerouted, thus incurring additional airfare or additional ground expenses, is the manager authorized to pay this? Or is each passenger to pay at the time?
- *The agency's attitude toward this tour*—is this a deluxe tour on which the manager should spend a little, if necessary, to keep everyone happy? Or is this a tightly budgeted tour, on which the manager has little financial leeway?

SPECIAL THOUGHTS FOR CRUISES

For a cruise (or if a short cruise is included as an integral part of the trip), the tour manager should be especially informed about the following.
- *Meal seating*—has it been arranged for the group to sit together, and, if so, at an early or late seating? Or have the passengers selected individual meal seating, perhaps at different times and at different tables?
- *Welcome-aboard party*—does the budget permit one? If so, has it been prebooked or is the tour manager to set it up with the ship's cruise director after boarding? Is it paid by the cruise line as an additional amenity for the group or is the manager to pay for it on his or her shipboard bill and tip the waiter out-of-pocket?
- *Shore excursions*—how are they being handled? Have they been prebooked (either for the group as a whole or for those individual

passengers who have purchased these options)? Or are passengers to purchase their own shore excursions as the cruise moves along? What about the manager's own shore excursions—are they complimentary or is he or she to pay for them if the cruise line does not grant a complimentary at each port?

- *Wine or other festivities*—is any budget built in?
- *Cabin locations*—has the manager been given a deck plan to take along and a list of the passengers' cabin numbers?
- *Shipboard gratuities*—what arrangements have been made, if any, for gratuities to the shipboard personnel at the end of the cruise? Are passengers to tip on their own, and if so, have they been advised in the information bulletins what the appropriate amount is? Or have gratuities been costed-in to the cruise cost and is the tour manager to tip on behalf of the entire group at the end of the cruise? Either way, the manager's shipboard gratuities will have to be paid. Have they been costed-in to the trip? Or will the manager have to pay his or her own?

## Everything Is Ready

If everything listed here has been thought of, the tour manager has been prepared and briefed as well as possible. The manager has received all necessary materials, and has been informed about the behavior appropriate to agency policy in certain situations. The tour manager should now be able to go home, pack a suitcase, and prepare for departure, confident that he or she will fulfill the agency's expectations.

## 11

# Managing the Tour Enroute

When the tour manager has received all departure materials and instructions from the company—early enough, it is hoped, to allow time for careful review—any questions should be resolved with the company before departure. Now is the time to read all correspondence with suppliers, check to be sure that all necessary materials and lists are available, and spend a little time reading about the passengers—their names, interests, health problems, and so forth. The manager might also check to see if any of the passengers have birthdays or anniversaries for special celebration enroute. And, of course, the tour manager will want to do some background historical reading on the countries to be visited if not extremely conversant with them. If the company has not sent out adequate preparatory materials to the group members, the tour manager may wish to gather or make up handouts, such as maps, currency converters, phrases in foreign languages, articles, and fact sheets on some of the countries to be visited.

Everything should be packed as efficiently and compactly as possible, separate from personal apparel. It should not be necessary to search enroute for the Paris city maps among the dirty laundry. The tour manager will also want to call the departing airline to verify departure times and to check whether or not the agency has arranged for a group check-in lane, preassigned seats on the aircraft, and other special services.

## At the Airport

BEFORE THE PASSENGERS ARRIVE

It is important for the tour manager to arrive at the airport *before* the tour members arrive. Therefore, if the passengers have been advised to check in one and one-half hours before flight departure, for example, it is best for the tour manager to be there at least two hours before flight time.

On arrival, the tour manager should go to the check-in counter and ask to see the flight supervisor on duty. After presenting his or her business card and a copy of the group's flight manifest, one can then discuss with the supervisor how flight check-in will be handled so that there is no chance of giving conflicting information to the passengers as they arrive for check-in. Here are some of the things that should be discussed:

- How seat assignments are being handled—are passengers in the group free to select their own seats throughout the aircraft? Or is a certain area blocked off for the group and are they to select their seats within that block?
- How many people are in the group boarding this flight and of the total how many are to be in smoking and how many to be in nonsmoking sections of the aircraft.
- Whether there will be a special check-in lane for the group.
- Airport to which all luggage is to be checked. Are any interline tags needed? (If so, perhaps they can be prepared at this time to facilitate the entire process.)
- Full details of the flight itself; for example, boarding time, gate number and location, departure time, expected in-flight meal service and times, in-flight movies, if any.

Before the group's arrival, the tour manager should check in, selecting an aisle seat so that it is easy to get up to attend to the group in flight without constantly having to climb over passengers. It is also a good idea to be prepared to answer typical questions that the passengers may ask, such as where the airport restrooms are located, if there is a duty-free shop and if it is open, or where the coffee shop is.

## As the Group Members Arrive

When the group members start arriving, the tour manager takes the initiative—approaching them and introducing himself or herself (wearing a name badge and perhaps carrying a clipboard so as to look official). Members of the group should be identifiable, because they should be using the tour name badges and luggage tags. If several members of the group are standing around, the manager should again take the initiative and assume the role of host, introducing them to one another. They should then be alerted to get out their air tickets and passports and to go to the counter. The tour manager should not interfere between the tour members and airline personnel during the check-in procedure. The airline agent will handle the actual check-in—seat assignment, baggage tagging, review of passport and visas, if any, and will return to the passengers their air tickets, baggage claim stubs stapled into the ticket jacket, and boarding passes.

The tour manager can then tell the group members that they are free to roam the airport, have a cup of coffee, or visit the duty-free shop, and that the group will reassemble at the boarding gate. Tour members should be reminded of boarding time and gate number, and of the importance of proceeding to the gate sufficiently early because of the necessity to pass through security check. In some cases, passengers may check in and check their luggage at the counter, but may still have to go to the gate to get their seat assignments and boarding passes. In such cases, it is important that they do so early and not assume that because they have already checked in at the counter and because the tour manager knows that they are present they are all taken care of. *They are not really on board until they have a boarding pass and a seat assignment.*

As the group moves along from country to country, one will find that some airline personnel overseas prefer to hand the tour manager the boarding passes and seat assignments for the entire group, asking the tour manager in turn to distribute them. If this is the airline's policy, it is important to be aware of it ahead of time.

The basic idea of this entire predeparture procedure is to get each individual member checked in as quickly and efficiently as possible and then away from the check-in area. Tour members should know that they are to board the aircraft as independent travelers even if they do not see the tour manager at the gate, and that the tour manager will find them later on board after takeoff. This frees the tour manager to wait for any last minute passengers and to thank the airline personnel who have helped the group with check-in.

Passengers should have been given or mailed their tickets beforehand so they can bring them to the airport rather than the tour manager carrying the entire group's tickets to the airport. In this way, should the tour manager be delayed, passengers can check in on their own. Also, if passengers have their own tickets, should they miss an inbound flight connecting to the group flight, they can go directly to the airline counter and ask airline personnel to rebook or reissue as necessary to catch up with the group.

NO SHOWS

If it is departure time and a tour passenger has not arrived, there is no alternative but to go on without the passenger. The tour manager's basic responsibility is to the group as a whole and not to any one individual tour member. Quite frequently, when a passenger has not shown up, it turns out that he or she bypassed the lobby check-in counter and went directly to the gate, or perhaps checked in early before the rest of the group arrived and is browsing around the airport. On the other hand, the passenger may have called the agency office to tell them of an emergency and the message may not have been passed on to the tour manager. If possible, the tour manager should call the office and advise them of the missing tour member, or if it is so late that calling will cause the tour manager to miss the plane, should give the airline flight supervisor the office phone number and ask him or her to call.

## In Flight

ON BOARDING

Once aboard, the tour manager should introduce himself or herself to the head flight attendant, then sit down, see that the group settles in, and make sure that they stay seated until after takeoff. Inflight personnel will not appreciate a tour manager who blocks the aisles socializing with tour members at this particular time. Of course, if it appears that there is a problem, the tour manager should be as quietly helpful as possible, asking the flight attendant for assistance if necessary.

## AFTER TAKEOFF

Once the flight is airborne and the seat-belt sign has gone off, it is then time for the tour manager to get up and circulate through the plane, locating tour members, reintroducing himself or herself, and chatting with this one and that one. The tour manager is the host and should set the tone and take the initiative—not just sit and wait until someone comes by with a question. *Visibility is important,* particularly during the first twenty-four hours when tour members feel insecure.

At some time during the flight, depending on flight schedule and meal service, the tour manager may collect air tickets and baggage claim stubs from each member of the group. This can be done efficiently by going down the aisle with a list of tour members and with two manila envelopes—one envelope marked "Air Tickets" and one marked "Baggage Stubs."

*Air tickets.* The tour manager should then strip down the air tickets (returning to the passenger the ticket jacket and any typed flight itinerary or other miscellaneous loose papers), keeping the air ticket only, checking it off against the passenger's name on the manifest. Then, after all tickets are collected they can be alphabetized, counted to be sure that they are all there, and double checked to be sure each flight coupon is intact at the time of picking up the ticket (a double check that a flight coupon has not been erroneously pulled by airline personnel at check-in or at the time the ticket was issued). There is nothing worse than suddenly finding out, ten days later somewhere enroute, that a flight coupon is missing. In such a case, the passenger in question may not be allowed to board a specific flight without paying out of pocket for the missing sector. The group's air tickets should then be bundled together with a rubber band. The tour manager should carry them for the balance of the trip until just before the last flight home, when they should be redistributed to the tour members, who can then check in individually for their homeward flight.

Air tickets are negotiable and, if lost, may require payment for a replacement ticket at the time, since filing for refund of a lost ticket can take months to process. Therefore, it is important that tickets be guarded carefully, not left lying in an unattended briefcase or flight bag; they should be checked in a safety deposit box at the hotel each and every night enroute. If, at any time, the package of air tickets is turned over to airline personnel or reception operator employees for the purpose of reconfirming onward flights, the tour manager should be sure to get a receipt for the number of tickets. When they are returned, they should be counted again to be sure that they are all there. Similarly, it is wise for the tour manager to check that all flight coupons are intact each time the tickets are returned. This should not wait until everyone is in the bus enroute to the airport to check the tickets; it is too late then to do anything if one is missing!

*Baggage claim stubs.* While chatting with the passengers, the tour manager should verify how many bags they checked through, write that number down next to their names on the flight manifest, and pick up the baggage claim stubs. The passenger's last name should be written in black marking pen on each stub and then the stubs can be dropped into the manila envelope marked "Baggage Stubs." Hand luggage should not be included in the count. The count should include only those bags that the passengers actually checked in with the airline, and for which they should have baggage claim stubs. After collecting all the stubs and adding the tour manager's own stubs, a total count should be made to be sure that the number of stubs in the envelope equals the total of the numbers written down next to each name on the manifest. Then the envelope can be sealed and the total written on the outside ready to hand to the reception operator, who will be meeting the group on landing.

JUST BEFORE LANDING

About thirty minutes before landing (but before the plane begins its descent and before the seat belt sign goes on), the tour manager should circulate again, explaining to tour members what documents they should have handy on landing, such as passports or tourist cards. The members should also be told that the tour manager will precede them to make contact with the operator meeting the group, and that they should follow as individuals through immigration and out to the customs area on the other side, where all will convene.

## On Landing

Immediately on landing, the tour manager should go as quickly as possible ahead of the group. The next step will depend on the government regulations in the country concerned. Some countries will permit the reception operator who is meeting the group to go inside the customs area and greet the group there. In some cases, the reception operator might be permitted inside the immigration area to help the group through immigration and customs. Other countries will not permit anyone inside the immigration/customs area and the tour manager will have the responsibility of shepherding the group through, locating porters, getting the luggage counted and loaded onto carts, and going through customs with the group and the luggage. In some cases customs officials may wave the group on through or merely spot check the luggage. In other cases, all passengers may be asked to open their suitcases, so all tour passengers should stand by readily available with their luggage keys. Once through customs and immigration, the reception operator should be waiting to direct the group to the motorcoach for loading. The tour manager should ask that all luggage be lined up on the sidewalk outside the coach and that all passengers check to see that their luggage is there as they board the coach. This may cause a short delay in departure while waiting for the luggage to be loaded after boarding, but it is the best way to be absolutely sure that no luggage has gone astray or, if it has, to determine at what point it may have disappeared.

While the passengers are boarding the coach and double checking to see that their luggage is there, the tour manager should ascertain the name of the representative meeting the group and that of the driver, so that these individuals may be introduced to the group once everyone is aboard. The tour manager should also ask to see a copy of the local itinerary or any other material that the representative plans to hand out to the group, to be sure that it agrees with what was promised. This is a good time to catch any errors before material is distributed to the group. Sometimes these hand-out materials are standardized by the ground operators, and may mention things not pertinent to one's particular group. For example, they may mention that airport departure taxes or farewell tips to the local guide are not included in prepaid tour arrangements. In actuality, perhaps this tour company has costed-in for the tour manager to tip the guide on behalf of the group, or to pay the airport tax. Quite often these standardized materials may try to sell optional tours that the tour manager does not want offered to the group. (Perhaps the options spend a great deal of touring time at stops to ensure commissions to the local guides—a financial fact of life in many countries where the local guides work on a miniscule base salary with the expectations of tips and commissions to augment their earnings. Or perhaps the passengers are too tired and need some free time instead of additional tours. Or the tour manager may simply feel that the options offered are not a good value or are a duplicate of something that the group did in a previous country.)

After all passengers and luggage are aboard, the tour manager should board, and do a head count to be sure that everyone is present. He or she should then take the microphone and formally introduce the driver and greeter/guide, and should then turn the microphone over for the greeter's welcoming comments. This makes it clear to the local company that the tour manager is in the leadership position and is in control—yet the local personnel are graciously invited to take over in the area of their expertise. If the tour manager simply boards the bus with the group and sits down, control has been automatically relinquished to the greeter guide.

## On Arrival at the Hotel

As the group arrives at the hotel, the tour manager should either ask the group to remain in the coach a minute (if traffic conditions permit this) or ask them to proceed into the hotel and sit down in the lobby, perhaps asking one tour member to act as a focal point around whom the others should be seated. The idea is to make them comfortable but not to permit them to gather at the registration desk. The tour manager needs freedom to speak with the hotel front-desk people in private without the pressure of the group standing impatiently nearby.

The tour manager should present a business card and the tour/rooming roster at the desk and ask the hotel personnel how they plan to handle check-in. The check-in procedure will vary from hotel to hotel. Some hotels will have a special group desk where keys are laid out ready in alphabetical order. Others may have the keys ready at the main desk and may ask the tour manager to distribute them. A few hotels may be totally disorganized and not have the rooms assigned or the keys ready—in fact, the rooms may not even be cleaned and made up. It is important that the tour manager work with hotel personnel patiently and insistently until all rooms are assigned and all keys ready. This is the time to check for any special needs—any connecting rooms requested by families or friends traveling together, any room near the elevator for a passenger who has difficulty in walking, any double beds mistakenly assigned instead of the twin-bedded rooms promised.

If there are any errors, or if room changes are necessary, they should be handled before handing out keys, if possible, not after. Of course, there always may be the passenger who is dissatisfied with a room after seeing it and who comes down to the lobby afterward requesting a change, but at least a few of these changes may be avoided by checking room assignments *prior* to distribution of the keys. If two strangers are sharing a room (and particularly if this is the first night of the tour when roommates do not yet know each other), it is a nice gesture to formally introduce roommates and to ask the front desk for two room keys, because usually hotels hand out only one key per room.

Before distributing the keys and dispatching people to their rooms, the group should be gathered for any announcements. One could say something such as "I'm going to hand out your keys now, folks. Please go directly to your rooms and carry your hand luggage with you; your big suitcase will be sent up just as quickly as possible but it may take some time, so please do not be concerned. Do not tip the hotel bellboy when he brings your bags; we are tipping for you. If you wish to walk around the hotel you may do so; you do not need to wait in your room for the bellboy. If you need me, I will be here in the lobby for a while until I get everything settled, and afterward my room number is 302. Remember, per your itinerary, we will all meet here in the lobby at 7:30 p.m. for dinner. Dress is coat and tie for the gentlemen, short dinner dresses for the ladies."

Wherever possible, the above speech (or any announcements at departure times, for that matter) should be given over the microphone in the motorcoach. This is not only because the group is a captive audience at the time, but also for security reasons. There is no reason to announce to the whole world in a hotel lobby what time the tour members are leaving the hotel, giving a listening thief no doubt as to what time the tour group's rooms will be empty. For this same reason, it is not smart to post departure time announcements in hotel elevators or on lobby bulletin boards, as many tour companies seem to do.

As soon as tour members are on the way to their rooms, a number of things remain for the tour manager to do before relaxing:

- Help expedite the delivery of luggage to the rooms, perhaps translating foreign-sounding names to the bellboys or assisting them in marking room numbers on baggage tags.
- Take out a safety deposit box and place the group's air tickets and any other valuables there (double check the access hours so that things can be taken out when needed).
- Get a list of the room numbers assigned to the group or work with the front-desk personnel in writing down on the master list each person's room number.
- Familiarize oneself quickly with the hotel so as to be knowledgeable when directing people in the group to the money exchange, pharmacy, coffee shop, and so forth.

- Check for mail for oneself and the tour members.
- Visit the coffee shop and dining room and note the hours that they normally serve. If possible, meet with the *maitre d'* and discuss what the group's meal plan is, how signatures and tips are to be handled, what meals are on the master tour account and what are on the client's own personal account, which they must clear individually when they check out of the hotel. If a meal plan is included for tour members, verify which meal items are in the meal plan and which are considered extra items that the passengers must pay for on their own. Some hotels restrict group meals to certain hours, certain dining rooms, or a specified monetary amount. Most tour passengers are understanding if they know about this in advance; if they find out after they have eaten the steak and received the bill, they are furious.
- Ask to meet the sales manager or front-office manager for public relations purposes and to be sure that instructions have been transmitted from the sales division to the hotel cashier as to how the group's bill is to be handled. It is important to avoid any financial surprises at check-out time, surprises such as the cashier having no record of the deposit or no knowledge of a complimentary for the leader or not providing a breakdown analysis of the total bill.

Once all of the above are taken care of and all luggage has been delivered to the rooms, one can relax. But it is important not to go off duty until personally seeing to the last of the luggage. Often, well-meaning bellboys will delay group luggage delivery to attend to new arrivals as they walk into the hotel unless the tour manager is there watching.

**Orientation Meeting**

One of the first and most important events of any tour is a good orientation meeting. This is the time when the entire tour gets together for introductions and a discussion as to how the tour will be operated—the tour manager's opportunity to give members the "rules of the road." Some tour operators like to give a welcome cocktail party as a place for introductions and loosening up first, then often giving a short briefing, followed by a period of hype and selling optional tours. Others prefer not to have the briefing follow a cocktail party because they know it is important that the tour members be attentive and be listening carefully to what is being said. Later on, if certain passengers are consistently late and a sightseeing tour goes off one morning and leaves them behind they may become angry and abusive. However, if the tour manager can say "Remember, I told you at the briefing that we would leave for sightseeing on time and I would not wait for latecomers," they will realize that everyone else heard it at the briefing and they are not being singled out for punishment. It is best to hold this briefing within the first twenty-four hours of the tour if possible, because it sets the right tone. It is a good idea to wait until all tour members are present, although if some are joining the tour three days late this is not always feasible. If a problem develops with a passenger later on tour, often the one who did not attend the briefing is the culprit.

One of the best briefing times is a breakfast briefing. Passengers do not expect cocktails at that hour and it starts the tour off on the right foot. If there is no budget in the tour for breakfasts, sometimes the hotel will grant a meeting room free of charge for an hour or so if you order coffee and sweet roll service. A nice icebreaker is to ask the tour members to stand one by one and give their names, home town, profession, and the reason they came on this tour. If there are people in the group who have made previous trips with the agency, this is an excellent time to mention this and give them a bit of recognition. After introductions, it is nice for the tour manager to introduce himself or herself, providing some personal background information, and then to introduce any VIPs or service personnel in the room, such as the local reception ground operator, guides, hotel personnel, or whomever. After these niceties, it is time to discuss important points of the tour.

POINTS TO COVER

- *Departure on time*—The group will not wait for habitual latecomers; it is the individual's personal responsibility to get up on time in the morning, get to breakfast on time, and so forth. The tour manager is not responsible for waking people or ordering group breakfasts. Stress that repeated tardiness is a discourtesy to the other passengers and indicate that breakfast service in the dining room may be slower than that to which they are accustomed at home, so they should allow sufficient time.
- *Coach seating*—Everyone paid the same for the tour and therefore everyone is entitled to a chance at the front seats. Passengers are expected to behave as adults and automatically rotate their seating positions. They are also expected to follow any stated policy on smoking.

- *Courtesy to others*—Passengers are expected to be gracious and courteous to one another, no matter how tired or out-of-sorts they may be, and to the local people with whom they come in contact—be they guides, waiters, hotel personnel, customs officials, or immigration officials. Unkind behavior on the part of group members will not be tolerated no matter what the circumstances, even if the other person is in the wrong.
- *Attention to guides*—The local guides have a great deal of information to give to the group and it will be appreciated if the group give undivided attention to the guide when he or she is speaking. A passenger should not chat with a seat mate or run off to take photos in the middle of the presentation.
- *Appropriate dress*—Members will be advised adequately in advance as to what the expected dress code is for a given event and are expected to comply. There will be certain activities where coat and tie are a must or where Bermuda shorts or short shorts are not acceptable.
- *Dissatisfaction on tour*—It is anticipated that there may be certain times in the coming days when the group members are upset or unhappy with something. They should go directly to the tour manager with the complaint, rather than internalizing it or circulating it around among the other tour members.
- *Reminder about valuables*—Passengers are urged to check valuables in a hotel safety deposit box, to keep an eye on their cameras, know where their passport is at all times, and never leave watches or valuable jewelry in their hotel room or at the beach or pool. Men should keep their wallets inside their jacket, not in a rear pants pocket, and women should keep their purses zipped and worn close to the body at all times.
- *Luggage reminder*—The tour manager will always advise the group of the time to have their luggage ready for pick-up and will appreciate their complying. If a passenger should lose a baggage tag, the tour manager should be notified immediately, since the bellboys and airport porters are instructed to pick up only those bags with the company baggage tag. Members must be responsible for their own hand luggage. If they add or subtract a bag they should advise the tour manager so there is no confusion over the count.
- *Review of tipping policy*—A reminder should be made of specifically which tips are included in the tour and which are not, and

a suggestion as to appropriate amounts when the participants must do their own tipping. It is helpful to read out loud the tour brochure statement on tipping and then explain it in more detail. Participants are entitled to know specifically which of the following tips are included or not included: waiters, *maitre d'*, room maids, airport porters, hotel bellboys, local sightseeing guides, and, if a cruise is involved, cabin steward and dining room personnel.

- *Water and food*—The safety of local water and food, advisability of buying bottled water, peeling fruit, and staying away from raw vegetables and salads should be discussed. Mention the local foods that are particularly good and that tour members may want to try. Remind them of the high cost of imported wines and liquors and suggest that they stick to domestic drinks. Also mention local meal hours and any dining customs pertinent to the area.
- *Hotel check-out procedure*—The importance of each tour member checking out of the hotel individually to clear any extra charges with the cashier and turn in the key should be stressed.
- *The tour manager's availability*—Some parameters of when participants may feel free to call the tour manager's room should be laid out. A good policy is for the tour manager to be available from 8:00 a.m. to 10:00 p.m., but if group members are ill or have a real emergency they should feel free to call any time, even in the middle of the night.

## Leadership and Planning

Leadership is not just a coincidence. Granted, there are some who are better at it than others but there are skills that a tour manager can develop to appear as a true leader. The following outlines crucial advice to tour managers:

- *Be visible*—look like a leader. If necessary, count, carry a clipboard or checklist, circulate, and oversee. Do not just sit and wait for things to happen.
- *Plan ahead*—has someone called ahead to the restaurant to remind them that the group is coming and advise how many are in the party? Has someone doublechecked that the coach will be on time? Is the right change available next day for departure tips? Has the bell captain been reminded of tomorrow's check-out time and given an up-to-date list of room numbers? Think twenty-four hours ahead!

- *Be early*—do not be the last one down to the lobby. Be there ahead of the group. Check—has the guide arrived? Has the motorcoach arrived and, if so, where is it parked and which hotel exit will be used?
- *Make announcements when the group is together*—preferably on the coach when all are "captive" and the microphone can be used. Do not wait until after some participants have gone to their rooms and then ask others to pass the word. The "word" usually becomes garbled.
- *Anticipate problem situations*—announce them and ask for passengers' help (if there is a particularly difficult passenger, put this individual to work assisting you). People are usually cooperative if they know in advance what the problem may be. No need, however, to tell them of every little thing that is going wrong: many of these problems will be solved as the tour goes along.
- *Announce what is going to happen when leaving the coach*— always tell the group where and at what time they are to reboard, whether the coach will be locked or not, and whether they may leave things on board or not. It is always a good idea to remind group members of the coach number and tell them where the coach will be parked so that if someone wanders from the group or does not feel well, it is possible to locate the tour manager back at the coach.
- *Circulate at group meals*—and see that everyone has ordered and is being waited on. Be aware of situations in which perhaps meal service could be expedited. Be sure that passengers know what items on the menu are included in their tour and what items are at additional cost to them. Many times a restaurant will offer a drink, wine or coffee, only to present tour members with the bill afterward, much to their surprise.
- *Do not be afraid to enforce the "rules of the road"*— these were outlined at the orientation meeting. Although speaking up may anger the offending tour member, it will gain the tour manager the respect and support of the remaining tour members. Remember, the tour manager's main duty is to the group as a whole, not to any one individual, no matter how much of a VIP that individual may be.

DEALING WITH LOCAL GUIDES

A local guide can be a real gem and can contribute immeasurably to the success of the tour. Conversely, an unsatisfactory guide can detract from the quality of the tour and can even cause a disaster if one has to depend on this person for a long period. Therefore, it is wise to establish a good working relationship with the guides, formally introducing them to the group, letting it be known that they are appreciated, and trying to bring out the best in each guide assigned to the group as the tour moves along. However, if despite all one's efforts, a particular guide does not work out, a tour manager may feel free to tell the local reception operator and ask for a replacement,

Guides come in all sizes, shapes, ages, and levels of competency and intelligence. In countries such as England, Greece, and Israel, for example, most tour managers agree that local guides are some of the most knowledgeable and educated individuals in the world. In other cases, one may work with guides whose only interest is in getting the group into the carpet showroom. Over the years, however, experienced tour managers have developed their own personal expectations of a professional guide; these include the following:

- A guide who reports ten minutes or so before departure—not breathlessly at the last minute.

- A guide who has checked with the motorcoach dispatcher the night before to be sure that the order is on record, and who checks again the next morning to be sure that the coach is ready and waiting.

- A guide who is neatly dressed and groomed.

- A guide who is organized, departs on time, and maintains the pacing of the day's activities so as to get in everything that was promised.

- A guide who supervises the coach and driver—checks that the driver knows the route, has sufficient fuel, and keeps the coach clean; makes sure that the public address system is working, and assists passengers to board and alight.

- A guide who keeps control of the group, maintains their attention, and announces in advance what is going to happen.

- A guide who does not continually solicit for optional events, shopping, and other activities on which a commission may be made.

- A guide who can give more than just dates and historical facts, who has a good cultural understanding of a given city, country, or an era, who is attuned to the interest of the group and sensitive to the amount of information that the particular group can absorb.

## Hotel Check-outs

One of the most difficult times for a tour manager can be the departure—getting out of a hotel and to the airport on time. The best procedure, of course, is to leave sufficiently early to allow extra time for the unexpected—the lost suitcase, the flat tire, the late bus, the bureaucratic airline check-in clerk, and so forth. It is helpful to start preparing for check-out the night before by walking through the next day's departure mentally. Details that should be checked the night before might be the following:

- Does the bell captain have a list of room numbers and does he know what time all bags are to be pulled?
- Will the dining room be open sufficiently early for breakfast before departure? If not, is it possible to arrange for coffee and rolls at the hotel? Or can the group leave earlier and have coffee at the airport?
- Does the tour manager have correct change for tipping bellboys, the bell captain, *maitre d'*, or others who have been helpful to the group during their stay?
- Has the cashier been advised of the check-out time and alerted to present an itemized bill? (The tour manager should not accept a lump sum bill, but rather a bill that breaks down the number of twins, singles, complimentaries, tax, and so forth.) Perhaps the hotel will permit the tour manager to pay the bill the night before departure to alleviate the crunch in the morning.
- Has the group been properly advised as to baggage-call time? Have group members been reminded to have their passports on them, not locked in their luggage, to be sure to pay the cashier for any extras on their bill, and to turn in their keys?
- Is there an airport departure tax the next day? If so, who is paying it? If the tour manager is paying on behalf of the entire group, it is important to have the right amount of cash in local currency and in the right denominations. If passengers are to pay individually, they should be so advised. If the local ground operator pays it, he or she should be reminded.

To be sure that things go smoothly on departure day, it is best for the tour manager to be visible down in the lobby ahead of the group. He or she should be sure that luggage is coming down and should do a bag count *before* it is loaded on the motorcoach or baggage truck.

Everything should be taken out of the safety deposit box, including the group's air tickets; the coupons for that day's flight should be pulled and all put together ready to turn in at the airport. The tour manager should check with the cashier and settle the master bill (double checking that all passengers in the group have paid their personal hotel bills and turned in their key), should tip all the appropriate hotel personnel, say goodbye, and thank those who were helpful, such as the sales manager or front desk manager. If unable to locate them, it is a nice gesture to leave one's business card with a personal thank-you line or two. On boarding the coach, tour members should be reminded not to leave anything behind and to be sure that they have their passports. Last but not least, before leaving for the airport the tour manager should do a head count or roll call to be sure that everyone is on board!

## Personal Comportment of Tour Manager

One of the most sensitive subjects is that of the tour manager's behavior on tour. When is he or she working and when on free time? What about friendships or personal involvements enroute? Should gratuities, gifts, or free drinks be accepted? In fact, should the tour manager drink at all? These questions and many others have plagued those in the travel industry for years. Most travel professionals have come to realize that there is a certain unwritten code by which to operate. Some elements of this unwritten code are outlined below:

1. A tour manager should give equal time and attention to all, never playing favorites. This means dining, dancing, sitting with all, not just a select few (even if they are more fun, more enjoyable, more beautiful, more available).
2. A tour manager is on the trip in a professional role, that is, working, not on vacation.
3. A tour manager should not upgrade some participants and not others on flights or designate certain passengers as VIPs. (However, if someone gets a bad room one night, it is a good idea to compensate a bit the next night.)
4. A tour manager should go places in groups—never appear to be going off with just one person in the group. Others should be invited to participate.
5. A tour manager should not become personally involved with a tour member.

6. If the tour manager wishes to see local friends along the way, he or she should do so quietly and discreetly away from the group after the day's tour activities.
7. A tour manager should not hustle a group into stores or activities to make a personal commission.
8. A tour manager should have an understanding with the tour company before the trip begins as to whether he or she may receive gratuities from the passengers at the end of the trip. If so, the tour manager should accept them graciously but not constantly remind the group as the trip moves along that a tip is expected.
9. A tour manager should feel free to accept small token gifts, poems, songs, and emotional protestations of undying loyalty and affection from tour members.
10. A tour manager should not drink to excess, but should feel free to have a before-dinner cocktail or wine with meals if the group, or most of them, drink. If this is nondrinking group, the tour manager should refrain.

## Safety of the Tour Manager

It usually comes as a surprise to first-time tour managers to learn that they are seen as potential crime victims. Yet, when tour managers get together, many can relate stories of attempted robberies, holdups, or rape. As the leader of a group, a tour manager is seen by outsiders as the individual likely to be carrying large amounts of cash, travelers checks, negotiable air tickets, and perhaps the group's passports (valuable on the black market in some countries). Once it is known that a group is in town, the tour manager may be approached by everyone from jewelry fences to black marketeers eager to buy dollars. To avoid unnecessary risks, a tour manager should dress with decorum, not give out his or her hotel room number, and scrupulously safeguard all tour documents and valuables.

## Some Problems Enroute

Many tours run smoothly with never a ripple on calm waters. These are the tours that almost anyone can escort, since the tour manager's expertise or lack thereof may never be put to the test. However, most tours do encounter some problems enroute, and it is in these problem areas that true leadership ability comes to the fore. The group looks to the tour manager to resolve difficult situations; yet, he or she may not know any more about a problem than the group does. It is here that common sense and the ability to think on one's feet come into play.

Some problems might be passenger oriented, such as tour participants who are always late, complainers, or just generally unpleasant people. Also, passengers become ill, lose their passports or their money. Other problems may be operational in nature—the reception operator who does not show up at the airport to meet the group, the lost or damaged luggage, the delayed flight, or a bad hotel room. Still another category, and a totally unforeseen one, is what is termed "acts of God" or force majeure—the typhoon, civil war, strike, or accident. One could write an entire book on handling enroute emergencies, but the following are a few of the most commonplace problems.

PROBLEMS WITH PASSENGERS

Most of these problems are personality-related—often involving personality traits or difficulties that cannot be solved during the duration of the tour. A tour manager probably cannot cure somebody of inconsiderate behavior, complaining, anxiety, kleptomania, alcoholism, hypochondria, or nymphomania in the course of a tour. What the tour manager must do, however, is *control* the problem. *Step One* is to give a good, strong briefing, outlining at the outset of the tour the behavior expected. *Step Two* is to call negative behavior to the attention of the offending individuals privately and quietly, drawing them aside from the group and reminding them. *Step Three* is to use the rest of the group as leverage; peer pressure often will bring an offender into line. Asking the entire busload to boo loudly when a tardy passenger boards the bus can work wonders. One can also appoint a "sergeant at arms" for the day. At the beginning of the day's tour, the tour manager announces on the microphone: "Since I don't like the image of a 'bad guy,' today I'm going to appoint you, Mary, as sergeant at arms. You have my permission to reprimand anyone who is tardy or who hogs the front seat or who talks while the guide is talking. Now, did you all hear me? I don't want any of you to get mad at Mary if she comes up and says something to you, because she's doing it in my name."

*Dropping a tour member.* *Step Four* is to threaten to remove someone from the tour. A tour manager would do this only after several warnings, and nine times out of ten such a threat usually will jolt the person into correcting the behavior.

Dropping someone from a tour is a serious matter, a matter that could bring a lawsuit against the agency. It is not something that one does on a whim. If a tour manager does decide to drop a participant, he or she must be sure to be on strong legal ground. The company should have a statement in the brochure declaring that it does have the right to drop someone. The tour manager should document in a journal as the tour moves along the difficulties encountered with the passenger in question and the attempts that have been made to have him or her correct the offending behavior. Also, at the time the decision is made to remove an individual, a brief statement should be written as to what has occured and why the individual is being removed from the tour, and then the entire tour group should be asked to sign it. It is also a good idea to get any other witnesses, such as the hotel manager or local reception operator, to sign the statement.

Dropping someone should be considered only for major offenses, for example: stealing, repeated drunkeness, involvement in drugs, smuggling, or other behavior illegal under local law. Whether or not the passengers agree with a local law, they are expected to abide by it as long as they are guests in that particular country. One cannot afford to have the safety of a group and the reputation of one's agency jeopardized by one individual.

The author once had two couples on tour in Spain who chartered a fishing boat for the day in Marbella and then refused to pay the full amount that they had agreed on, since at the end of the day they did not believe that they had received what they had bargained for. The entire group was horrified that night when, at their elegant farewell dinner at the hotel, the Spanish National Guard tracked the couple down and came to arrest them. They paid up quickly! One cannot afford to have incidents such as this happen.

*Illness or injury.* It is a rare tour that makes it through to the end without some injury or illness. Of course, one of the best ways to avoid this is preventative care—advising passengers about food and drink, warning them of the dangers of air conditioning and subsequent travelers' bronchitis, asking them to get enough sleep and take care of themselves. Often they are so excited at being on vacation that they want to see everything, do everything, and not miss anything, to the detriment of their health. However, despite care, there will always be the passenger with a gastrointestinal problem, a twisted ankle, or even a broken leg. In these cases it is important that professional medical help be obtained immediately. Usually the hotel's house physician is the first recourse.

One should be wary of practicing home cures on the patient—there may be legal repercussions. It should be understood from the outset of the trip that any medical bills incurred enroute are to the passenger's individual account. Often passengers are surprised when they discover what the charges are for a doctor's call to their hotel room. In fact, one of the major problems that one may encounter is the passenger who refuses to see a physician, not wanting to spend the money or disrupt the day's activities and then finding out later (usually in the middle of the night or the middle of nowhere) that a physician should have been consulted after all.

Of course, if an individual is seriously ill and needs hospitalization or surgery and must leave the tour, the matter takes on a new dimension. It is here that using a top-notch reception operator can make all the difference in the world. Since the tour manager will have to continue on with the group to the next city or country, leaving an ill person behind, he or she must depend on the local operator to handle all details, such as visiting the tour member in the hospital, arranging for follow-up care, packing up luggage and personal belongings, reissuing the air ticket (either to catch up with the group when recovered or fly home), notifying family at home, and so forth. When this happens, the tour manager should cable or telephone the agency regarding the circumstances, advising them that he or she is proceeding with the group and leaving the passenger in a certain hospital giving the name of the physician under whose care the passenger is. The author still has a strong sense of loyalty to a certain reception ground operator in Bogotá who helped her through a difficult situation such as this. Even though other operators have since come to the fore offering very attractive and less-expensive reception operator services, the author has not switched her allegiance.

*Lost passports.* A lost passport can be a frightening and disruptive experience and one that can be solved only by the consulate, because the passenger cannot continue to the next country on the group's itinerary until a substitute passport has been issued. It may even mean the passenger's missing the group flight and remaining in the country independently until the new passport is issued. If the tour manager has the number, date, and place of issue of the missing passport, this will expedite matters. Even with this information, the individual will have to go to the consulate *in person* and, here again, the local operator can be of assistance in providing transportation and perhaps a guide to accompany the passenger. Of course, any such expenses will be on the individual's own account and it may mean the passenger's missing certain tour activities while attending to this important matter. If there were visas for upcoming countries stamped in the lost passport, it will be necessary to obtain new visas (from the consulates of the countries concerned) once the new passport has been issued.

OPERATIONAL PROBLEMS

These problems occur between the tour manager or the group and those who are providing services, for example, airlines, hotels, reception operators, guides, and motorcoach companies. Since the tourism industry is basically a service industry, no matter how well things may be planned in advance, a great many things can go wrong in providing services. In fact, since the service depends on so many diverse people, from the manager to the busboy, it is often a miracle that things go as well as they do! A few areas in which problems can occur are the following:

*Lost or damaged luggage.* It is important that lost or damaged baggage be reported immediately to the airline or other source presumed to be responsible. Although this may delay the group slightly, it often is impossible to locate the bag and to service the claim unless a formal written claim form is completed right away. The tour manager should write down the name of the individual with whom the claim was placed and the telephone extension at the airport so that he or she can follow up with phone calls later. This is another area in which the local reception operator can be helpful. The tour manager may be busy with the group and not be able to call the airline repeatedly or drop everything to go to the airport. However, the tour manager and the passenger will have to stay in close touch, since it may be necessary for one of them to produce the claim check and the key and go to the airport personally to claim the bag if customs clearance is necessary. In other cases, the local operator may be able to arrange to have it delivered to the hotel.

If the bag remains lost, everyone on the tour will usually be willing to pitch in and lend the victim pieces of clothing from their wardrobes; however, some purchases of essential items will be necessary. If the bag does not arrive in short order, the tour manager should begin to pressure the airline to give the passenger immediate financial assistance. If the bag is merely damaged, it should be ascertained immediately from the airline as to the quickest procedure for repair and reimbursement, since the tour may not be staying in that city long and the suitcase may not hold up for the next flight unless it is fixed.

*Delays.* There are often delays in flights, trains, or other transportation—delays that are beyond the tour manager's control. They simply must be endured. When these delays occur it is (1) important to check periodically as to what is happening and report back to the group, keeping them informed; (2) work on the group's behalf in obtaining free meal or drink vouchers from the airline; (3) be sure that the group knows that if they are missing any tour activity because of the delay, their itinerary will be rearranged in the city to give them everything promised, or a substitute activity for anything missed. If it becomes evident that the delay may be lengthy, causing the tour to arrive at the next city extremely late, it is important to cable ahead to the hotel and reception operator meeting the group telling them that the group is going to be late but that they are surely are coming. This may prevent the group's hotel rooms from being given away.

*Strikes.* Sometimes a strike will occur with absolutely the worst timing in the world—just when the group arrives. Many tourists have had to make their own beds when the hotel staff walked out or have had to make do with a cold dinner when the kitchen help closed down the kitchen. These situations try one's patience and test one's ingenuity, but it is amazing what can be done when one has to. The author has stopped the bus at a supermarket and staged an impromptu picnic. She has paid private citizens to drive groups to the airport in their own cars when taxis went on strike. Groups have made their own music with bottles, pots, and pans when the band walked out. Other groups have gone from France to England via Belgium when the French dock workers were on strike. These are situations in which one must often solve the problem through quick thinking—and with cash. A voucher or a company check means nothing, so tour managers must have emergency funds available for situations such as these.

*Nonappearance of reception operator.* Occasionally a group will deplane, the tour manager will go through immigration and customs, go out into the waiting area and discover that no one is there to meet the group. The first thing to do in such a case is to get the entire group to sit down in one area and remain there. The tour manager then may ask airline officials if they have seen a representative from the company that is supposed to meet the group. If not, the airlines may be asked to page. Quite often the representative will be there but may have wandered off to help a passenger or to get a cup of coffee on the assumption that the group would take longer in clearing customs and immigration than was actually required. However, if no one shows up, the next step is to call the company if they are open (one reason to have the name and phone number handy when arriving, as well as some change in local currency). Perhaps the person is on the way to meet the group but has been caught up in a traffic jam or has been involved in an accident.

Whatever the case may be, if fifteen minutes or so have gone by and the tour manager has not been able to locate anyone, there is no alternative but to put the group into taxis and get them to the hotel as quickly as possible. By now, the tour members are tired and perhaps out of sorts, so it is best to consider their needs first. The tour manager should try to treat the matter lightly and vent his or her anger on the local operator later, not on the passengers. The tour manager should pay for the taxis and get receipts from the taxi driver. He or she should have sufficient money in local currency in order to pay the various drivers and to pay tips to the airport porters and hotel bellboys. After the group is settled into their rooms, the tour manager can find out what really happened.

When leaving this city, if the tour manager is paying the local operator for services rendered or is turning in a voucher or is signing an invoice, it is important to make a notation that the group did not receive the arrival transfer service and payment for it is not authorized.

**Acts of God**

Acts of God encompass a number of natural disasters, such as earthquakes or storms, and man-made disasters, such as war, civil disturbances, or riots. Each one has to be dealt with in the best way that one can at the time. When in doubt as to the best procedure to follow, the tour manager may call the embassy and be guided by their advice. Often the group may be in a perfectly safe place but may have heard of a problem in the next country on the itinerary. The decision then is whether to proceed as planned or whether to try to avoid the affected area—perhaps overfly it or turn back. If, after consulting with the embassy and reaching a decision, the tour manager decides not to proceed, he or she may be faced with a passenger who says, "I'm going on in. I've spent all this money to come this far and all my life I've dreamed of going there and now, by God, nobody is going to stop me." In this case, the individual should be allowed to go, but the tour manager should ask for a signed statement to the effect that the individual is doing so as an independent traveler and against the tour manager's better judgment. The reverse may happen: the tour manager may have decided that it is safe to go on, but there may be an individual who feels uncomfortable doing so. A person should never be forced to accompany the group. Instead, the local reception operator may be asked to rearrange this individual's itinerary to stay where he or she is for a longer period of time and then catch up with the group at a later stop. Of course, if the group is traveling on a group airfare, such as a GIT, an individual wishing to deviate might have to pay the supplemental airfare involved, unless the airline will make an exception. If the tour manager is truly in doubt as to what to do, he or she may call the home office long distance. A call to almost anywhere in the world can be made for $12 or so, and having the backing of the agency will reassure the tour manager about any decision.

## Dealing with the Airlines Enroute

On a lengthy trip involving fifteen or twenty different flight legs, each of these legs must be reconfirmed as the tour goes along. In some cities, the tour manager may do this personally; in other cities, the reception operator will offer to do it, with the tour manager turning the air tickets over to the local office and getting them back before the next flight. Whoever does the reconfirming, it is still up to the tour manager to be sure that it gets done! Reconfirming flights can turn up some amazing information—no record of the group's reservations, an oversold flight where the airline has arbitrarily bumped the group to another flight or even another day, changes of flight scheduling, and a number of other unexpected possibilities. Therefore, it is wise to reconfirm as early as possible to be assured that all will go smoothly and to provide ample time to do battle if it becomes necessary.

## Special Hints on Cruises

Escorting a group aboard a cruise ship is somewhat different than escorting an air/land tour. Since virtually everything is done for the members by the cruise personnel or shore excursion operators, the tour manager's role is really that of a host or hostess, following up what the cruise and shore staff people are doing to be sure that the group is getting the best, getting efficient handling, getting special service.

This, in effect, puts the tour manager in the position of go-between—relaying messages, instructions, tickets, and so forth between the group and the cruise staff. In one sense, it is easier than managing a regular tour with its daily traumas of flights, transfers, and guides. In another sense, it is more difficult, since the tour manager really has little decision power. If the sightseeing tour in a given city spends three-fourths of its time in a shop buying emeralds, the tour manager cannot really say anything because it is not his or her tour. However, there are a number of things that one can and should do to establish leadership, loyalty, and control of the group, such as the following:

- If a tour manager has not been on a particular ship before, immediately on boarding, he or she should make a quick tour in order to know where everything is—the dining room, purser's office, pool, sauna, and so forth. One should have brought a deck plan from home and circled in red the cabin numbers of the group.

- Soon after boarding, the tour manager should go around and meet the key staff people, because developing a good rapport with them is all important to the success of the trip. These are the purser, the director of the shore excursion desk, the cruise director (social director), and the *maitre d'* (head dining room steward).

- It is a good idea always to hold a welcome party and a briefing, even if there is not much on which to brief the group. It makes them feel special, apart from the regular passengers.

- Shortly after boarding, the tour manager should double check seating arrangements in the dining room with the *maitre d'*. If the agency has requested group seating ahead of time, it should be determined if this is being provided as requested. Some agencies like to provide group seating. Others prefer to let the passengers select early or late seating and take their own chances on table mates. There are advantages and disadvantages to each approach. If possible, the single women should not all be seated together. If there are birthdays or anniversaries in the group, the *maitre d'* should be advised early so that a special cake or festivity can be arranged the appropriate day.

- If the tour manager does not know all of the tour members well, ask them to wear their name tags—at least for the first few days. Sometimes it is difficult to recognize them the second day when they have changed clothes, and one ends up greeting everyone on the ship for fear of snubbing one of the group. Once, in Yucatán, the author spent an entire evening at dinner seated with a charming couple that she assumed was part of her group, only to find out over dessert and coffee that they were not on her tour at all. She had simply seated herself with them in the dining room assuming they were in her group.

- The tour manager should try to arrange special shipboard tours during days at sea—for example, a tour of the bridge, the galley, or the engine room. Quite often this is done for the regular passengers. They may start talking among themselves, and the group members will wonder why it is not being done for them. To beat them to the punch, a tour manager may announce to the group at the briefing that he or she is working with the cruise staff to arrange special shipboard tours for their group, and they will be informed when these will take place.

- The tour manager should act as a catalyst, getting people to know one another, to mix, to enter into activities. Group members might be invited to join him or her in, say, a swim at 2:00 p.m. or bingo at 11:00 a.m.
- The tour manager may decide to talk up the usual cruise costume party—helping the reticent ones plan their costumes. Maybe a group theme could be worked out. For example, the author once saw an entire group of thirty plus from Salt Lake City twirl onto stage dressed in tiny white tulle skirts, billing themselves as the "Salt Lake Swan Lake Ballet."
- The tour manager may try to arrange with the shore excursion manager to assign the group together in one particular motorcoach for sightseeing. This is not always possible if different people in the group are buying different optional shore excursions, but if the entire group is taking the whole package, sometimes it can be worked out. In this way, the group will not have strangers disrupting their good habits.
- The tour manager should circulate every day and be visible, working, and available, perhaps carrying a notebook and pen even when on the sundeck in a bathing suit! One might consider stipulating a certain time and place on board to be found every day if needed.
- If the cruise line has a departure briefing on the last day to give passengers information on baggage pickup, transfers to the airport, and flight reconfirmation, the tour manager can expedite this for the group so that they do not need to have to stand in long reconfirmation lines. They may assume that because they are in a special group they should get this special service and may resent having to line up with everyone else.
- The tour manager should try not to spend a lot of time in front of the group with the officers or other passengers or groups. One's group may become possessive, convinced that they have paid for a tour manager, and some may resent the time and attention paid to outsiders.

As can be seen, the basic thought behind all of the above hints is to make a group feel special so that if they book another cruise or tour they will want to book through the same agency. The cruise line will do everything possible to secure their loyalty and participation in future cruises aboard their ships; what a tour manager must do is augment that loyalty to booking through his or her agency. After all, if group members are getting exactly—and only—what every other passenger is getting, they could just as easily have booked independently through any travel agency.

## Those Last Twenty-four Hours

Just as the first twenty-four hours were all important in setting the tone of a trip and pulling the group together as a unit, so the last twenty-four hours are important in leaving a good taste in the mouth, warm feelings, good friendships. If possible, and if the tour budget permits, it is a good idea to have a farewell party of some sort. If nothing else, perhaps an after-dinner drink and a few good songs and laughs can be shared together. The author often writes an epic poem about the group and reads it at the last night's function, trying to bring in a verse about each of the individuals in the group. Here again, it is not always money that does the job—it is the feeling of personal warmth and togetherness.

On that last flight homeward, it is preferable to have each person check in at the airport as an individual passenger (usually much to the dismay of the local reception operator). This individual check-in is for two reasons. First, usually by the last flight home, the tour members have become pack rats and are carrying twice the luggage that they started out with. If they all pool their luggage together and the entire pool is over the allowable amount the tour manager will be given the bill. However, if they check in individually, each pays for his or her own overweight or perhaps teams up with someone in the group whose weight is under the limit. Second, when the group members arrive at the return gateway city, they can claim their luggage and go right on to their connecting flight to their home town. If, on the other hand, the tour manager has all the baggage claim stubs for the group and has to wait for the entire group to claim luggage and go through customs as a group, someone in the tour may miss a connecting flight. The tour manager should remain with the group members to the end, seeing to it that the last passenger has located his or her luggage, has gone through immigration and customs, has been given a farewell hug, and has gone happily into the night.

# 12
# Posttour Wrap-up

As soon as the tour returns, there are six things that must be taken care of before the project can be considered closed, as follows.

1. Debrief the tour manager.
2. Send the tour participants a welcome-home letter and a questionnaire to solicit their feedback on the trip.
3. Close the tour financially, completing any unpaid bills, collecting any accounts receivable, and looking at a profit-and-loss statement on the project.
4. Pack away all operational files and client correspondence in an orderly fashion for future reference.
5. Add tour members' names and addresses to the agency's permanent mailing list of clients.
6. Look to the future.

**Debriefing the Tour Manager**

A tour manager will return weary at first, but then eager to talk at length about what went right and what went wrong on the trip. Whether the manager was a staff person, a paid professional, or the organizer, this person feels emotionally attached to the tour and is anxious to share with the agency both the successes and the problems encountered along the way. On the one hand, the tour manager is looking for the agency's support, a pat on the back saying "You did right" or "You did what we would have done in such and such a situation." On the other hand, if things went wrong, the tour manager is in a defensive position, wanting the agency to know what transpired *before* passengers start to call in with complaints.

Therefore, it is wise to plan a period to debrief—in short, to listen. If other groups are leaving shortly, the tendency is to put the tour manager off or speed up the debriefing session and perhaps not give him or her the time and attention deserved. This can be a mistake. Even if the tour manager is totally wrong in some aspects, this debriefing session can be a learning experience for the agency. After all, the tour manager is the person who was closest to the tour, to the participants, to the hotels, to the various servicing companies—he or she knows what was done well, what was lacking, and what improvements could be made were the trip to be repeated next year. It is not enough just to elicit negative feedback, such as that a hotel was terrible. Can the tour manager make a positive recommendation as to a better one?

One of the best arrangements for a debriefing session seems to be to invite the tour manager to come to the office in the morning and be told that there will be an hour or so to spend together in consultation. Then a desk should be made available for the balance of the morning so that he or she may complete financial accounting (Figure 12.1), type up the posttour report (Figure 12.2), and meet with the accountant/bookkeeper to turn over the financial report and return any unspent monies.

This will ensure that the tour manager's report gets proper attention, that the financial report is turned in quickly after the tour rather than letting it drag on, and that a complete recap report is submitted in writing—a report that can be referred to later as needed. This written report can be particularly important when booking next year's tour or if filing a claim with a supplier, or even in forming a base should a legal problem develop. If the tour manager is an outside professional who is paid by the day, most better agencies pay the daily salary for both the pretour briefing day and the posttour debriefing day, and cost the two days' salary into the tour.

## Contacting the Tour Participants

One of the things that should be done right after the group returns is to write to the members to welcome them home and to ask how they enjoyed the trip. This serves several purposes:

## TOUR MANAGER'S EXPENSE REPORT

Name of Tour: **Rosemont Country Club**  Currency: **French francs**
Departure Date: **September 6, 1985**  Number of Passengers in Group: **27+1**
Tour Manager's Name: **M. Kimberly**

| DATE | PLACE | EXPLANATION | REC. NO. | MEALS | TIPS | ENTRANCE FEES | MISC | TOTAL |
|---|---|---|---|---|---|---|---|---|
| Sept. 10 | Paris | Rail station porterage 56 bags x 3 Fr | | | 168 | | | 168 |
| " | " | Guide tip 27 x 5 Fr | | | 35 | | | 35 |
| " | " | City tour driver tip, 27 x 3 Fr | | | 81 | | | 81 |
| " | " | Extra driver tip, unloading bags | | | 150 | | | 150 |
| " | " | Meurice arrival porters, 27 pax x 2 bags x 2 Fr | | | 280 | | | 280 |
| " | " | Own dinner, service included | | 120 | | | | 120 |
| " | " | "   " , small extra tip | | | 15 | | | 15 |
| Sept. 11 | " | Upfront tip to maitre d' | | | 60 | | | 60 |
| " | Versailles | Entrance, palace, 27 x 8 Fr | | | | 216 | | 216 |
| " | Paris | Local guide tip half-day, 27 x 5 Fr | | | 135 | | | 135 |
| " | " | Driver tip, half-day, 27 x 3 Fr | | | 81 | | | 81 |
| " | " | Own lunch at cafe, incl. service | | 80 | | | | 80 |
| " | " | Small extra tip at lunch | | | 10 | | | 10 |
| " | " | Taxi to Air France to reconfirm, RT | | | | | 60 | 60 |
| " | " | Own dinner, incl. service | | 100 | | | | 100 |
| " | " | Small extra dinner tip | | | 5 | | | 5 |
| " | " | Lido. Maitre d' tip for good tables | | | 90 | | | 90 |
| " | " | Evening - Lido bus driver tip | | | 60 | | | 60 |
| Sept. 12 | " | Upfront tip to maitre d' | | | 60 | | | 60 |
| " | " | Louvre entrance fee, 27 x 8 Fr | | | | 216 | | 216 |
| " | " | Own lunch at hotel, incl. service | | 100 | | | | 100 |
| " | " | Small extra tip at lunch | | | 10 | | | 10 |
| " | " | Dinner including guests: Rosemont Country Club Pres & husband, incl. tip | 1 | 400 | | | | 400 |
| " | " | Roundtrip taxi for above | | | | | 40 | 40 |
| Sept. 13 | " | Upfront tip to maitre d' | | | 60 | | | 60 |
| " | " | Meurice Hotel - incidentals bill | 2 | | | | 315 | 315 |
| " | " | Meurice Hotel chambermaids 28 x 3 Fr | | | 84 | | | 84 |
| " | " | Concierge tip, flat amount | | | 75 | | | 75 |
| " | " | Hotel bellboys 28 x 2 bags x 5 Fr | | | 280 | | | 280 |
| " | " | Departure transfer tip to bus driver | | | 60 | | | 60 |
| " | " | Porters CDG Airport, 28 x 2 bags x 3 Fr | | | 56 | | | 56 |
| " | " | Misc. Newspaper, gum | | | | | 50 | 50 |
| TOTALS IN LOCAL CURRENCY | | | | 800 | 2,090 | 432 | 465 | 3,787 |
| AT AVERAGE EXCHANGE RATE OF: 7.90 PER U.S. DOLLAR, EQUIVALENT IN DOLLARS | | | | | | | U. S. | $479.37 |

**Figure 12.1** Tour manager's expense report form, to be used for out-of-pocket payments. A separate sheet would be used for each foreign currency, and receipts (numbered) attached for each item over U.S. $25. Hotels, motorcoaches, and local reception operators are not listed, as they would probably be paid by voucher or company check or be prepaid.

## TOUR MANAGER'S EVALUATION REPORT

NAME OF TOUR MANAGER _____

NAME OF TOUR _____ _____

DEPARTURE DATE _____

1. ON AN <u>OVER-ALL BASIS</u>, HOW SUCCESSFUL DO YOU FEEL THIS TOUR WAS?

   ☐ Very Successful;   ☐ Successful;   ☐ Moderate;   ☐ Poor;   ☐ Very Bad

2. <u>AIRLINE(S)</u>. Give us names of airlines on which you flew and your opinion, good or bad of each.

   _____
   _____
   _____

3. <u>HOTEL(S)</u>. Any hotels not up to par? Where and why? _____
   _____
   _____
   _____

   Any hotels particularly outstanding? Where and why? _____
   _____
   _____
   _____

4. <u>RECEPTION GROUND OPERATOR(S)</u>. Specify wherein particularly good, wherein not up to par (in which case, how would you improve it?)

   _____
   _____
   _____

5. <u>LOCAL COURIERS OR GUIDES</u>. Names of any couriers or local guides who were particularly outstanding and whom we should try to use again?

   _____
   _____

   Any couriers or local guides who were not good and why _____
   _____

6. COMMENTS ON SPECIAL EVENTS. Any special tour events you would add or delete and why.

_____
_____
_____

7. COMMENTS ON PASSENGERS. Any passengers whom you feel may prove to be potential problems for the company? Any who need post-tour followup servicing from our office?

_____
_____
_____
_____
_____
_____
_____
_____
_____
_____

8. ANY COMMENTS ON PRE-TOUR PREPARATION OF TOUR MANAGER'S MATERIALS? Were materials given you correct, adequate quantities, etc.? Any suggestions for improvement?

_____
_____
_____
_____

9. ANY MAJOR PRICING/BUDGETING ERRORS WE NEED TO KNOW ABOUT? Places wherein you found our anticipated expenditures too high or too low, for our planning purposes the next time 'round.

_____
_____

**Figure 12.2** Tour manager's evaluation report form.

- It shows that the agency is interested—not only in selling them a trip and taking their money before the tour leaves, but also in being sure that the trip lived up to expectations.
- It makes them feel needed, that their opinions are valuable and helpful in improving the trip for future travelers.
- It gives the agency a reason to keep the relationship open—it is hoped with an eye to future business.
- It may provide referrals—friends or organizations who might travel with the agency in the future.

The welcome-home letter should be warm and friendly (Figure 12.3). Enclosed with the letter should be a questionnaire (Figure 12.4) about the trip and a stamped return-mail envelope. A nice gesture is to send everyone a group photo of their tour (if the tour manager took such a photo). However, if getting the photo developed and copies made for everyone is going to delay the letter, the photo can wait until later, because it is important to get the welcome-home letter out quickly.

The letter should indicate that the agency would appreciate their taking a few minutes to fill out the enclosed questionnaire, since their opinions are valuable in planning future trips. The questionnaire should be fairly specific if specific answers are wanted. For example, instead of asking "How was the airline service?" One might ask "Which airlines do you believe did the best job? The worst?" In short, guide and direct them into being specific.

Sometimes the tour participants will not answer certain questions for fear of hurting someone's feelings or getting someone into trouble, particularly if a question pertains to the tour manager or organizer. They may be afraid that if they make a negative comment about someone, the person may see their complaint and be angry with them. One effective way of getting around this is to have the welcome-home letter go to the passenger directly from the agency president with the return-mail envelope marked "Personal."

Of course, this all assumes that travel professionals have broad shoulders and can take a certain amount of criticism. Anyone who has ever organized or managed tours in the field has been criticized—sometimes unjustly by an impossible-to-please or misinformed tour participant. Professionals must expect this, learn from it, but not let it totally undo them.

If one already knows of a definite problem that occurred on the trip, perhaps the best solution is to mention this in the letter. For example, if the flight home was delayed six hours, bringing everyone in late and

LSI TRAVEL AGENCY, INC.

Welcome Home!

We presume that by now you have had time to "settle in" ... to unpack, catch up on jet lag and adjust to life at home again ... reality.

However, while your travels are still fresh in your mind, could we ask you to spend a few minutes and give us your opinion of the trip? Our staff does travel frequently to keep up to date, but it simply is not possible for us to be everywhere at all times, so we particularly value the suggestions of tour participants like yourselves.

A questionnaire is enclosed along with a postage-paid return-mail envelope. You will note it is to be returned to me personally, so you may feel free to make whatever comments you wish with the assurance that they will be confidential.

You have now joined the ever-growing family of LSI travelers and we hope to see you on many a future tour with us. To that end, we are placing your name on our permanent mailing list to receive notices of new trips as they develop and first offerings of exciting tours and cruises.

Thank you for traveling with us, and I look forward to hearing from you shortly.

Sincerely,

Frederic Schmidt

Frederic Schmidt, CTC
President

FS/s
enclosures: Questionnaire
Postage-paid envelope

**Figure 12.3** Welcome home letter.

disagreeable, one might say "We already have been advised about the unfortunate delay you encountered on the way home with XYZ airline and we have asked for a full report from airline management in this regard." This will deflect their anger somewhat so that it does not color the entire posttour report.

One helpful marketing technique is to have a place on the questionnaire asking them where they would like to travel next, a place for referrals of friends whom they believe might enjoy a similar tour, and a question asking if they belong to any clubs or organizations that travel as a group.

LSI Travel Agency, Inc.

P O S T - T O U R   Q U E S T I O N N A I R E

NAME _____

ADDRESS _____

TOWN _____ STATE _____ ZIP CODE _____ TELEPHONE _____

NAME OF TOUR _____

1. WHAT PROMPTED YOU TO JOIN THIS TOUR? _____
   _____

2. ON AN OVERALL BASIS, HOW WOULD YOU RATE THIS TOUR?

   ☐ POOR    ☐ LESS THAN AVERAGE    ☐ AVERAGE    ☐ GOOD    ☐ SUPERIOR

3. WHAT DID YOU ENJOY THE MOST? _____
   _____

4. WHAT DID YOU ENJOY THE LEAST? _____
   _____

5. HOW WOULD YOU RATE THE AIRLINE SERVICE YOU RECEIVED? SPECIFY WHICH AIRLINE(S) BEST AND WHICH WORST AND WHY _____
   _____
   _____

6. HOW WOULD YOU RATE THE HOTELS, IN GENERAL?

   ☐ WHAT I EXPECTED    ☐ LESS THAN EXPECTED    ☐ BETTER THAN EXPECTED

   WAS THERE ANY PARTICULAR HOTEL WHICH WAS NOT GOOD AND WHICH YOU WOULD DEFINITELY NOT RECOMMEND OUR USING AGAIN FOR A FUTURE TOUR?

   ☐ NO    ☐ YES    Specify _____

7. GENERALLY, HOW WOULD YOU RATE THE LOCAL SIGHTSEEING GUIDES?

   ☐ POOR    ☐ LESS THAN AVERAGE    ☐ AVERAGE    ☐ GOOD    ☐ SUPERIOR

   WAS THERE ANY PARTICULAR GUIDE OR CITY WHERE YOU FELT THE LOCAL GUIDE WAS OUTSTANDING AND WHERE YOU FEEL WE SHOULD REQUEST THIS SAME GUIDE AGAIN BY NAME ON FUTURE TOURS?
   _____
   _____

   WAS THERE ANY PARTICULAR GUIDE OR CITY WHERE YOU FELT THE LOCAL GUIDE WAS NOT AS GOOD AS YOU HAD HOPED AND WHERE YOU FEEL WE SHOULD NOT USE THIS GUIDE AGAIN?
   _____
   _____

8. WHAT IS YOUR OPINION OF YOUR TOUR MANAGER? STRONG POINTS? WEAKNESSES?
   _____
   _____
   _____

9. HOW WOULD YOU RATE THE PRE-TRIP SERVICE AND ASSISTANCE YOU RECEIVED FROM OUR OFFICE --
   INFORMATION BULLETINS, ANSWERS TO YOUR QUESTIONS AND SO FORTH?

   ☐ POOR     ☐ LESS THAN AVERAGE     ☐ AVERAGE     ☐ GOOD     ☐ SUPERIOR

10. IF THIS TRIP WERE TO BE REPEATED, IS THERE ANYTHING YOU WOULD LIKE TO SEE ELIMINATED
    FROM THE TRIP? _____

    ANYTHING ADDED? (EVEN IF IT INCREASES THE PRICE?) _____
    _____

11. WHERE HAD YOU TRAVELED BEFORE THIS TRIP? _____
    _____

12. WHERE WOULD YOU NEXT LIKE TO TRAVEL? _____

13. DO YOU BELONG TO ANY CLUBS, CHURCHES, BUSINESSES OR ORGANIZATIONS WHICH DO GROUP
    TRAVEL -- FOR PLEASURE, BUSINESS, STUDY, CONVENTIONS OR MEETINGS? _____
    _____

14. NAMES AND ADDRESSES OF FAMILY OR FRIENDS WHOM YOU FEEL MIGHT ENJOY KNOWING ABOUT OUR
    TRIPS

    (a) Name _____
        Address _____
        Town _____ State _____ Zip Code _____

    (b) Name _____
        Address _____
        Town _____ State _____ Zip Code _____

    (c) Name _____
        Address _____
        Town _____ State _____ Zip Code _____

15. COMMENTS (ADD SECOND SHEET IF NEEDED) _____
    _____
    _____

**Figure 12.4**  Posttour questionnaire.

## Financial Closing

Now comes the important day of reckoning—the day when financial facts must be faced. Did the tour make money or not? It is as simple as that. Did it make as much as was anticipated? Was it priced adequately? Or in retrospect, were many expenses overlooked?

Before one can reach these decisions, it is necessary to close out any financial matters pending. The following are some of the areas to be looked at.

- Has the tour leader's salary (if any) been paid?
- Have all promotional expenses been paid? The brochure? Flyers? Advertising? Promotional evenings?
- Are all suppliers' bills settled? Hotels, airlines, cruise lines, motorcoach companies, ground operators?
- Are there any sales fees or donations still to be paid to the organizer or sponsoring club?
- Are there any refunds due that the office has not yet received?
- Were there any override commissions promised by the airlines, cruise lines, or other suppliers and has the agent formally applied for these?
- Are all client payments completed?

If all of the above are settled and if all deposits and payments on this tour were accurately credited or debited to the accounting code number assigned to this tour at the outset, the company's accountant should be able to supply an accurate profit/loss picture fairly quickly.

The results should be assessed honestly. It is easy to make excuses and say "If Mr. and Mrs. Smith hadn't cancelled at the last minute we'd have had the twenty participants we planned on and we would have made money" or "If we hadn't had to do that second promotional mailing we would have made so much." The figures should be used as a learning experience for the future. Perhaps the next time, plans for a last-minute cancellation or an extra promotion can be costed into the tour from the outset.

## Packing Away Files

Once all pending matters have been settled, the tour files can be packed and filed away. Taking an hour or two to put the tour files in order will make it possible for anyone on the staff to locate needed information later. This could be for booking the tour again in the future. It could be for looking up a client's financial record if he or she is being audited by the Internal Revenue Service and asks for help. It might be in referring to the tour manager's report with suggestions for the future.

Certainly all things financial should be filed together—the original costing and the posttour profit/loss statement, so that if a similar tour is planned in the future these costing sheets can be used as reference.

One master file of all sample form letters and information bulletins that were sent out to the participants should be kept. The samples may be used in modified form for a different tour to a different destination. Samples of all ads, invitations, and so forth pertinent to the project should be retained. And, before throwing away supplies of surplus brochures, a supply should be set aside for reference or for use as an interim sales piece until next year's brochure is printed, if there are plans to repeat the tour.

## Adding Names to Mailing List

Assuming that the agency maintains a mailing list of all clients who have traveled with the company, the names and addresses of these tour participants should be added to that list at this time. If the agency does not maintain such a list, now is the time to start one. Such a list makes it possible to do a couple of important things.

- To send out periodic mailings to past tour participants, thus keeping a rapport going with each client. These mailings could be future tour or cruise announcements, perhaps a company newsletter, or an invitation to a promotional evening.
- To refer to the client's travel history with accuracy should he or she book with the agency again. For example, if a previous tour member books again, the welcome acknowledgment letter could be modified to read: "Welcome aboard your third tour with LSI Travel. It's nice to have you along again and we hope this trip will prove as enjoyable as the Europe one did back in '82." This makes the client feel remembered and important.

If these records are kept alphabetically in a card index file, personnel can be trained to check the file each time a booking comes in to see if the client is a repeat customer or not. The alphabetical card index file (see Figure 12.5 for a sample card) can include such information as

```
Name:    Wing, Mr. Elliott / Mrs. Marilyn
Address: 2433 Brown Derby Road
City:    Rosemont         State: IL   Zip Code: 60018
Source of booking:   Elaine Whittaker
                   name of organizer, outside sales rep etc.

Name of Tour/Cruise and Destination          Year    Leader
Rosemont Country Club - Europe               '85     Kimberly
Sun Line Orinoco Cruise                      '84     Corley

See continuing card for more ..........................
Comments: Experienced travelers, but Mr. Wing
has heart condition.
```

**Figure 12.5** Past participant client file card.

name and address, tour and year, destination, and name of the tour manager. The index card can also be used to write in little comments for use in the future, such as "Difficult tour member—do not solicit again" or "good prospect for the Orient."

In fact, if this information is readily accessible, an agency can develop some interesting marketing and sales ideas, such as forming a travel club and giving each tour participant a membership card after the first trip with the agency. Another idea is to give past tour participants a discount on future tours or a discount against their own tour if they bring along a friend who has not traveled with the agency before.

Of course, depending on the size and volume of group tours in the office, some system is needed for getting these names onto a mailing list. Agencies with large lists employ a computer company. At the completion of each tour, the names and addresses of the tour participants are sent to the computer company to add to the agency's list. Then, the computer company can run off mailing labels when they are needed, sorted by zip code rather than alphabetically (thus making it possible to use the lower bulk mail rates, which are not allowable for small lists or for lists sorted alphabetically).

Small agencies that have few group tours prefer to keep the alphabetical card index and then also type up each tour list of passengers alphabetically on plain white paper (three rows, eleven names and addresses to the vertical row), thus suitable for running off on photocopy label sheets whenever a mailing is planned. The disadvantage of this method is that the names are not listed by zip code nor are they integrated alphabetically with other tours. Each tour list stands alone.

## Looking to the Future

Now is the time (while pleasant tour memories are fresh in the clients' minds) to start the wheels in motion for the future. If this was a tour for a private club or organization, a meeting with the club organizer or president is advisable to assess the success and/or problems of this last tour. Of course, if this same person also acted as tour manager, this would already have been accomplished at the debriefing session. Whatever the case, in preparation for this meeting it is good to have two or three new destination ideas in mind with ballpark figures as to price and suggestions for time of year. Often, if the club is left to its own devices, to its own inner politics of election of new officers, and so forth, by the time it is ready to book the next tour or cruise, it is too late! The club officials need to be prodded with the assumption that of course, they are going to do another tour and, of course they are going to do it through the same agency. And the decisions regarding next year's tour must be reached now while the same club officers are involved in the decision-making process, not delayed until a new Board of Directors comes into power (perhaps with its own travel plans, own travel agent, and own vested interests).

One thought that might be planted is the idea of having a tour reunion to show films, relive the happy memories of the trip, and enjoy the camaraderie of new-found friends. This sort of reunion often can be a springboard for future trips, announcing next year's tour at the reunion and giving past participants first chance to sign up for a new trip. One might even want to invite each tour participant to bring a friend, if it will not change the spirit of the reunion and alter the group dynamics. It can also be effective if one of the tour participants acts as host and catalyst for the reunion, with the agency representative and/or the tour manager attending as invited guests.

All in all, by the time the tour files are packed away and the agency moves on to other things it should: (1) have a new nucleus of happy tour members; (2) have decided whether to repeat the same tour next year for a new clientele; (3) have decided whether to offer a new tour next year, but to this same clientele; (4) have a financial picture of the tour; (5) have learned a lot—both from the successes and from the mistakes encountered on this tour.

# 13
# Incoming Group Tours

Once an agency has some experience in operating an outgoing tour program, it may be time to consider opening an incoming tour division as well. In this sense, *incoming* means handling groups of foreign visitors or groups from other parts of the United States. An agency could, of course, elect to be simply a local reception operator providing local transfers, city tours, and the like. But the money is to be made by becoming a full-service reception tour operator—handling a complete "Visit U.S.A." package. Under such an arrangement, one combines hotels, sightseeing, motorcoach transportation, meals, social events, tour manager, and technical visits all into a total package, adds a markup and then offers it to a tour operator or travel agent overseas (or in the United States) for sale to his or her specialty group.

Under this arrangement, the selling agent or tour operator overseas is often called the *producer,* since this is the company producing the group or clientele. Conversely, the agent or tour operator in the United States who puts together the components of the package and operates the tour is often called the *supplier* or the *reception operator* or sometimes the *ground operator*. In other words, the roles are now reversed; the agent is no longer the agent.

A company that can offer a good incoming specialty tour product and promote it properly over three or four years should find it possible to build an operation of twenty incoming tours or so per year, earning $4,000 to $5,000 minimum per each small-size group.

In many countries, travel agencies and tour operators regularly handle two-way travel. However, in the United States, most travel agencies and tour operators have concentrated on outgoing tourism and have left incoming traffic to incoming specialists. Agents with some group expertise have now begun to look at incoming tourism as a new market, a new product, a new source of revenue. And with 1980 as a watershed year, the first year the United States received as many foreign tourists as it sent abroad, it is high time for this change in attitude.

Incoming tourism is not a business for the inexperienced. Nor is it a stable business since it usually fluctuates with the strength of the United States dollar. When the dollar is strong on foreign markets and North Americans find it a bargain to travel overseas, at the same time it is very difficult for foreigners to buy dollars with their weak currencies and a vacation in the United states is totally out of reach financially. Yet, for the company with solid group operational know-how, incoming tourism should be looked at for a number of reasons.

## Reasons to Consider Opening an Incoming Tour Department

- As a balance to outgoing business, filling weak seasons in the office.
- As an additional source of revenue, particularly important if outgoing business is down during an economic slump.
- As a means of generating balance of payments. Foreigners spending money for United States packages are infusing money into our economy, money that circulates and provides jobs in tourism in the United States—often jobs at the lowest end of the economic spectrum, where they are needed most. Visitors to one's city or state make purchases and support local restaurants, shops, and businesses.
- As a method of diversifying an agency so that it does not have all its eggs in one basket should any one segment of business take a downturn.
- As a means of developing a new area of business that, except for start-up promotional monies and some cash flow for deposits, does not take a great deal of new investment capital. Also, it does not require a lot of new personnel *if* the agency already has a good group department.

## Designing an Incoming Tour Product

Probably the easiest way to start with incoming tours is to develop a specialty tour that can be marketed both overseas and in other areas of the United States. The agency may want to start out small and not try to compete with large-volume operators who can easily underprice the small operator, nor should one try to sell to the extremely large producers who may expect to be carried financially for ninety days or longer.

Therefore, it would be best to appeal to the moderate-size operator and to design a special-interest tour or tour service that someone else does not appear to be doing. A tour for European women visiting American families, homes, and schools? Tours of the Southwest stressing Indian culture, the desert, and turquoise jewelry? Horseback trips, rock climbing, or backpacking into our National Parks? Decide what the agency staff knows the best. Theatre? Opera? Fashion? Perhaps check with the local convention and visitors' bureau to see what they believe is lacking and, conversely, to see what is already being done and what the competition would be.

The next step is to put together and price a few *sample* itineraries. Remember, these itineraries will probably not be sold as is, but will serve as a showcase for overseas tour operators. In actuality, the final itinerary custom-designed for a group may bear no resemblance to the original sample. But the sample will serve as the catalyst, as food for thought. The overseas tour operator, upon seeing these samples, may write or telex and request that a similar tour be custom-designed for his or her clientele.

Once the sample itineraries are drawn up, the agency should produce an attractive brochure that can be used as a sales piece for the trade. Rather than listing tour prices right in the brochure, it is best to print a separate tariff insert sheet. In this way, the tariff can be updated and reprinted annually, or as needed when prices change, without having to reprint the basic brochure. Each tour may be priced on two different levels: one based on standard hotels and one on more deluxe properties.

Remember, if marketing overseas, that many foreigners are not knowledgeable about distances within the United States or the length of time it takes to get from one city to the next. Quite often, if left to their own devices, they will ask to travel too far in one day at a pace that would exhaust their passengers if one complied. A brief day-by-day sample itinerary (or several) in the brochure, illustrated with a good route map, can be an immense help in their planning a realistic schedule for their group.

The brochure should answer other important questions. Who is the agency, how long has it been in business, what are its credentials, and who are its credit and banking references? What are payment policies? It is helpful to state that a minimum deposit is expected in order to begin reservations proceedings for a tour. A request for, say, $500 per tour group does not seem unreasonable. Final payment schedule should be explicit. A suggestion would be to indicate that payment in full, in United States dollars, is due thirty days before the tour begins to enable one to prepay hotels and other suppliers in adequate time. If this is not stipulated, final payment may not arrive in time to provide the cash flow needed, In fact, the incoming group tour may even arrive with payment in foreign currency cash in a flight bag!

Once the brochure and accompanying tariff are published, where does one begin to look for clientele? Remember, the buyer is the overseas or domestic tour company or travel agent selling groups, *not the individual traveler*. Promotional monies or efforts would be wasted on the general public. After all, one wants incoming groups that another agent or tour operator forms and which arrives as a group entity. One does not want individual clients. These prospective client groups are going to need a local travel agent or tour operator in their country or city to process their bookings, handle their air reservations to the United States, assist in securing their visas, publish a brochure in their language for promotion in their country, and so forth, just as if the situation were reversed and a group were being formed here to send to their country or city.

**Promotion**

Promotional efforts for incoming groups may be directed to several areas:

- *Tour operators and group-oriented travel agents overseas and in the United States* that the agency particularly wishes to cultivate. Start with those that the agency may be using to receive its groups overseas; they are already friends. Then expand. One can obtain a list, for example, from *Travel Weekly's World Travel Directory*.
- *Our embassies,* particularly the department pertinent to the agency's specialty tour operation. For example, if specializing in theatre/ballet/opera tours, one might contact the Cultural Attaché at each United States embassy, alerting them to this specialty prod-

uct so that they can refer any local inquiries they may receive to the agency in the United States.

- *Airlines.* Bear in mind, local airlines sales managers do not receive revenue from business *into* their territory, only on tickets sold *from* their territory. Therefore, the local airline sales office personnel have nothing to gain by helping an agency promote an incoming tour division. But, if an agency acknowledges this fact and simply asks for help getting in touch with the airlines' various sales managers overseas, they may give that help. Then, the agency can write a letter of introduction to these overseas airline managers directly, describing the incoming tour product and asking them to call it to the attention of tour operators and travel agents in their country when the airline staff makes sales calls. Sometimes overseas airlines sales people are looking for exciting new products they can bring to the attention of their travel agents and tour operators. Perhaps, if a travel product is distinctive enough, it will catch their eye.

- *United States Travel and Tourism Administration.* An agency may contact the regional offices overseas, alerting them to the product and asking them for referrals. There are offices in six countries: Canada, Mexico, The United Kingdom, Germany, France, and Japan.

- *Join Travel Industry Association of America (TIAA).* Although this organization will not actively go out and promote or refer an agency's products, it is helpful to be a member of the club. This is the organization that sponsors the annual Pow Wow trade show (see below). It also publishes a newsletter and a directory of members, and can be helpful in terms of networking or providing background information. Membership fees for travel agents and tour operators run between $100 and $500 per year, based on the gross sales volume of the company.

- *Trade shows, such as Pow Wow.* Trade shows are probably one of the most effective promotional methods, since it is possible to meet several hundred potential clients within a three- to four-day period. Pow Wow is sponsored by TIAA as a once-a-year marketplace, bringing together American suppliers and overseas buyers. The meeting is held in a different United States city each year and agency representatives are prescheduled, by computer, for an appointment with a different overseas tour operator or travel agent every twenty minutes.

In addition to Pow Wow, which covers travel suppliers from the entire United States, one might first attend one of the smaller, less hectic shows; for example, the Foremost West Show, promoting the five Western states of Arizona, Colorado, Nevada, New Mexico, and Utah. Then, after really learning to work a trade show, one might attend the Big One, the International Tourism Bourse (ITB), held every February in Berlin. It is pointless to waste valuable promotional monies on trade shows that are open to the public, giving away free brochures, free trips, free time, and energy. It is better to select only those shows that are for the travel trade itself, being selective even there.

To attend these trade shows, an agency preregisters and rents a booth for the duration of the show. In addition to the booth registration cost, there is an enrollment fee for each staff member who attends and works in the booth. For example, a small booth at Pow Wow costs about $1,175, another $1,125 for enrolling three employees (three at $375 each), and roughly $200 for miscellaneous booth furnishings. This does not include personal staff expenses, such as airfare to the city of venue, hotel, and some meals (sometimes many meals and festivities already are included in the enrollment fee). Attendance at these social events is an excellent way to meet potential clients informally.

When attending one's first trade show, it is possible to go equipped with no more than brochures, tariff sheets, a sign to identify the agency, and a good supply of business cards. Later, the agency may have a professional booth backdrop made, which should fold down that it can be shipped from show to show. Such a backdrop, complete with lighting, can run as high as $4,000, but it is a promotional investment that can be amortized as a capital investment over several years.

Also, as agency representatives attend more shows, they may wish to carry other handouts besides brochures: perhaps a one-page synthesis of the agency's operations translated into several different languages, perhaps a tabletop slide presentation. At the first show or two, it is a good idea to take time and visit the other booths to get ideas.

## Operational Setup

If the promotion is a success, the agency may suddenly receive requests for quotations and itineraries. The office should be prepared to move

quickly when this happens. The same general requirements would apply as for an outgoing tour department (see chapter 2), that is:
- A separate room or a work area away from office traffic.
- Adequate insurance.
- Personnel adept with group operations.
- Photocopy machine.
- Separate phone line(s).
- An accounting system to separate out expenses and income for each different tour.

In addition, incoming business has some special requirements all its own. These are:
- *Ability to respond immediately* to requests for quotes and suggested itineraries. Someone able to do this should be in the office at all times. All of the incoming staff should never be away at the same time. The client who has to wait a week for an offer will go elsewhere. Often such producers are under pressure to get back to their own clients quickly with a suggested itinerary and rough price estimate, or lose the business themselves to their local competition.
- *Telex.* At first, it is possible to get by without this magic machine, but most overseas producers expect an agency to have one and once the agency staff has become accustomed to relying on a telex, it will seem impossible to manage without one.
- *Accessibility to multilingual tour managers and translators.* Although it is not mandatory that an agency's in-house staff be multilingual, it is helpful. But it is mandatory that an agency be able to contract with good, professional, freelance tour managers who can conduct a tour in the foreign language concerned and with native-speaking translators who can put the itineraries and other written materials into various languages. This usually means being located in a large urban area or in a university town.
- *Ability to work with minute details.* In outgoing tourism, one usually is working with an overseas reception operator who is responsible for the day-to-day details like making luncheon reservations, checking mileages, and reminding the bus company to pick up the group on time. When the situation is reversed, and the agency becomes the reception tour operator, it carries the same

responsibility. Someone on the staff must have a fine eye for detail, to be sure that nothing slips by.
- *Staff availability twenty-four hours a day.* Tour managers must be able to reach someone from the agency when out in the field with a tour in case of problems encountered enroute. There is no such thing as being unavailable on weekends or evenings.
- *Necessity to understand foreign traditions,* viewpoints, dietary likes and dislikes, and so forth.

## Costing Incoming Tours

The principles of costing, be they for incoming or outgoing tours, are basically the same (see chapter 5). Individual variable expenses and fixed group expenses must be separated out just as they are for outgoing tours. But there also a few differences:

- *No air commission.* Remember, all earnings must come from markup on ground expenses. The passengers' flights most likely will be booked and ticketed by their local tour operator or travel agent (the producer) who will then, obviously, get the air commission.
- *No promotional expense.* There is no need to cost-in for promotional efforts. The producer takes the risk for promoting the trip and foots the bill for printing the brochure (perhaps in a foreign language), advertising the tour, and so forth.
- *Graduated rates.* The producer will expect a quotation on graduated prices, based on the volume produced. For example:

    $800 per person, basis 40 paying passengers and one complimentary (expressed $800 pp 40 + 1)
    $875 per person, basis 30 paying passengers and one complimentary (expressed $875 pp 30 + 1)
    $950 per person, basis 20 paying passengers and one complimentary (expressed $950 pp 20 + 1)

It is the producer, not the reception operator who is taking the risk, so it is the producer who gets the price break for producing volume. Regardless of how many tour members they produce, they still will charge their tour members the same price; they will not lower the price to their customers as their tour fills. But as their tour fills, they realize an escalating profit.

Overseas quotations should always be made in United States dollars, letting the overseas producers convert into their local currency. Also, an agency should be sure to quote net and state that rates are net, noncommissionable, when making the offer. The overseas producers will add in their promotional expenses and markup before establishing their selling price.

Even if the overseas producer specifies that the agency quote on, for example, 40+1, it is wise to also quote prices on thirty, twenty, and so forth. This forces the producer to face the fact that they may not actually produce forty passengers and, therefore, should be conservative and price their tour on thirty or twenty. If graduated prices are not given at the start, later, when they have only sold twenty or twenty-five they may try to pressure the reception operator to honor the price quote that was given them based on forty, and may, in fact, become angry when they are then quoted a higher per person price based on only twenty in the group at that late date.

As many tour managers and complimentaries as needed must be priced in. If, for example, one complimentary is allowed by the hotels and it is used for the tour manager, the agency will need to cost-in another complimentary for the incoming group leader or maybe two, depending on the producer's request. Since the group size probably will not warrant a hotel's granting that many complimentaries, the extra complimentaries will have to be prorated over the clients booked, so that each client actually absorbs part of each additional complimentary required.

Do not try to bid too low. Many larger operators can easily underbid a smaller concern; many of them do so, hoping to make their profit by selling the tour members optional trips after the group arrives. Instead, one can offer a quality tour with many private functions on which a financial value cannot be placed, functions such as private receptions, home hospitality, meetings with key leaders, access to private clubs or businesses. Do be prepared, however, for the producer's trying to negotiate to bring the price down; it is best to have a small extra margin in there that can be given away if necessary. The first offer should state that the prices are estimates only, that final and firm prices will follow after the agency has been given the go-ahead to book and after the final price confirmations have come in from the hotels, from the motorcoach company, and so forth.

BOOKING

Once the agency has been given the go-ahead to book and, has collected a nominal good-faith deposit from the producer, the next job is to secure all necessary reservations—the hotels, the motorcoach, and perhaps to start looking for a bilingual tour manager. The finishing touches (such as meal reservations, social events, and so forth), may be added later, when it is certain that the group is really materializing. However, these items should be costed in now, and adequately so, even if each and every menu is not actually booked at this stage.

MOTORCOACHES

One of the most important decisions to be made is the selection of the motorcoach company with which the agency will deal. Good or bad motorcoach services can make or break a tour. Everything can go well on a trip, but a coach that breaks down, a public address system that does not work, an air-conditioning unit that fails, or a rude, disagreeable driver can ruin an entire day. Therefore, when it comes to motorcoaches, it pays to get the best, not necessarily the least expensive. Here are some important things to remember when leasing motorcoaches.

- Be sure that the company selected has all the necessary licenses, both intrastate and interstate, if the group will be traveling over state lines. Also be sure that it carries adequate insurance and that it has permission to pick up and drop at any airports that the group will be using.
- Specify the equipment desired—air conditioning, lavatory, public address system.
- Give the coach company exact details on where the group is going, number of hours the coach will be needed each day, and so forth, so that they can calculate time/mileage charges. The tour manager must be told later how the coach is priced so that he or she does not run up extra time and mileage charges while on tour and authorize sending the bill to the agency after the fact.
- Verify the number of seats available for sale. One seat should be set aside for the tour manager, one for the incoming group leader, and perhaps additional ones as needed for local city guides or hosts if these will be used. The producer should be told from the outset the maximum number of seats that he or she may sell to avoid an oversell situation. An agency may not want to sell the back-row seats, or those over the rear wheels. And if a coach with a lavatory is ordered, the two seats across from the lavatory may be better left vacant. In the United States, most Greyhound coaches are forty-three seaters. Trailways has some larger forty-six seaters. A

problem may be encountered when the group size is small, say fifteen to twenty. Not many small coaches are available, particularly for interstate use, and when using a van or minibus there are problems with luggage storage space and with driving long distances, particularly over mountains.

Also be sure the producer understands that if one coach is oversold and a second one must be operated, it may be more expensive. A group of eighty (two forty-three-seat coaches with forty passengers each) is economical; a group of fifty (two forty-three-seat coaches with twenty-five passengers and eighteen empty seats each) is not.

- Verify the coach company's equipment points (places where they service their equipment or have other coaches available). Obviously, a company with many equipment points around the state or the country and the ability to get a replacement coach immediately in case the original one breaks down is of prime importance.
- Verify if the coach company is charging deadhead charges, that is, charges for driving the coach back to home base empty. If so, the itinerary might be redesigned, or one might wish to look for a company that is large enough not to charge deadhead mileage or dropoff charges.
- Verify availability of the coach and put in a formal reservation order. Do not wait, because many coach companies book up their equipment, particularly during peak periods. If not reserved in advance one might have to locate a coach through another company, perhaps at a higher rate, wiping out a substantial part of the agency's profit just to keep faith with the overseas customer.

HOTELS

An agency planning to handle incoming tours will have to become familiar with hotels in the immediate area and across the country. At first, this seems like a formidable undertaking, since there are so many. Perhaps the best way to start is to make a hotel inspection in one's own city, trying to locate two or three properties in a moderate price category and another two or three in a more deluxe category. Remember, one cannot always count on first choice being available, so it is best to have several and to build a rapport with the sales managers of these properties.

In selecting properties, the same criteria would apply as in selecting properties for outgoing tours (see chapter 4), such as bus loading zone, dining room, meeting rooms, ambience, and efficient group handling.

But, in addition to these criteria, some other criteria may prove particularly important in dealing with foreign groups:

- Will the group feel comfortable in the atmosphere of the hotel?
- Do front-desk personnel speak foreign languages? In short, is the hotel geared to the foreign market?
- Is there a concierge to help foreigners who do not speak English or know the city?
- Is there a money exchange facility at the hotel (or nearby)?

If the itinerary is a full one, with most free time taken care of, the above factors may not be so important. But if tour participants have free time on their hands and must make independent arrangements for dinner reservations, shopping, and optional sightseeing activities, it can be extremely important. If there are no such services in the hotel, the agency may end up having to run a hospitality desk or having the tour manager on call around the clock to assist members who do not speak English.

SIGHTSEEING

While the group is trekking along through the countryside, enroute sightseeing and commentary probably can be handled by the tour manager, assuming that this individual has been well selected and has done some homework before departure, reading up on areas to be visited.

However, no matter how educated and well read this tour manager may be, the agency cannot expect such a person to know the history, facts, and figures of each and every city on the itinerary. Therefore, a more formal type of sightseeing may be arranged in some of the major cities—either by prehiring a local guide to give the sightseeing tour aboard the group's coach, or by letting the coach rest for a day here and there and hiring a local sightseeing company to tour the group, complete with its own coach and driver/guide. For example: Greyhound is a coach company only; its drivers are not guides. Gray Line, on the other hand, is basically a sightseeing company. Its drivers are also guides and will give a tour as they drive. However, many are not bilingual, in which case they give the tour in English and the bilingual tour manager translates—a lengthy and not totally satisfactory solution. It is preferable to contract for the tour to be given directly in the language of the visiting group and to work with a sightseeing company that can provide this service. In pricing the tour, check to determine if entrance fees to museums, public buildings, and other places listed on the itinerary are included. And what about the guide's tip? It will be necessary to cost these miscellaneous items in to assure a quality tour.

AIR

Arrival and departure flights will be handled by the producer, not by the reception operator. But domestic flights *within* the itinerary as part of the tour, are not so clear. If coming from overseas, it may be best for the passengers to purchase these domestic flights overseas in conjunction with their international ticket. In other cases, it may be more financially advantageous to the passenger for the reception operator to do it and include the United States domestic flight segments in the land tour package.

Perhaps the best solution at the outset is to take the initiative and book the group flights within the itinerary that seem best for scheduling purposes. One can then advise the producer of the flight schedule and price of the domestic air portion and offer to release the group flight space to the producer for ticketing at time of tour finalization.

TRANSFERS

The agency will have to book transfer service to and from airports in conjunction with the tour, assuming that the group is arriving and departing as a unit. If involved with a group in which participants are arriving individually, it probably is best to have the tour start officially at the hotel the first night with a hospitality desk check-in. In costing transfers, compare the prices of sightseeing companies versus motorcoach companies. It is not unusual to find that sightseeing companies, which charge a flat transfer fee, may be less expensive in some cases than a motorcoach charter, which often requires a five-hour minimum.

## The Wait

Once the agency has quoted a price to the producer and has been given booking go-ahead, it will reserve all space, get final confirmations and price quotes, and then get back to the producer to advise of hotel confirmations and final prices (which should not differ too much from the original quote once the agency staff becomes adept at pricing).

During the next six months, the file probably will be dormant while the producer is busily promoting and selling the tour. This can be one of the most frustrating periods for the reception operator, as the success of the project rests totally in the hands of this producer; there is nothing one can do to help. When dealing with outgoing tour business, during this period the agency would be promoting and selling and would have a feel as to how the tour is progressing and would know what the outlook is for success. But when the situation is reversed, one is excluded during this important period. Nevertheless, during this waiting period, the agency should require periodic progress reports and should telex requesting them if the producer does not take the initiative and send them on.

At sixty days before the group's arrival, it is time to begin to cut back some of the space if it appears that it will not all be used. It is important to play fair and square with the hotels and other suppliers, if the agency is to build credibility with them. The producer should be reminded that at thirty days before arrival final rooming lists and final payment are expected. This gives one time to turn around and send rooming lists, payments, and final instructions to the hotels, motorcoach companies and other various suppliers involved.

## Finalizing the Tour

At thirty days before arrival, it is time to finalize with the various hotels, motorcoach companies, sightseeing companies, the tour manager, guides, and others servicing this tour. At this point the agency cancels any unsold space, formally commits to the tour manager, and goes into high gear in the finalization process just as on an outgoing tour. It is at this time that rooming lists and payments to hotels should be sent out, finishing touches put on social events, and menus for group meal functions selected. At this time one should mentally walk through the tour day by day, hour by hour to be sure that nothing has escaped attention.

The staff will also be busily preparing information packets to be distributed to the group as they arrive—their day-by-day itinerary (translated into the native language of the arriving group), perhaps a map showing the route that they will be following, dining suggestions for meals on their own, and other goodies that may be helpful. Perhaps it will even be necessary to provide name tags or baggage tags if the producer is not doing so; double check to verify.

As arrival time draws near, the tour manager should be brought in for briefing. All documents and background information must be turned over to him or her for reading and clarification. And travelers checks and other funds must be prepared.

Once the group arrives, the tour should be operated on a day-by-day basis in the field by the tour manager. If one has selected a good manager, most problems can be solved as the tour moves along without frequent call-ins to the office. However, no matter how qualified the tour manager may be, there will be times when quick assistance is required from the office—if a tour member is ill, if someone's flight schedule must be changed, if the group's return flights must be reconfirmed, and so forth.

While the group is in town it might be helpful to the future business relationship to make a special effort to spend an evening with the group personally or to invite the incoming leader to dinner. It may even be prudent to accompany the group personally for a day or two or to invite the entire group for an evening of home hospitality. This is strictly a management decision to be made on the basis of the importance of the account. When accompanying such a group for however a short a period of time, it is important *not* to erode the leadership position of the tour manager; he or she must remain at the helm throughout.

## Frustrations and Problems

Although incoming tourism can be one of the most satisfying and profitable segments of the travel industry, it can also be extremely frustrating at times, with more than its share of problems and areas of misunderstanding. Let us look at a few of these:

- *Travel agents or tour operators overseas who do not operate as professionally as one would like,* not sending in booking reports, rooming lists, or payments when due, requiring constant follow-up and sometimes requiring harsh treatment to get the job done when it is supposed to be done.

- *Difficulties in obtaining visas* to come to the United States. Many times, foreigners wishing to visit us encounter lengthy delays when applying for tourist visas or are made to feel like immigrants rather than welcome guests when they approach our embassies overseas.

- *Misunderstanding on the part of the tour members and the incoming leader* as to what services are to be provided and how the itinerary is to be followed. One's commitment to the producer may have been perfectly clear, but perhaps it was not conveyed properly by that agent to the incoming leader or to tour participants. For this reason, it is wise to hand out a detailed itinerary and list of included services in the tour member's arrival packet.

- *An underdeveloped incoming tourism industry* in the United States. Hotels without staff with foreign language ability. Hotels with no money exchange. Assumption in most public places that everyone speaks English. Encounters with some unsophisticated Americans who may not know a foreign group's country, history, customs, or sensitivities and who may, perhaps inadvertently, cause hurt feelings or tensions.
- *Incoming tourists who do not wish to follow the program,* preferring to strike out on their own to shop, cherchez la femme, and so forth—some without the courtesy to advise the tour manager that they will not be attending certain functions.
- *Participants who are not always easy to get along with,* perhaps continually late, not thoughtful of their fellow tour participants or of those hosting them, perhaps critical of the United States and its way of life.
- *Dependence on the economic and political climate.* The fluctuations of foreign currency versus the United States dollar, inflation, and international disputes can have an undue influence on incoming tour business—something over which an one has absolutely no control. A Falklands crisis, the invasion of Afghanistan, or a Middle East incident can totally undo plans for an expected group on which much time and money have been spent.
- *Last-minute group bookings.* Overseas agents who sell a group first, then telex for help in booking it at the last minute—a nightmare! Of course, they want Yosemite Park in midsummer, Hawaii at Christmas, Las Vegas over Thanksgiving weekend or some other equally impossible request.
- *Agents who want partial services only.* They want a reception operator to provide the technical program or social events or other services in which it specializes (and on which it makes no money), but they want to book their own hotels and tour services directly. Learn to say no!

But, all in all, the positive outweighs the negative. Developing an incoming tours segment of the business can be a satisfying and positive addition to the agency's mix if approached in a professional way with knowledgeable staff, a promotional plan, nominal startup monies, adequate cash flow, and without pressure to produce a group or a profit immediately. One must not look at it as an immediate solution to a business downturn in other areas of the agency, since the first group will probably not come in for well over a year. One should look at incoming tourism as an exciting way to diversify a travel company's operation.

**Some Helpful Contacts**

International Tourism Exchange (ITB)
c/o U.S. Travel and Tourism Administration
Ross Markt. No. 10 600
Frankfurt/Main West Germany

International Tour Management Institute
P.O. Box 3636
San Francisco, CA 94119

Travel Industry Association of America
1899 L Street, N.W.
Washington, DC 20036

United States Travel and Tourism Administration
United States Department of Commerce
14th and Constitution N.W.
Washington, DC 20230

# 14

# And... for the Experienced Group Operator

Once the agency has had several years' experience in groups, it may be ready to handle some more difficult assignments, such as meetings, seminars, conventions, trade missions, and incentives. Also included in this category would be academic overseas study programs and special-interest travel such as opera tours, wine and gourmet trips, trekking, and the like.

Make no mistake, all of these are for the sophisticated group operator with a strong background—a background in group operations, costings, and promotion. They are for the operator with excellent knowledge of suppliers within the industry, with heavy in-the-field tour-operating and tour-managing experience. They definitely are not the kinds of tours with which to experiment as learning experiences or with which to break into the field of group travel.

A brief look at the idiosyncracies of some of these more sophisticated trips will make them more easily recognizable, and will help the group operator know when to attempt them and when they are out of the agency's league.

## Meetings, Seminars, and Conventions

An area drawing a great deal of interest and being attempted by a number of newer, smaller agencies is the area of meetings, seminars, and conventions. For many agencies, this is an offshoot or logical development of their regular commercial business.

Unfortunately, a number of agencies simply assume that volume business automatically means volume profits, and many new agents become terribly excited at the prospect of handling such big business. The truth of the matter is that unless the potential exists for packaging the trip (and thus costing-in a markup), the venture may not prove to be as profitable as hoped, regardless of the numbers of clients traveling.

If the meeting is at a destination within driving distance, and if the organization basically wants nothing more than hotel or resort accommodations for a couple of nights, some meeting room space, and a meal function or two, it is somewhat difficult to package it and make any real money other than commissions. If, however, the agency can include air, sightseeing, and transfers in the basic package and may also package an optional post-meeting tour (or perhaps sell a group cruise), it may become a viable project.

Many agencies prefer not to handle such meetings here at home, but do become involved when the meeting is offshore. For example, a meeting in Honolulu can be packaged quite successfully with a basic program of roundtrip air transportation, convention hotel, lei greeting, arrival transfer, hospitality desk, meeting room space, and a social event or two such as a luau. If the meeting is no more than three to four days, usually many of the group will extend their trip to include one or two additional islands as short post-convention tours. A number of operators are successful also in packaging their own trips even farther afield as to Japan or Tahiti, for example, as extensions. Quite frequently the bulk of the profit is to be made from the post-convention trips, with only minimal earnings realized on the basic package.

Large conventions are best left to the specialty handlers in this field. Such large events have requirements all their own that the small to average size retail agency may not be prepared to meet. These requirements include the following.

- Computer programming capability of inventory control that can automatically pull up rooming lists for each hotel, flight manifests for the many different flights from various gateways, membership lists for each optional post-convention tour, and so forth. Computerized invoicing and computerized documentation are also musts.

- Financial ability to make sizable deposits or handle other up-front expenditures if necessary.

- Necessity to reorganize the office and staff around the project—perhaps hiring and supervising a great many temporary employees to meet the crunch. The author has been involved in some conventions where it actually was necessary to lease additional office space, put in extra banks of telephones, and print separate stationery and document supplies.
- Necessity to spend time, money, and entertainment on the organization. This undoubtably would involve inviting their decision-makers on an inspection trip to the convention site to see the hotels, meet the local managers, and generally gain confidence in the selection of the convention site and the agency.

**Trade Missions**

The trade mission is group travel in a business format. This is the group from a given industry, company, or city making a trip abroad to ascertain the potential of the overseas market, to show off its product, or to meet with prospective overseas importers.

Samples of these would be a group of California vintners traveling to the Orient and hosting wine tastings for restaurateurs and hoteliers in Hong Kong, Taiwan, and Manila as part of an effort to induce them to feature California wines instead of European wines on their menus. Or a cooperative of cotton growers visiting China after United States-China relations were first normalized to investigate the possibilities for selling United States cotton to Peking. Or a city to city or sister city type of visit by a government delegation. It could be a city's port authority directors visiting with comparable port authority officials in their respective countries—the purpose being to induce more shippers to use its port facilities.

The trade mission takes many forms, but all are dominated by a common thread—*the basic purpose of the trip is to engender business,* be it short-range purchase of a product or service or long-range development of an elaborate scheme for business cooperation. Some of the characteristics of this type of travel might be:

- Shorter lead time than the normal vacation tour, often responding to a sudden economic or political need.
- Usually a short, snappy trip with a purpose—bearing in mind that those participating often are business or political leaders who cannot justify being away for long periods.
- The financial tab for the trip rarely being paid by the individual participant. Usually it is picked up by his or her company or a

government entity; or perhaps it may even be an invitational trip by a sponsoring organization here at home or by an overseas entity.
- The travel agent is often subject to pressure from certain participants—participants who may think that because of their status in the community they can get it wholesale or can persuade certain airlines or other segments of the travel industry to donate their services.
- Spouses frequently do not participate in the trip; if they do, they do so at their own expense.

Since this is essentially business travel—although business travel on its highest plane—it must be approached from the standpoint of business and not vacation travel. Handling a project of this nature requires *strong control* on the agency's part, a willingness to spend a great deal of extra time involved in the project (often outside the office attending frequent directors' committee meetings), and a tremendous amount of tact and graciousness, since one often is dealing with community and business leaders who have a strong sense of their own importance. The attitude that usually works best with this type of project is one of extreme professionalism, presenting oneself as a professional peer, business person, and adviser to the project—not as a clerk who simply takes instructions on providing air and hotel reservations.

A typical package to present for such a trip (after a preliminary consultation to determine the needs) might include the following:

- *Round-trip airfare* (wherever possible, a group fare to ensure the participants staying together as a group and not each one doing his or her own thing, thus deteriorating into a group of thirty FITs).
- *Hotel accommodations throughout.* Note that many business groups require all single-room accommodations rather than share-twin arrangements.
- *Quick early breakfast* at the hotel each morning.
- A *tour manager* to handle all business details of the trip as it moves along, thus leaving the group director and members free to conduct their own business and not be bothered with behind-the-scenes tour problems.
- *Round-trip transfers, baggage handling, and tipping* in and out of all overseas airports and hotels.
- *Printing of a roster* of participants with photos and biographical sketches of those on the trip. This can be designed as an insert

for a wrap-around cover that serves as the brochure and carries the IT number, responsibility clause, and other requirements to qualify the tour as a bona fide tour with an IT number.
- *A kickoff meeting and meal function* overseas—the first chance for the group to be together, make introductions, review the operational plan for the rest of the trip, and ask questions.
- *Perhaps meeting room space,* product display rooms, or other public room space.
- *Perhaps motorcoach charters* for days of field inspections, moving the group around from one point to the next for rapid business meetings.
- *Perhaps an interpreter* to accompany the group to various business and related social events.
- *Perhaps air freight charges* if the group plans to ship samples and demonstration items, projectors, and films—more than will fit into the standard two suitcases per person limit.
- *Perhaps certain other meals or social meal functions,* often banquets or cocktail receptions hosting overseas guests. (If the group is visiting several cities on the itinerary, this function might be repeated in each city with a new set of overseas guests at each party.)
- *Occasional sightseeing,* primarily on weekends, as incidental features or to augment the basic business nature of the tour—never preempting the business format.

Note that just as on a pleasure vacation tour, the product should be presented as a *whole package,* with a flat all-inclusive per-person rate (based on a certain stated minimum number in the group, on which the package has been priced). It is not presented in breakdown fashion—so much for air, so much for hotels, and so forth. The agency will be working with net rates and adding its markup, just as is done with pleasure tours.

It is important to have a clearly written statement of specifically what is included in the package and, conversely, what is not included so that there is no misunderstanding. It often is a lifesaver to cost-in a small contingency (say $50)—an extra amount to cover those things that the organizers somehow forgot to mention—the extra guest(s) for dinner, the extra tips that you will have to pay to secure the real service these people have grown to expect, the storage charge for displays sent on ahead.

It is also important to mention the number of daily hours for which motorcoach charters are contracted. Groups of this nature have a way of extending on-site inspection days well beyond the allotted coach time. This is particularly true if they are working with overseas laymen hosts who may map out their day's activities with no real understanding of just how much can be squeezed into a day when moving a group, often resulting in long and arduous days running well into the night.

In addition to the statement of what is and is not included in the trip, it is important to have a clearly worded *conditions statement* covering such things as final payment date, last date to make any changes in individual travel plans, and financial penalties for cancellations, changes, or breaking away from the group.

Although vacation tour travelers have grown accustomed to the need to adhere to certain group restrictions, the independent business traveler is accustomed to changing travel plans frequently as business needs dictate. Those in the travel industry who work with commercial accounts are well aware of business travelers who may change their travel arrangements, request refunds, and rebook almost daily. Many of these same business travelers, on joining a group project, are surprised to learn that they may be penalized if they make changes or cancel. The author has worked on projects of this nature where participants have notified her virtually on the eve of departure that they are not going and are sending a substitute from their firm. They seem genuinely amazed when it is pointed out to them that their visa and their APEX air tickets are not transferrable!

## Overseas Study Programs

Arranging study tours, overseas campuses, or other such educational travel projects is an exciting venture into a new arena—an arena into which most travel agents have not stepped—that of academia.

Perhaps they are convinced that there is no money to be made in this arena, under the illusion that all students are nineteen years of age and travel with a backpack or that all professors are shopping for the cheapest deal in air fares and Eurail passes and nothing more.

Fortunately for those who have entered this field, these perceptions are not necessarily true, Although overseas study tours or in-residence campus programs are not carriage trade oriented, many of them do attract a moderate-income participant. This is usually the participant who is looking for a trip or overseas living experience with educational overtones. Often it is the client who is well read and somewhat traveled, now looking for a new experience. Many want to stay in one city or country for a while and experience it in depth rather than join another three-week whirlwind rat race. Many are interested in one particular field, be it art or theatre or learning a foreign language.

Some are teachers or educators themselves, anxious to increase their knowledge, to give themselves a new reservoir of material with which to return home and face the new academic year or to earn salary increments. Still others may simply be those adults wishing to expand their travel and intellectual horizons but not quite knowing how to go about it on an independent basis.

The possibilities in this field are endless. For example:

- *The small, privately escorted tour,* revolving around one key academic person, often a professor or noted expert, selling to his or her own following.

- *A complete series of tours for a local college or university,* officially sponsored by the college. These tours are often to a variety of destinations and draw on instructors from a variety of academic disciplines. Usually the success of such a program requires a fairly sizable off-campus promotional campaign to attract sufficient numbers. Typically, such a program will fall under the jurisdiction of the college's summer session or continuing education division and will be announced in the appropriate catalogue of courses, with the bulk of the participants coming from throughout the country, not necessarily from a local market, much less from a local professor's following.

- *The overseas campus.* Just as in the example above, this, too, may be under the auspices of one academic institution in the United States but will draw its clientele from across the country. But, rather than being a moving tour, it will feature an in-residence program in one place overseas—perhaps actually on campus, utilizing off-season dormitory space or a private home residence program.

Some programs may be for the summer months only. Others may be for a full semester or even the full academic year. Most carry academic credit through the sponsoring educational institution in the United States. Such programs usually involve weekly classes while overseas, with weekend field trips and then optional post-session tours.

Attempting to work in this market requires a strong understanding of the world of academia and that one feel comfortable discussing undergraduate versus graduate units, salaries of full professors versus associate professors, and the whys and wherefores of out-of-state tuition fees, transferral of academic credits, or ADA (average daily attendance) funds. It is helpful to have an understanding of academic institutions' financial needs to provide programs that generate revenue for them. It is also helpful to understand how such a successful travel and study program can enhance the reputation of an academic institution and excite faculty wishing to be affiliated with it.

In this type of program, as in the trade mission, the agency will become the true business adviser to the project. Business people, who make up the bulk of trade mission programs, are aware of the needs for a business-like arrangement, for promotion, and for upfront financial expenditures. But academia often is blissfully unaware of many of the business and financial facts of life behind a successful travel-study program. They may assume that all they have to do is announce the project in their college catalogue and it will sell itself. They may be genuinely amazed to learn that a promotional campaign is necessary, that the agency has to supply upfront monies on their behalf for ads and brochures, and is in fact investing in a risk venture on their behalf. In fact, some may even be offended if the agency asks that they share in this financial risk.

Typically, handling such a project means individual client counseling (usually by phone and correspondence) with each of the participants. Although the college sponsors the project, at least from an academic point of view, its personnel do not have the time or knowledge to counsel or sell prospective passengers. And although the agency will want to refer specific academic questions to the college, all other client handling will fall to the agency, including individual billings, information bulletins, and liason with the college to mail out preregistration materials, reading lists, and other academic materials. Therefore, strong and detailed backup personnel in the office will be needed, since one is not dealing with one entity, one client (the college), but rather with many.

## Incentives

The incentive trip is totally different from the previously discussed groups. Here there is one client only—the corporation buying the agency's services. Although ultimately there may be several hundred travelers in the group, still the overhead corporation is the only client. It makes the decisions. It pays the bill.

An incentive trip is given by a corporation to its top producers as recognition for a job well done. Here is the insurance company sending its hundred top salespeople on a seven-day cruise. Here is the automobile manufacturer inviting the fifty top dealers and their spouses to Hawaii. It is called an incentive trip because the trip is the carrot dangled in front of the salesperson (and often the spouse) all year long as the *incentive* to do a better job. This better job may be to sell more units, to increase overall production figures a certain percentage over the preceding year, or to reach a certain monetary sales volume. In other words, the terms of the contest may vary but the contest always exists.

For years, large corporations sponsored such incentive trips for their sales force, and these trips usually were handled by the giant incentive houses such as The E.F. MacDonald Company, Maritz, S & H Motivation and Travel and others. In fact, incentive travel was only a small percentage of the total incentive picture; by far the biggest portion was in merchandise—stereos, televisions, cars, and furniture.

But travel is becoming more and more the preferred carrot to the salesperson. Qualifying for the trip brings recognition among one's peers, labeling the winner as successful. Travel is a benefit that endures for life; it is not like the car that is surpassed by a newer model next year or the household gadget that has broken down by the time next year's sales contest rolls around.

Travel is seen more and more as a motivating force; also, it is no longer associated with just the larger corporations. Many small corporations now consider travel as its annual sales motivation tool and are open to proposals for interesting and innovative trips. Moreover, many travel agencies, once they have had a thorough grounding in other types of group travel, are venturing into these waters.

If one is attempting to attract incentive travel business, it is good to remember that one will not only assume the role of business consultant and travel agent to the project, but that of marketing expert par excellence. The agency's job is not just to put together an exciting, attractive travel package within the client corporation's budget and ultimately to operate it successfully in the field. The prime job is to act as marketing and motivational leader throughout the entire campaign. If the salespeople are not inspired to get out there and sell more insurance or more cars or more whatever (thus earning their corporation the necessary additional profits out of which to pay the tab for the trip), the trip does not stand on its own financially. The corporation has bought the idea only because it is convinced that the revenues from the additional sales or productivity within the corporation will more than cover the cost of the prize(s)—that is, the trip.

This kind of business is just right for the travel counselor with a high sense of theatre, innovative thinking, and creativity. To keep salespeople selling insurance over a year's time, through thick and thin, ups and downs takes some doing. They need to be revved up, patted on the head, coerced, seduced, and convinced that they can make it—that success lies just around the corner, that this trip is something that they (and their spouses) really want in the worst way and cannot buy elsewhere.

It will mean preparing endless promotional mail pieces, perhaps showing films or even doing a song-and-dance act. The author has sent chopsticks (with instructions on how to use them) to groups striving for Hong Kong. Talk with anyone in the incentive field; they will tell stories of mailing out giant fortune cookies with custom-written messages inside, of sending singing telegrams, or of mailing hundreds of postcards postmarked from the overseas city of the incentive destination. A fertile imagination and many extra hours of involvement are musts for the success of an incentive project.

**Special-interest Tours**

Perhaps, in a sense, all the kinds of travel projects mentioned in this chapter may be seen as *special interest* in that none of them is your straight "If It's Tuesday, this Must Be Belgium" tour.

Yet, to the trade, *special interest* has come to mean those tours that truly revolve around a very special interest and are marketed to those with that interest. In this category would fall wine and gourmet tours, agricultural tours, opera and theatre trips, and certainly adventure travel. The last has almost become a case of the tail wagging the dog, and most catalogues of special-interest tours today are dominated by treks in Nepal, white-river rafting in the western United States, and backpacking in Peru.

There seem to be four strong characteristics of special-interest trips and the companies and people who operate them. *First* would be that the trip revolves totally around the interest, whatever it may be. The special interest is strong, almost all-consuming, and transportation, accommodations, and other tour services wrap themselves around this paramount interest. Rarely is it the other way around, wherein occasional special-interest activities are merely dropped into a regulation tour. In fact, that is often a sign of a phony special interest tour.

*Second,* most special-interest tour companies are the outgrowth of the efforts of one or two key individuals, often idealists with a great love for a certain sport or activity—individuals who want others to share in the experience. Often they have learned the travel business merely as a means of bringing their particular interest or philosophy or passion to others, be it skindiving, love for the opera, or fine cuisine.

Perhaps the founder of a west coast tour company specializing in opera tours had no intention of going into travel, but as a lecturer on Wagner, he found that forming groups of opera buffs and taking them to European opera festivals was a natural outgrowth of the teaching process. Similarly, the founder of one of the early skindiving specialty tour companies found a way to combine his great love for Tahiti and diving with a background as a retail travel agent. Another individual started organizing South Pacific tours that stay in villages and live with the local people—an idealistic and personal experience in which he once had participated and wanted to make available to that limited segment of the travel public that would appreciate the close human contact involved in such a travel program. These three typify those who are behind many of the special interest travel companies which have come to the fore.

*Third,* the key person in most of these companies is an expert in the special interest, able to answer the client's most sophisticated questions about types of ski boots or diving equipment and able to train staff to do likewise, thus not having to depend on outside experts for the answers.

*Fourth,* many of these companies have elected to sell directly to the public as well as through travel agencies rather than relying solely on retail travel agencies for their success. They find that a great many retail travel agencies do not handle individual client sales well on special-interest trips, since the agency sales staff may not have the necessary background in hiking, Wagner, French wine vintages, or whatever the tour specialty may be.

Because of this, if there is someone on staff who is truly an expert in a given field one may very well want to attempt using that person's expertise and putting together a special-interest tour. If not, it is best to book through an operator who is familiar with the particular field in question.

One word of caution—since these special-interest tours revolve around the interest, it is of prime importance to be able to provide what one promises. Just because an agent is an opera buff and has gone to Bayreuth every year, if he or she does not know the ropes for securing seats to the festival there and cannot truly come through with the tickets, it is best not to attempt it in the first place! Many a knowledgeable, well-meaning operator has virtually been ruined by not being able to provide the Super Bowl tickets or seats to La Scala or grandstand positions for the Carnival in Rio parade that his or her brochure offered.

## The Future?

It is obvious that the market is rife with possibilities and exciting kinds of travel projects. We have seen incentives and special-interest programs, nostalgia cruises promising Big Band dancing to music of the '40s, and overseas professional meetings with a flair. Group projects have been developed to attend foreign cooking schools, to learn to sail in Caribbean waters, or to ride horseback and cook out in the backwoods.

What will be next no one really knows. But an imaginative and innovative person with a good solid group tour background may have the ideas that will be the next contribution to this constantly-changing travel industry. The industry will welcome these ideas.

# Glossary

**accordion fold**  A method of folding paper so that it opens like the pleats in an accordion. May be used for a tour brochure or a direct mail letter if the printer has the neccesary equipment.

**account executive**  Person responsible for the management of a client's account. Often used today in place of "sales representative."

**acquisition cost**  The cost of acquiring something. For example, the cost of acquiring an inquiry regarding a tour might be the advertising cost divided by the number of inquiries the ad generated, resulting in the advertising cost per inquiry.

**addon**  A supplementary charge, as for example the extra airfare charged from the home city to the published tour gateway city.

**adjoining rooms**  Rooms or cabins sharing a common wall, not necessarily connected by a common door. See also **connecting rooms.**

**affinity group**  Membership organization, such as schools, businesses, trade associations, religious groups, clubs, and numerous other organized membership entitities, which may sponsor group travel programs.

**after-the-fact monies**  Promotional monies received by a tour operator from a supplier only if a tour project has materialized.

**air/sea**  Travel programs or itineraries using some combination of both air and sea transportation. In cruises refers to flying the passengers to/from the ship, which is stationed elsewhere.

**à la carte**  Each food item on a menu is prepared, priced, and ordered separately. As opposed to limited choice, a fixed menu, or table d'hote. Usually an indication of a higher priced, deluxe tour.

**allotment**  In tourism, a certain number of rooms, cruise cabins, airplane seats, etcetera, which the tour operator may retain for free sale until a specified date, at which time the operator must submit a manifest of names and release unsold space. Does not imply responsibility to sell the entire allotment. See also **block; bulk buying.**

**amenity package**  A cluster of special features, for example, complimentary shore excursions, bar or boutique credit, or wine at dinner offered to clients on a given tour or cruise, usually as a bonus or extra feature. Usually used to induce clients to book through a particular travel agency or organization.

**American plan (AP)**  Hotel accommodations including three meals per day in the price of the room. Usually means breakfast in accordance with the custom of the country concerned, plus full lunch and dinner, which may be set menu or may be limited to a specific monetary value. The hotel may require meals to be taken in certain dining rooms or only at certain times. See also **full pension**.

**APEX (Advance Purchase Excursion airfare)**  Special promotional roundtrip airfare. It must be paid for and issued within a stated time before departure, and cannot be cancelled, changed, or reissued without penalty. Other restrictions often apply.

**ARC (Airlines Reporting Corporation)**  Membership organization made up of United States domestic airlines. An administrative body, appointing sales agents (travel agencies and others), making available the area settlement bank for airline ticket sales reporting/payments, and many other functions previously administered by the Air Traffic Conference (ATC), which was eliminated January 1, 1985. See **ATC**.

**arunk (arrival unknown)**  Often used in a passenger's airline itinerary to refer to a surface segment or noncontiguous sector for which no flight is provided.

**ASTA (American Society of Travel Agents)**  Trade association of United States travel agents and tour operators, which includes international and allied memberships for trade-associated industries.

**ATC (Air Traffic Conference)**  Formerly a division of the Air Transport Association responsible for setting standards and establishing agreements regulating activities of domestic airlines among themselves, with international carriers, and with the travel industry in general. Eliminated January 1, 1985. See **ARC**.

**back-to-back**  A series of tours or charter flights wherein one group leaves as the next one arrives. The group operator uses the carrier in both directions, thus avoiding deadhead expenses.

**ballpark figure**  A rough, advance financial estimate, not to be interpreted as final or as a commitment.

**blackout**  A period during which a certain fare, rate, or offer is not valid, as for example during the Christmas holidays or some other peak period.

**bleed**  A term signifying that the printed image or color extends beyond the final edge of the paper. More expensive than a "nonbleed" because paper must be over-sized and then trimmed down.

**block**  A number of rooms or seats reserved far in advance, usually by wholesalers or group tour operators, who intend to sell them as components of tour packages. See also allotment.

**blow-up**  A larger version of an illustration, particularly a photo.

**body copy**  Basic printed information in a tour brochure or ad, as opposed to the headlines, photos, or art.

**boldface**  A heavier, darker type, often used for headlines or paragraph subheads in a tour brochure or ad.

**breakage**  Expenses budgeted for in a tour but not used or expended, thus resulting in additional profit to the tour operator. For example, meals budgeted but not consumed, currency fluctuations in favor of the tour operator, or the tour selling much larger numbers of passengers than anticipated.

**brochure**  Printed promotional literature offered by a tourism business. Usually implies a printed, folded piece as opposed to a one-page flyer or poster.

**bulk buying**  Buying in quantity. Often implies assuming risk for selling an entire block of seats, rooms, etcetera.

**bulk fare**  Net fare contract for a specified number of seats. The tour operator contracting for these seats assumes the risk of selling them, as in a charter.

**bulk mail**  Third class mail, requiring a special bulk mail permit number, zipcode sorting, and a certain minimum number of pieces.

**CAB (Civil Aeronautics Board)**  The United States government regulatory body designated under the Federal Aviation Act to consider aviation matters affecting the public convenience and necessity, including supervision of routes, passenger and cargo fares, conditions of service, and schedules. Phased out January 1, 1985.

**cabin assignment**  Actual assignment of a client's specific cabin location on a cruise. Gives deck and actual room number. Normally assigned by the cruise line close-in to departure date as opposed to previous guarantee of space by category and price only.

**cabin category**  Cruise line's division of the various cabins on its ship into pricing categories, so that all cabins within a given category carry the same tariff. May vary by deck or aft/fore location, with tub or merely with shower.

**calendaring**  The act of carefully posting important dates on one's calendar so that no task related to the operation of a group travel program is overlooked.

**capacity-controlled**  Space on a given flight apportioned among different fare bases with a limited number of seats for sale in each fare category.

**caption**  Copy accompanying and explaining photos or illustrations.

**cash flow**  Monies available to meet the tour operator's daily operating expenses, as opposed to equity, accounts receivable, or other credits not immediately accessible.

**charter**  To hire by contract the entire capacity of an aircraft, motorcoach, cruise ship, or train.

**classified advertising**  Small print ads, listed by category, and usually without illustrations, as in the "classified" ad section of a newspaper or magazine. See also **display advertising.**

**CLIA (Cruise Lines International Association)**  An association of cruise lines seeking to promote cruises by offering promotional materials, training guides, and educational programs for travel agents. Also administers the functions previously administered by the Pacific Cruise Conference (PCC) and the International Passenger Ship Association (IPSA), such as appointments of new travel agencies.

**client load**  The number of clients one travel counselor can reasonably and effectively handle at a given time.

**clip art**  Pre-prepared art that can be used in preparing ads or tour brochures. May be purchased from an art service or sometimes obtained from a supplier, such as a cruise line or airline.

**clipping service**  A subscription service that keeps track of and clips samples of the client company's ads and editorial mentions in newspapers, magazines, and other publications. Often a function of a public relations firm.

**closeout**  Finalization of a tour, cruise, or other similar group travel project, after which time no further clients are accepted, any unsold air or hotel space is released, and final lists and payments are sent to all suppliers.

**coach**  (1) in railroads, a car for ordinary daytime short-haul travel; (2) in airplanes, the economy class section as opposed to first class or business class; (3) a motorcoach or deluxe bus.

**cold list**  A mailing list untried by a particular advertiser, as in a direct-mail list of names and addresses that a travel agency might purchase to solicit group tour or cruise clients.

**complimentary ("Comp")**  Free. A product or service (for example, a night's lodging, a drink, or a dinner) given without charge, in recognition of past patronage, a promise of future patronage, or to rectify some mistake. In group business, usually the free trip accrued with the airlines, hotels, and other suppliers as a result of producing a given number of passengers in the group, may be passed on to the tour organizer.

**concierge**  Employee in many major hotels, especially in Europe, often multilingual, who is in charge of personalized guest services such as dinner reservations, theater tickets, letter mailing.

**connecting rooms**  Rooms or cabins which share a common wall and connecting door. See also **adjoining rooms.**

**continental plan**  Hotel room that includes both the use of the room and a light breakfast consisting of a beverage, toast or rolls, and sometimes juice.

**convention**  (1) business or professional meeting, usually of large numbers of people. The term *congress* is a common term outside the United States; (2) an international agreement on a specific matter, especially the outcome of a meeting.

**co-op advertising**  Arrangement in which a supplier and a tour operator or travel agency share the cost of placing an ad.

**copy fitting**  Determining what copy will fit in a certain amount of space. When writing a tour brochure, writing the copy to fit the particular space and layout restrictions of a shell or original brochure.

**costing**  Process of itemizing and calculating all costs the tour operator will pay on a given tour. Usually the function of the operations manager. See also **pricing.**

**crop** The process of selecting the most interesting portion of a photo or illustration for impact and eliminating the rest.

**cruise** Voyage for pleasure rather than for transport, often departing from and returning to the same port.

**DBA (Doing Business As)** Used wherein the business name differs from the corporate name. For example: LSI Travel Agency, Inc. DBA Specialty Tours Abroad.

**deadhead** Aircraft or transportation vehicle operating without a payload of passengers or cargo. Usually done to reposition the vehicle.

**deck plan** Visual layout of each of the decks of a cruise ship indicating location of various public rooms as well as various cabin numbers and their layout.

**demi-pension** Half board. Hotel rate including bed, breakfast, and a choice of one other meal—lunch or dinner. Breakfast is in accordance with the custom of the country concerned (not necessarily full American breakfast). Lunch or dinner is usually on a set menu or table d'hote basis, not a la carte. The hotel may require that meals be taken in certain dining rooms or only at certain times.

**deregulation** The act of deregulating the travel industry, specifically the Airline Deregulation Act of 1978, amending the Federal Aviation Act of 1958. Provided for the end of the CAB's regulating authority over domestic airlines on January 1, 1985, for removing travel agency exclusivity, thus paving the way for carriers to appoint and pay commissions to nontravel agents, and for removal of antitrust immunity for travel agents.

**direct mail** A form of advertising that reaches the individual through the postal services, usually third class.

**display advertising** A form of advertising distinguished from classified advertising by the use of illustrations, white space, headlines, and other attention-getting devices.

**double** Sleeping room provided with a double bed. Sometimes erroneously used to mean any room accommodating two persons, as in a twin-bedded room. See also **twin.**

**double double** Hotel or motel room with two double beds. Found mostly in the United States.

**double occupancy** The rate per person if sharing a twin-bedded room. The usual published tour price.

**downline** All segments (legs) of an itinerary after the originating flight.

**draw** (1) a famous name or individual who will attract or draw clientele to the travel program with which he or she is associated; (2) an advance of funds to a commissioned sales person against later actual sales and commissions.

**dummy** The layout for a brochure or booklet. Also sometimes called a mockup.

**duotone** A photograph reproduced in two colors, usually black and one other color. An effective way to give additional depth or warmth to a photo in a tour brochure.

**errors and omissions insurance** Coverage should an agent's staff make an error causing a client great hardship or expense. Travel agent's equivalent of malpractice insurance. Referred to as E and O.

**ETA** Estimated time of arrival.

**ETD** Estimated time of departure.

**European plan (EP)** Hotel accommodations with no meals included in the price of the room.

**ex** Out of, departing from. As in ex SFO or from San Francisco.

**fam trip** Familiarization trip/tour. Trip or tour offered to travel writers and travel agency personnel by airlines, cruise lines, and other suppliers as a way of informing the customer and influencing segments of the industry.

**final documents** Final materials sent to a client after payment in full, enabling him or her to make the trip. May include air tickets, cruise tickets, rail tickets, tour vouchers, baggage tags, name badge, departure instruction bulletin, list of participants in the tour, and mailing lists to leave with friends and family.

**finish** The texture or feel of paper to be used for tour brochures or other printed promotional pieces.

**FIT (Foreign Independent Tour)** An international preplanned, pre-booked, and prepaid trip with the itinerary and components planned to the traveler's specifications. Custom-designed itinerary, as opposed to buying an existing travel package.

**fixed expenses** Expenses related to the tour as a whole, which do not vary with the number of passengers in the group. For example: promotional costs, tour manager's expenses, charters, and so forth. See also variable expenses.

**float** Amount of money represented by checks outstanding, in process of collection.

**flop** To print a photo so that it is the mirror image of the original. Particularly pertinent to using photos in tour brochures or ads so that the photo faces inward, directing the reader's eye to the brochure or ad rather than facing outward to the edge.

**flush** To set printed copy even with other copy, that is lined up vertically. Flush left means that the left edge of the copy is aligned, but the right edge (ragged right) may not be. A solid even box of copy would be flush left and right. Flush right means that the right edge of the copy is aligned.

**flyer** Printed advertising distributed to potential customers by hand or by mail. Usually fairly simple in format, as opposed to a brochure, which is more complex and detailed.

**force majeure** From the French, literally a stronger force. In the context of a tour operator's responsibility clause, referring to something beyond one's control as in an act of God.

**four-color process** A printing process that produces full color photos, art, and graphics. Allows the designer to make full use of all colors of the rainbow in the design and to use color transparencies instead of black and white photos. Most expensive brochure method; usually beyond the budget of the average small tour operator.

**full pension** Full board. Hotel rate including bed, breakfast, and two principal meals. Breakfast is in accordance with the custom of the country concerned (not necessarily full American breakfast). Lunch and dinner are usually on a set menu or table d'hote basis, not à la carte. The hotel may require that meals be taken in certain dining rooms or only at certain times.

**galley proof** Initial printer's proof, often in long column or "galley" form, as opposed to a "page proof," with type laid out as it will appear on the finished page with headlines and illustrations indicated.

**GIT (Group Inclusive Tour)** Prepaid tour allowing special airfares to a group and requiring that all members must travel on the same flights roundtrip, and must travel together on the same itinerary during their entire time abroad. The GIT airfare may not be sold apart from the prepaid land package, and is a restricted airfare with limitations on such things as the number of days, stopovers permitted, and minimum numbers of passengers in the group.

**glossy finish** A shiny finish, coated paper stock, as opposed to a matte finish.

**gross** Rate prior to deducting the commission. See also **net, net net.**

**group desk** Desk or department within an airline that handles group reservations. Not to be confused with the airline's tour desk.

**guide** Person licensed and employed to take tourists on local sightseeing excursions. Not to be confused with the tour manager, escort, leader, or director.

**halftone** Printer's term for a photo or illustration. Refers to a method of rephotographing the photo or illustration through a screen so it may be reproduced.

**Hotel and Travel Index** Quarterly publication listing over 30,000 hotels, resorts, motels, guest ranches, and lodges world- wide. Includes their addresses, telephone contact, and published rates. Published by Ziff-Davis Publishing Co., 1 Park Avenue, New York, NY 10016.

**IATA (International Air Transport Association)** World-wide trade association of international airlines. The IATA conference promotes a unified system of air transportation on international routes, sets fares and rates, safety standards, conditions of service, and appoints and regulates travel agents to sell international tickets. Due to be replaced by the Passenger Network Services Corporation sometime in 1985.

**incentive tour** Group travel program rewarding a client company's successful sales people with a bonus in the form of an expense-paid trip. Distinctive from other kinds of tours in that the entire bill is paid by the client company, not by the individual travelers. Such tours are usually short, to a single or limited destination, and may feature convention or learning activities such as classes, seminars, unveiling of a new product, awards, and so forth.

**incidentals**  Items understood to be excluded from most tours, cruises, or pre-packaged travel programs. Examples: cocktails, laundry, phone calls.

**independent contractor**  Person contractually retained by another to perform certain specific tasks. The other person has no control over the independent contractor other than as provided in the contract. In the context of group travel, a tour manager or tour brochure designer/writer might be retained in this capacity.

**in/out dates**  Refers to arrival/departure dates in a hotel/motel. To avoid error, used in lieu of the term *from date x to date x*.

**interline**  Used in conjunction with another word to describe anything involving two or more airlines, such as interline itinerary, interline reservation, interline stopovers. See also **online**.

**inventory control**  System enabling the tour operator to keep track of the inventory of hotel rooms, flight reservations, and other suppliers' products he/she is holding for resale.

**IT number (itinerary number)**  Code number identifying a published tour that has been submitted and approved by IATA and that allows travel agents to obtain the additional 3 percent commission for air transportation sold as part of such approved tours.

**ITX (Independent Tour Excursion airfare)**  Special promotional airfare available only in conjunction with a prepaid land package. Similar to the GIT fare, but available to passengers traveling independently.

**layout**  Final arrangements of matter to be reproduced by printing. A detailed plan, on paper, as a guide to a typesetter or printer, as for example a tour brochure or layout. Sometimes called a mock-up.

**lead time**  Advance time, length of time between initiating a tour and its departure date.

**leg**  Sector, segment of an itinerary.

**lowercase**  Small letters, as opposed to capital letters or uppercase. Signified by the initials l.c. when marking copy or reading printer's proofs.

**manifest**  Final official listing of all passengers and/or cargo aboard a transportation vehicle or vessel.

**M**  Thousand, as in 5M means five thousand.

**margin**  Spare amount, measure, degree allowed for contingencies or special situations.

**market segment**  A limited portion of the total consumer market.

**markup**  Difference between the cost and the selling price of a given product. Difference between the net rate charged by a tour operator, hotel, or other supplier and the retail selling price of the service. Generally a percentage of the net rate rather than a fixed amount, as in a 20 percent markup on the net.

**matte finish**  Rough or unglossy finish on a paper stock.

**meet and greet**  Prepurchased service for meeting and greeting a client upon arrival in a city, usually at the airport, pier or rail station, and assisting the client with entrance formalilties, collecting baggage, and obtaining transportation to his or her hotel or other destination. Often includes an arrival gift such as a lei. Often associated with arrival transfer service. Sometimes referred to as meet and assist.

**modified American plan (MAP)** Hotel accommodations including breakfast and either lunch or dinner in the price of the room. Usually means breakfast in accordance with the custom of the country concerned, plus one principal meal, either lunch or dinner, which may be set menu or limited to a specified monetary value. Originated in beach resorts in the western hemisphere where the clientele did not wish to dress for lunch. It may be required by the hotel that meals be taken in certain dining rooms or only at certain times to qualify for the MAP plan. See also **American plan, demi-pension.**

**montage** Combination of several pictures or parts of pictures into a single unit. May also be a blend of pictures plus art.

**motorcoach** Bus designed to carry passengers in comfort; often includes a bathroom, air conditioning, microphone, and wrap- around windows for maximum viewing.

**negotiate** To confer with another so as to arrive at the settlement of some matter. In a group travel context, usually refers to discussions between tour operator and suppliers to obtain most favorable rates and conditions.

**net** Rate after deducting the commission, but prior to adding applicable tax and service charge. See also **gross, net net.**

**net net** Gross less commission plus applicable tax and service charge. Actual out-of-pocket amount to be paid for a given service or product. See also **gross, net.**

**net rate** Confidential, wholesale rate that must be marked up by the travel agent for resale to the customer. See also **gross, net net.**

**networking** The act of using an interconnected or inter-related chain, group, or system. A method by which members of the travel profession become known among their peers for mutual self-help in referrals, locating new positions, locating worthy employees, making themselves visible and their talents known. Female version of the "Good Old Boys" club.

**news release** Typed story about a forthcoming tour or travel program, submitted to various newspapers and magazines with the hope of receiving free publicity. Also called a press release.

**no-name** Practice of holding a space on a given flight, tour, or hotel room without giving the supplier a client's name. Usually means asking the supplier to hold the additional space "on faith" for a short period of time to allow you to sell it and submit the passenger's name, since once the space is released, it may be difficult to obtain it again.

**OAG (Official Airline Guide)** Monthly publication of flight schedules. Two versions available in the United States: Worldwide Edition and the North American Edition. Annual subscriptions available from Official Airline Guides, Inc. 2000 Clearwater Drive, Oak Brook, IL 60521.

**OHRG (Official Hotel and Resort Guide)** Three-volume worldwide directory of hotels, resorts, and motor hotels, edited especially for travel agents and related industries. Listings in geo-alpha order provide a description of the property, location, facilities, basic tariffs, commissions paid, rating information, and reservation information. Published by Ziff-Davis Publishing Co. Ordered from OHRG, P.O. Box 5800, Cherry Hill, NJ 08034

**occupancy rate** In hotel/motel industry, the percentage of total number of available beds or rooms actually occupied. Derived by dividing the total number of rooms occupied during a given time period (night, week, year) by the total number of rooms available for occupancy during that same period, to arrive at the occupancy percentage.

**online (intraline)** Used in conjunction with another word to describe anything over one airline only, such as online connection, online stopover, or online itinerary. See also **interline.**

**operations** Performing the practical work of operating a tour or travel program. Usually involves the in-house control and handling of all phases of the tour, both with suppliers and with clients.

**operations manager** Individual in charge of performing the practical and detailed work of tour operations. See **operations.**

**option date** Date by which an extended offer will be withdrawn. For example, a tour space held on option for a client until a specified date may be released if the client has not paid a deposit by that date. Conversely, hotel space held on option for a tour operator may be released if the operator has not paid a deposit by the stated option date.

**originating airline** Airline carrying a passenger on the first portion of an itinerary. In group international travel, usually refers to the first international airline, also sometimes called the sponsoring or controlling airline of the particular tour group.

**override** Extra commission paid by suppliers such as airlines, cruise lines, and so forth to group tour operators as an incentive for group and volume business

**overtonnage** Phenomenon in the cruise industry in which there are too many ships in a given area or market. For example, overtonnage in the Caribbean in winter, or in Alaska in summer. Implies a competitive atmosphere.

**pacing** Fullness or emptiness, fastness or slowness of a tour itinerary. The scheduling of activities within an itinerary to make for a realistic operation and to give certain balance of travel time, sightseeing, social events, and free time and rest.

**package** (1)(Noun) Pre-arranged combination of elements such as air, hotel, sightseeing, and social events packaged together and sold as an all-inclusive package price, not sold by component parts; (2) (verb) to package, meaning to combine elements as above into an all-inclusive package product, sold as such at a package price.

**PATA (Pacific Area Travel Association)** Membership organization of government and private business that seeks to promote and monitor travel to and within the Pacific area. In addition to the overhead PATA, which accepts only organizations and government members, there also exist local chapters of PATA to which individuals may belong.

**pax**  Passengers

**per diem tour cost**  Cost of the whole tour divided by number of days to arrive at an average per day cost. Often the land/sea price (published price less air), divided by actual number of hotel nights to arrive at an average per night land cost. A method used within the travel industry to compare the cost of seemingly similar travel products.

**Pied Piper**  An individual with a following. Used in the travel industry to refer to a person who may recruit a group. See also **draw; tour organizer.**

**plate**  Originally a very thin layer of metal on a surface of base metal, nowadays usually plastic, as in a credit card. Distributed by airlines to travel agents appointed to represent them and then used by agents when issuing airline tickets on behalf of the participating airline concerned. In group tours it is customary to use the plate of the originating or controlling air carrier for the particular tour in question, even though a great many other airlines may be involved in the interline itinerary.

**pre/post convention tour**  Extension of a convention tour whereby, for an additional charge, extra days or destinations may be added to the beginning or end of a basic convention itinerary.

**press release**  See **news release**

**pricing**  Decision-making process of ascertaining what price to charge for a given tour once total costs are known. Involves determining the markup, studying the competition, and evaluating the tour value for the price to be charged. Usually a management function, See also **costing**

**promotional assistance**  In travel industry terms, usually financial assistance from a supplier to the travel agency/tour operator. Can be in many different forms: cooperative advertising, free brochure shells, sharing direct-mail costs, and so forth.

**promotional fare**  Fare, lower in cost than normal fares, that may carry restrictions, be valid only on certain days, times, or flights, and require a minimum stay abroad or at the destination. Designed to attract passengers who may not otherwise travel, so usually aimed at the non-business traveler.

**promotional evening**  Social event to promote enrollments in a group tour, cruise, or other similar travel program.

**proof**  Sample of an ad, tour brochure, or other printed material supplied to the client prior to publishing so that the client may check for errors.

**property**  Hotel, motel, resort, or other place of lodging.

**prorate**  To divide, distribute, or assess proportionally.

**rack rate**  Regular published rate of a hotel or other tourism service.

**rate desk**  Department of an airline that fares various itinerary routes and issues written fare quotations to tour operators/travel agencies.

**reception ground operator**  Person, firm, or corporation providing vehicles, guides, or local services to a tour operator or travel agent. Sometimes called a local operator, receiving agent, ground operator, reception agency, subcontractor, or land operator. May be a division of a full-service retail travel agency, or only a reception ground operator without air appointments or full-service travel agency capabilities.

**reconfirm** In travel, usually refers to an airline's requirements that the passenger call to the continuing airline of each flight segment and reconfirm his/her intention to travel as planned.

**release** (1) (Noun) Signed form giving the tour operator permission to use a person's name, picture, or statement in a tour advertisement; (2) (verb) to release space, as in returning unsold air reservations, cruise cabins, or hotel rooms to the supplier who originally allotted them.

**responsibility clause** Detailed statement of conditions applicable to the sale of a tour package; one of the printed sections of a tour brochure.

**retroactive** Made effective as of a prior date.

**reverse** A white on black print, as for example white type on a black background.

**review dates** Dates on which the supplier will ask to review the inventory of space a tour operator is holding and perhaps take back part or all of the space if it is not being sold sufficiently quickly.

**risk monies** Funds that an agency would not recoup should a tour not materialize. For example: nonrefundable deposits to suppliers, promotional expenditures, printing expenses.

**room assignments** Placement of individual members of a tour group in specific rooms in a given hotel, resort, or other property. Usually, but not always, done by hotel personnel.

**rooming list** List of names of passengers on a tour or other group travel program, submitted to a hotel, motel, or similar. Names are not alphabetized as on a flight manifest, but rather room by room indicating who is rooming with whom. Twin-bedded rooms, singles, and triples are usually listed in separate categories.

**RT** Roundtrip.

**run-of-the-house rate** Flat rate for which a hotel or motel agrees to offer any of its available rooms to a group. Final assignment of rooms is at the discretion of the hotel.

**sales representative** The employee of an airline, hotel, tour operator, cruise line, or other supplier who calls on travel agents or group operators. See also **account executive.**

**sector** One part of a trip, travel between any two points on a multi-destination itinerary; also called a segment or leg.

**segment** One part of a trip, travel between any two points on a multi-destination itinerary; also called a leg or sector.

**seminar** Educational or informational meeting. Used in the travel industry to signify a one-time learning situation wherein one learns about new travel products. Often sponsored by suppliers or industry associations for travel agents/tour operators.

**service charge** Amount of money automatically added to the bill in many hotels, restaurants, and night clubs in lieu of the "voluntary" gratuity or tip. Usually determined by a percentage of the bill rather than a set monetary amount. More frequent in Europe than in the United States.

**shell brochure**  Brochure containing graphics, illustrations, or photos but no copy.

**shore excursions**  Planned land or air tours available for purchase by cruise passengers at scheduled ports of call.

**short sector**  Flight or segment of a trip of short distance or sector. A portion of a longer, continuing flight or journey. Often a sector on which it may be difficult to obtain space since blocking the short duration inhibits the carrier's opportunity to sell the longer, full journey.

**single supplement**  Additional amount of money to be paid by a client for single occupancy of a hotel room, especially when participating in a tour that specifies double occupancy accommodations. Calculated by the tour operator by subtracting the share-room cost per person from the single cost—the differential being the single supplement. Sometimes called the single room supplement.

**soft sailing**  Cruise sailing or departure date on which bookings are low or on which it is anticipated they may be low due to projections based on these dates in the past. A sailing on which it should be possible, therefore, to secure best possible rates and concessions from the cruise line.

**spec**  Term describing the "specifying" of type faces and sizes for a specific printing project. Usually done by the artist or designer planning the brochure or ad rather than leaving it to the discretion of the typesetter.

**special interest tour**  Prearranged, packaged itinerary designed to appeal to or respond to requests by a group of persons with unique interests. Such tours may focus on horticulture, law, gourmet dining, backpacking, music, religious events, sports, or any other specific field.

**spread**  Selection, as in a spread of cabins on a cruise, meaning a selection of cabins in each of the major categories on the ship.

**stock**  Name, weight, and finish of the paper or cardboard to be used for a given printing job.

**supplier**  Airline, railroad, cruise line, motorcoach company, or other entity offering travel-related services and products as component parts making up a package tour.

**tour**  Any prearranged (usually prepaid) journey to one or more destinations and returning to the point of departure. Usually includes transportation, accommodations, meals, sightseeing, and other components.

**table d'hote**  Fixed price meal. A complete meal as described on the menu for a set price, as distinguished from à la carte listings in which each item is priced separately. Usually a feature of full pension or demi-pension meal plans.

**tariff**  (1) Fare or rate from a supplier; (2) class or type of fare or rate; (3) published list of fares or rates from a supplier; (4) official publication compiling fares or rates and conditions of services.

**tour consultant** Individual within a travel agency selling and advising clients regarding a tour. Sometimes a travel consultant or sales person with particular expertise in group tour sales.

**tour desk** (1) Desk, table, or counter space often located in the lobby area of a hotel and staffed by a hotel employee or representative of a local travel agency or tour operator for the purposes of answering questions, selling local sightseeing tours and excursions, and providing information on things to do. In the case of conventions or large group tours may be combined with the hospitality desk; (2) desk or department at an airline staffed by an airline employee who sells the airline's own official tours and packages directly to passengers or to passengers through retail travel agents. Not to be confused with the airline group desk, which books group air reservations.

**tour manager** Person employed as the escort for a group of tourists, usually for the duration of the entire tour, perhaps supplemented by local guides. The term tour director, leader, escort, conductor, and in Europe, courier, have the same meaning and are used interchangeably.

**tour operator** Company that arranges tour packages by assembling the components such as hotels, air, sightseeing, and so forth and then markets them either through travel agents at a commission to the agents (a wholesale tour operator) or directly to the public or to a tour organizer (a retail tour operator).

**tour organizer** Person who locates and creates groups for a pre- paid tour. May be an outside sales representative of a travel agency. Often compensated with a free trip and/or named titular tour leader. Also called a "Pied Piper."

**tracking** Following. As in tracking which ad in which publication produces a given number of inquiries, and how many bookings result from those inquiries.

**trade mission** Group tour with a business rather than vacation purpose. Usually planned for business or government representatives traveling overseas to secure new business in foreign markets for their product, city, or other entity.

**transfer** Service provided for arriving or departing travelers to transport them from an airport or an air, sea, or rail terminal to their hotel or vice versa. May also be between one terminal and another. A standard element of an inclusive tour. Usually includes more than just transportation: meet and greet service and baggage handling.

**twin** Hotel or motel room having two single beds for use by two persons. Not to be confused with a double, which is one bed for two persons. See **double**.

**unable** Unable to confirm, not available.

**upfront** In advance, as in upfront expenses referring to monies expended prior to launching a tour or receiving passengers' monies. Monies at risk.

**uppercase** Capital letters, as against lower case. Signified by the initials u.c. when proofreading.

**variable expenses** Expenses related to the individual passenger and for which the tour operator will not be charged unless the passenger is present to use them. For example: hotel accommodations, meals, tips. See **fixed expenses.**

**VAT (Value Added Tax)** Government-imposed tax, based on the value added at each stage of the production and distribution of a product or service.

**velox** A particularly sharp photographic print suitable for reprinting. An effective means of sending the same tour or cruise advertisement to many different publications.

**waitlist** List of clients awaiting confirmation on a flight, cruise, tour and so forth that is currently sold out. Space is confirmed to waitlisted clients as cancellations of confirmed clients occur.

**white space** The part of an ad or brochure layout which has no copy or illustration, purposely left blank, often indicative of an elegant or more expensive product.

**wholesale tour operator** Company that arranges tour packages by assembling the components such as hotels, air, sightseeing, and so forth and then markets the total travel package through travel agents at a commission to the agents, rather than marketing directly to the public or a tour organizer. See **tour operator.**

# Index

Academic courses, 36
Accounting, 22
Accounting code number, 186
Acquisition costs, 133
Acts of God, 242-243
Admission fees, 90
Advance payment, 200-201
Advertising, 90-91, 129-136
  agencies, 129-131
  co-op, 136
  coupons, 133, 136, 137
  effective use of media, 132-133
  magazines, 131
  newspapers, 131
  radio and television, 131-132
  samples, 134, 135
Advertising agencies, 134, 135
Air carriers
  selection of, 59
Airfare, 12, 90, 216-217
  and itinerary, 38
  restrictions, 158
Airline account executives, 79
Airlines, 265
  dealing with enroute, 243
  finalizing, 188-190
  seating, 152-153
Airport, 220-222
Airport security, 152
Air reservations. *See* Group air reservations.
Air tickets, 171, 223
Almanacs, 36

Amenity packages, 55
American plan, 76
Annual programs, 5-6
Attorneys, 18-19

"Background Notes," 165
Background reading, 158, 219
Baggage, 155-156. *See also* Luggage.
  claim stubs, 224
  handling, 71
Balance, 40
Balance of payments, 262
Berth deposits, 55
Billing, 162-166
  accompaniments, 163
  format, 163
Boarding passes, 221
Bon Voyage cover letter, 173, 174
Bookings, 30-31, 48-82
  group air reservations, 60-64
  hotel, 66-70
  incoming group tours, 269-270
  letter to airlines, 60, 62, 64
  order of, 49
  reception operators, 78-82
  sample booking form and control sheet, 61
  sample hotel booking, 73
Briefing, 212-218, 228-229
  checklist, 212, 213-216
  on cruise, 244, 245
  points to cover, 229-231
Brochures, 35, 90, 100-114, 122, 263-

264. *See also* Shells.
  art, 107-108
  color, 105-106
  cover, 108-110
  and cruises, 54-55
  itinerary, 110
  layout, 104-105, 107-108
  maps, 108
  packaging, 97
  photos, 107-108
  printer's bid, 105-107
  reasons for printing, 102
  reservation form, 111-113
  responsibility clause, 113-114
  sample, 103, 109
  and tour price, 110-111
Budget, 24
  for promotion, 116-117
Bulletins. *See* Information bulletins.

Cabin locations, 218
Calendaring, 176-182
  review dates, 178-182
  typical dates, 177
Cameras, 152
Cancellations, 153, 162, 167-168, 169
Care of valuables, 157
Changing arrangements, 217
Charters, 92
Checklist
  final documents, 171-173
  30 day finalization, 181
Check-in, 221-222
Check-out, 231, 234-235
Clerical help, 30
Client handling, 142-175
Client records, 184, 186, 187
Coach seating, 229
Commissions
  and advertising agency, 130
  and cruises, 53-54
  override, 65-66
Companionship, 12
Community organizations, 10-11
Complaints, 230
Complimentaries, 54, 123, 203-204, 269
Computer programming capability, 279

Conditions statement, 283
Confidential tour roster, 190-191, 193-195
Confirmations, 62, 66, 82
  hotel, 72-74
Contract
  cruise line, 58
  with tour manager, 213
Control forms, 182-184
Convenience, 12
Conventions, 278-280
Co-op advertising, 136
Costing a tour, 83-99
  admissions fees, 90
  advertising, 90-91
  airfares, 90
  basic points, 84
  brochure, 90
  charters, 92
  decision making, 97-98
  direct mail, 91
  do's and don't's, 98-99
  fixed expenses, 90-92
  hotel charges, 85, 88-89
  markups, 92-94
  meals, 89
  miscellaneous lump sum expenses, 92
  organizers, 91-92
  other considerations, 95
  promotional evenings, 91
  sample, 94-95
  sightseeing, 89
  taxes, 90
  tips, 89
  tour manager, 91
  variable costs, 85, 88-90
  variable *v.* fixed costs, 85
  worksheet, 86-87
Costing *v.* pricing, 84
Costume party, 245
Coupons, 133, 136, 137
Courtesy, 230
Credit cards, 153-154
Cruise contracts, 56-57, 58
Cruise Lines International Association, 53
Cruises, 217-218
  advantages, 50-51

# INDEX

benefits to agency, 53-56
benefits to clients, 53-56
disadvantages, 51-52
finalizing, 201-203
handling a group, 50-57
negotiating with cruise lines, 52-53
roster, 201
special hints, 243-246
tickets, 171
Customs, 158-159

Defaults, 20
Debriefing, 247-248
Delays, 241
Departure bulletin, 171, 173, 175
Deposits, 142-143, 144-145
Deregulation, 64-65
Destinations, 12-13
*Dictionary of Tourism* (Metelka), 74
Dining, 217, 228. *See also* Hotels.
Direct bookings, 30-31
Direct mail, 91, 96, 118-121. *See also* Mailing lists.
  host club arrangement, 119-120
  nonprofit postage, 121
  personalized envelope, 120
  professional mailing house, 120
Draw, 121, 123-125
  letter of understanding, 123-124
Dress, 230

Emergencies, 216, 236-237
  expenses, 217
Encyclopedias, 35
Enroute problems, 236-237
Entertainment, 217
Entrance fees, 90
Envelopes
  personalized, 120
  prepacking, 160, 162
  return-mail, 167
Equipment, 27
Errors and omissions insurance, 19-20
Escrow account, 21-22
European Highlights sample tour, 42-47
European plan, 76
Evaluation report, 250-251
Evening activities, 40
Expense report form, 249

Film, 152
Final documents, 170-173
  checklist, 171-173
Finalizing, 188-204
  cruise lines, 201-203
  hotels, 190-191, 193-198
  reception ground operators, 198-201
Final payments
  acknowledgments, 170
Financial closing, 256
Financing, 22-23
Fixed cost *v.* variable costs, 85
Fixed expenses, 90-92
Flight bags, 170
Flight manifest, 189-190, 191
Follow-up flyer, 120, 141
Food safety, 231
Foreign currencies, 88-89, 113, 154-155, 276
Foreign Independent Tour, 33
*The French—Portrait of a People* (de Gramont), 166
Full pension, 76

Galley proof, 107
Giveaways, 128-129, 164-166, 219
Government tourist offices, 35
Graduated rates, 268
Greeter/guide, 226
Gross, 76
Ground operators. *See* Reception ground operators.
Group air reservations, 57-64
  booking, 60-64
Group business. *See also* Group travel.
  preparing to handle, 18-32
Group operations managers, 28-29
Group travel, 12-14. *See also* Group business *and* Tours.
  categories of, 11
  choosing the right business, 15-16
  for experienced agencies, 278-289
  finding group business, 9-11
  group ideas, 16-17
  group *v.* individual travel, 3-5
  last 24 hours, 246
  reasons for handling, 1-3
  types of groups, 14-15
  undertaking, 1-17

INDEX 309

viability, 8-9
why organizations sponsor, 13-14
Guides, 230
   dealing with local guides, 232-233
   expectations, 233

Half pension, 76
*Handobok of Professional Tour Management* (Reilly), 205
Handling of monies, 186, 188
Health problems, 158, 238-239. *See also* Emergencies.
Horizontal structure, 26
Host club arrangement, 119-120
Hotels, 271-272
   answers needed from, 72-74
   arrival, 226-228
   baggage handling, 71
   booking, 66-70
   booking with reception operators, 69-70
   chain sales office, 68
   charges, 85, 88-89
   check-in, 226
   choosing right group hotel, 70-72
   contacting directly, 67-68
   cover letter to, 196-198
   dining, 71
   finalizing, 190-191, 193-198
   handling group hotel space, 66-78
   hotel representative, 69
   image, 71
   loading space, 71
   lobby, 71
   location, 70
   pricing accommodations, 76-78
   requesting space, 72
   special facilities, 72
   terms, 75-76
   type of clientele, 71

IATA form, 114
*Iberia* (Michner), 166
Illness. *See* Health problems.
Incentives, 285-287
Incoming group tours, 261-277
   air flights, 273
   booking, 269-270
   contacts, 277
   costing, 268-269
   designing, 263-264
   finalizing, 274-275
   hotels, 271-272
   motorcoaches, 270-271
   operational setup, 266-268
   problems, 275-277
   promotion, 264-266
   reasons to consider, 262
   sightseeing, 272-273
   transfers, 273
   waiting period, 273-274
Individual insurance, 20
Inflight, 222-224
Information bulletins, 146-162
   accompanying bill, 163-166
   first bulletin, 150-159
   learning to prepare, 149-150
   purpose of, 146-147, 149
   standardizing, 159-160
Inhouse operations, 176-204
Injury, 238-239
Inoculations, 150
Inquiries, 142-144
   inquiry record card, 188, 189
   tracking, 188
Insurance, 19-21, 166-167, 173. *See also* specific types.
   for tour manager, 20-21
Interim mailings, 162
International Air Transport Association, 57
Introductions, 221
Invoices, 162-166
   cover letter, 165
   sample, 164
Itinerary, 110
   balance, 40
   charting, 39-40
   evening activities, 40
   first and last days, 40-41
   number, 102, 114
   one-night stands, 40
   pacing, 39
   planning, 37-47
   problem areas, 38-39
   sample, 36-37, 263
   sample tour, 42-47

Landing, 224-226
Lapel name badge, 171

# INDEX

Large v. small groups, 15-16
Lead time, 23, 37, 48-49, 280
*Legal Aspects of Travel Agency Operation* (Miller), 19, 20
Legal preparation, 18-19
Letters
   acknowledgment card, 146
   agency acknowledgment, 148
   to airline, 60, 62, 64
   Bon Voyage cover letter, 173, 174
   booking ground operator, 79, 81
   cancellation ackowledgment, 169
   cover letter to airlines, 190, 192
   cover letter to cruise line, 201-203
   cover letter to hotels, 196-198
   for draw, 123-124
   followup, 144
   form, 181
   to hotel, 72, 73
   inquiry reply, 143
   invoice cover letter, 165
   90-day review, 179
   60-day review, 180
   sponsoring club acknowledgment, 145, 147
   tour manager's ticket request, 204
   welcome-home, 248, 252-253
Liability insurance, 19
List of tour participants, 172
Luggage, 227, 230. *See also* Baggage.
   checking, 220
   count, 234
   lost and damaged, 217, 240
   tags, 156, 171

Magazines, 131
Mailing houses, 120
Mailing instuctions, 171, 172
Mailing lists, 5, 257-259
Malpractice insurance, 19-20
Maps, 108, 264, 172
Marketing, 115-141
   definition of, 115
   direct mail, 118-121
   marketing plan, 115-117
   mix, 116
   promotional budget, 116
   selecting segment, 116
Markup, 2-3, 92-94
   estimating, 93-94

noncommissionable items, 94
Master tour control sheet, 184, 185
Meals. *See* Dining.
Media
   effective use, 132-133
Medicare, 21
Meetings, 278-280
*Men of Mexico* (Magner), 166
Metelka, Charles J., 74
Miller, Jeffrey R., 19, 20
Mixed structure, 26-27
Motorcoaches, 152-153, 270-271
Modified American plan, 76

Name tags, 171, 244
*National Geographic,* 166
Negotiations, 52-53
   with airline, 64-66
Net, 76
Net net, 76
Newspapers, 131
90-day review letter, 179
Noncommissionable items, 94
Nonprofit postage, 121
No shows, 222

Office layout, 27
*Official Airline Guide,* 38-39
One-night stands, 40
Optional insurance, 20
Options
   on hotel space, 74
Operating procedures, 30-32
Operational problems, 240-242
Order of booking, 49
Organizers, 91-92
Orientation meeting, 228-229
Override commissions, 65-66
Overseas study programs, 283-285

Pacing, 39
Packaging tours, 3
Packing suggestions, 156-157
Page proofs, 107
*Pan Am's Encyclopedia of Travel,* 36
Passenger Network Services Corporation, 114
Passports, 150, 173
   lost, 239-240
Passport billfold, 171

# INDEX 311

Paying bills, 216
Per person rate *v.* room rate, 85
Personalized envelope, 120
Personnel, 28-30
Photographs, 107-108, 139-140
Pied Piper. *See* Draw.
Posttour wrap-up, 247-260
Pow Wow, 265-266
Press releases, 136-140
   do's and don't's, 140
   format, 138
   photos, 139-140
   samples, 139
Pretour reading, 158, 219
Price
   evaluating, 95-96
   ways to reduce, 96-97
Pricing
   hotel accommodations, 76-78
   a tour, 83-99, 110-111
Pricing *v.* costing, 84
Principal, 18-19
Printer's bid, 105-107
   spec sheet, 106
Problems with passengers, 237-238
Producer, 261
Profit, 2-3, 83-99
Promotion, 264-266. *See also*
   Promotional evenings.
Promotional budget, 116-117
Promotional evenings, 91, 125-129
   checklist, 127
   format, 127-128
   giveaways, 128-129
   preplanning, 126-127
   wrapup, 129
Punctuality, 229

Questionnaire, 160, 161
   posttour, 254-255

Rack rate, 75
Radio, 131-132
Reception operators, 78-82, 261
   finalizing overseas, 198-201
   nonappearance, 241-242
   tariffs, 79-80
Refunds, 153
*Register of Corporation Directors and Executives* (Standard & Poor's), 10

Reilly, Robert T., 205
Research aids, 35-36
Reservations, 144-145. *See also*
   Bookings.
   forms, 111-113
   group air, 57-64
   hotel, 66-70
   with supplier, 8
Responsibility clause, 18, 113-114
Review dates, 178-182
Rooming arrangements, 151-152
Rooming list, 190-191, 193-195
Room rate *v.* per person, 85
Run of the house, 76

Safety deposit box, 227, 235
Sales call hints, 11-12
Sample tour, 94-95
Seating
   airplane, 152-153
   assignments, 220
   on cruise, 244
   meals on cruise, 217
   motorcoach, 152-153
Seminars, 278-280
Service charge, 76, 88-89
Shells, 54-55, 100, 101, 102, 104
Shipboard gratuities, 218
Shipboard tours, 244-245
Shopping, 157-158
Shore excursions, 217-218
Sightseeing, 89, 272-273
Single room supplements, 88
60-day review letter, 180
Small *v.* large groups, 15-16
Smokers, *v.* nonsmokers, 189
Solicitation
   of group accounts, 29-30
Special interest tours, 263, 287-289
Spending money, 154
Stationery, 27-28
Strikes, 241
Structuring a group division, 23-27
Suppliers, 176-204, 261
   finalizing, 188-204
   review dates, 178-182
Supplies, 27-28

Tariffs, 35, 263-264
   reception operator's, 79-80

Taxes, 88-89
Taxes, 90
Television, 131-132
Telex, 267
Tipping, 89, 153, 230-231
Tour designer, 33-35
Tour files, 256-257
   client file card, 257-258
Tourist cards, 151
Tour manager, 91, 205-218
   agreement with, 211-212
   and airfare, 216-217
   at the airport, 220
   availability, 231
   changing arrangements, 217
   complimentaries, 54
   contract, 213
   on cruises, 243-246
   debriefing, 247-248
   definition of, 205-206
   emergency expenses, 217
   and entertainment, 217
   enroute, 219-246
   experience, 209-210
   free trips, 211
   gratuities, 212
   handling emergencies, 216
   insurance for, 20-21
   job description, 210-211
   language ability, 210
   leadership, 231-232
   and lost luggage, 217
   no-go date, 212
   paying bills, 216
   personal comportment, 235-236
   planning, 231-232
   qualities of, 206-209
   responsibilities, 211
   safety, 236
   salary, 211
   selection of, 211
   visibility, 223
Tours. *See also* Group travel.
   cancellation, 97-98
   designing for clientele and community, 5-6

   designing for specific groups, 6-7
   future, 259-260, 289
   large operator's approach, 7-8
   researching and designing, 33-47
Trade missions, 280-283
   conditions statement, 283
   packages, 281-282
Trade shows, 265-266
Translators, 267
Travel counselor
   group *v.* individual, 3-5
Travelers checks, 154-155
Travel Industry Association of America, 265
Travel insurance, 152, 166-167
Travel Insurance Services, 20
*Travel Weekly's World Travel Dictionary,* 264
Turnaround time, 163
Twenty-four-hour-time system, 62-63

United States Travel and Tourism Administration, 265
Upfront costs, 85
Upfront monies, 65

Valuables, 230
Value Added Tax (VAT), 76
Variable costs, 85-90
Variable cost *v.* fized costs, 85
Vertical structure, 23-26
Visas, 151
Volume, 279
Vouchers, 172

Waiting lists, 168-169
Water safety, 231
Weekly booking report, 182-183
Welcome-aboard party, 217
Welcome-home letter, 248, 252-253
Wholesalers, 30-31
Wholesaling
   to retail agents, 31-32
Worldwide liability, 19

Yellow pages, 10-11